MANAGEMENT AND OPERATIONS OF AMERICAN SHIPPING

MANAGEMENT AND OPERATIONS OF AMERICAN SHIPPING

ERNST G. FRANKEL
Massachusetts Institute of Technology

Auburn House Publishing Company
Boston, Massachusetts

Library of Congress Cataloging in Publication Data

Frankel, Ernst G.
  Management and operations of American shipping.

  Includes index.
  1. Shipping—United States.   2. Merchant marine—
United States.   I. Title.
HE745.F729   387.5'068   81-22873
ISBN 0-86569-100-2   AACR2

Printed in the United States of America

PREFACE

The American shipping industry has been the subject of controversy for many years. Some contend that there is little economic or strategic reason for continued government support (which is, however, essential for its survival); others maintain that a U.S. merchant marine of reasonable size is necessary for our national defense and economic wellbeing. Notwithstanding this long debate, it is a fact that the U.S. merchant marine, and particularly its international shipping capacity, is today at an all-time low since World War II. Among the reasons for this development are adverse conditions in the international shipping market, increasing protectionism by other shipping nations, and declining support by the U.S. government.

This book is aimed at the student of shipping and transportation as well as the shipping manager who requires a readable text that clearly defines the concepts of the organization, management, and operations of American shipping. This book is a companion volume to the author's *Regulation and Policies of American Shipping*. While an attempt has been made to provide comprehensive coverage of the subject, equal attention is given to the discussion of novel and often provocative concepts, based on the belief that the problems facing American shipping, management, and operations need new, imaginative, and possibly controversial solutions.

Increasing domestic deregulation, larger international protectionism, and declining government support to the industry provide new challenges and opportunities for American shipping management, which may in the future be able to act much more freely than in the past. This is a new experience for an industry which has largely survived, though not really prospered, under an umbrella of government regulations and aids.

The book is divided into eight chapters. Chapter 1 provides an overview and perspective of American shipping, while Chapter 2 discusses its organization. In Chapter 3 we review the framework in which American shipping operates. Issues affecting ship operations are covered in Chapter 4, with particular reference to the emerging impact of fuel prices and availability and the quality of ship operations. The discussion of ship management in Chapter 5 covers organizational structure, fleet and personnel management, as well as the increasingly important issues of information use and handling. Ship operating costs and shipping finance are covered in Chapters 6 and 7. Here we also discuss the opportunities provided for ship and equipment leasing under the Economic Recovery Act of 1981. Case examples using the terms of the Safe Harbor Clause of the Tax Act are presented as examples. Chapter 8 deals with the economics, opportunities, and challenges presented to American shipping and includes some provocative suggestions for future decision making. It is based on the premise that American shipping management will in the future have larger and more far-reaching decision making powers, introduced by the expected elimination of many constraints that have traditionally curtailed decision making in such areas as ship purchase and sale, type of ownership, route selection and service, manning, and ship financing.

Of the many people I wish to thank for their help and contributions in the preparation of this book, I would especially thank Ms. Patricia Read, who edited Chapters 1 and 2; Mr. John Cooper, who contributed the sections on bulk shipping management in Chapter 5; and Mr. Glenn Mahnken, who critically reviewed the manuscript. Most importantly, I would like to thank Mrs. Sheila McNary, who labored untold hours in typing and retyping numerous drafts of this book. Finally, my thanks go to my beloved wife Tamar and our son Michael for their patience, understanding, and support during the long hours that this book was in process.

E.G.F.

CONTENTS

CHAPTER 3
Framework of Shipping

CHAPTER 4
Issues in Ship Operations

CHAPTER 7
Shipping Finance   199

CHAPTER 8
*Economic Issues and Opportunities for American
Shipping* 229

LIST OF TABLES

LIST OF FIGURES

MANAGEMENT AND OPERATIONS OF AMERICAN SHIPPING

Chapter 1

PERSPECTIVE ON AMERICAN SHIPPING

American shipping management and operations have long been the subject of discussion, criticism, and often contradictory comment. Much of this is due, on the one hand, to the recognition of the pivotal role played by the American shipping industry in the U.S. foreign trade and national defense, and on the other hand, to the long-term dependence of the industry on government aid to or protective regulation of some major segments of the industry. This government support has provided mixed blessings at best. Similarly, the industry's role as an arm of U.S. defense suffers under lack of role definition and, what is worse, the long virtual disregard of American shipping by defense planners.

A major criticism has always been the emphasis the industry is said to place on the protection of parochial or vested interests; yet these "interests" are seldom defined. In fact there is really no proper definition of what constitutes American shipping. Does it include all U.S.-owned shipping, or only U.S.-registered shipping, or ships flying the U.S. flag? The definition of American shipping could similarly include all shipping under U.S. control during a particular time. Some countries include not only chartered-in tonnage but also space charters. Joint ventures in shipping involving multinational ownership or registry, shipping consortia, and other transnational shipping arrangements make defining the size of a merchant shipping fleet quite difficult. Therefore, before discussing the problems and challenges of managing and operating U.S. shipping, we must define it.

The U.S. shipping industry has been accused of emphasizing short-term issues instead of long-term and national goals. This criticism is usually applied to American shipping policymakers, management, and labor. U.S. policymakers have generally confined their concern

1

to U.S.-flag shipping in a narrow sense. Present U.S. regulation largely restricts U.S.-flag shipping ownership to U.S. citizens and limits any joint venture or consortia agreements with both U.S.- and foreign-flag operators.

The role of the U.S. merchant marine is variously defined as a purely business, commercial, strategic, foreign-policy, or military asset. As a result, policymakers have for long vacillated in their policy deliberation. Instead of devising new maritime planning with changing national roles and objectives, our maritime policy consists largely of amendments to the Shipping Acts of 1916 and 1920. We may surmise that indeed we have no real national maritime or shipping policy. At this time the same is also true of national transportation, energy, education, and even foreign policy. Shipping management, as a result, acts largely in a vacuum—a handicap at a time when an ever larger number of countries have adopted nationalistic shipping policies that often involve restrictive bi- or multinational agreements as well as various approaches to multinational collaboration such as joint ventures, capacity pooling, space sharing, and more.

Although shipping statistics, in defining national shipping, usually reflect registration and not ownership, an increasing number of maritime nations include chartered, jointly-owned, and other tonnage under their effective control in defining national shipping for the purposes of cargo- or revenue-sharing allocations. Similarly, the role of governments in shipping is also changing. Although the United States has no government-owned shipping engaged in commercial carriage, many other governments participate in the ownership of commercially operated shipping or own and operate shipping companies outright. In fact, in many countries, including all communist nations, all commercial shipping is government owned and operated. It is estimated that by the end of 1980 over 18 percent of the world tonnage and 26 percent of the number of ships were government owned and operated. Many of these government-owned shipping companies operate without the traditional profit objective of privately owned companies, and their pricing of shipping services is often influenced more by political or strategic than by commercial considerations.

Such government ownership has a major influence on world shipping, which has been a bastion of free enterprise and competition. Many countries without any substantial government ownership in shipping have introduced other measures to assist, protect, and promote national shipping. Although the United States was among the first maritime nations to provide government aids to shipping in the form of subsidies and protective regulation to liner and other sectors of national shipping, many foreign governments have devised arrays of new and original approaches to directly or indirectly assist their national shipping, while the United States has essentially stayed with the so-called "cost parity" subsidy programs for U.S. foreign trade liners (and since 1970 for bulk carriers as well). U.S. government loan guarantees and other financial aids, while useful, have at the same time been much more restrictive than the type of financial aids offered by other countries. Tax advantages to those building in U.S. yards hardly offset other differences.

The main problem, though, appears to be the lack of consistency in policymaking. The United States, for example, has generally been against international cargo-sharing agreements; yet for some time the United States has entered into bilateral agreements that stipulate the agreeing parties' entitlements to the shipping. Joint rate making and other anticompetitive agreements by operators have often been allowed—actions that would normally violate U.S. antitrust laws. Yet at the same time the Federal Maritime Commission (FMC) is maintained to prevent anticompetitive behavior, market abuses by liner conferences, and joint carrier arrangements.[1] Thus planning and operating become quite difficult for shipping management.

Another issue is the coordination of maritime policy. In the United States, much more than in most countries, a large number of diverse government agencies are involved in "interpreting or implementing maritime policy." They usually represent diverse interests that affect government policymaking. These agencies—the FMC, the Maritime Administration, the International Trade Administration, and others in the departments of Agriculture, Defense, State, Energy, Transportation, Commerce, and Justice—each have an active function, often stipulated by law, which affects maritime policy. This is how our democratic government functions. The executive branch has sometimes tried to provide some coherence or coordination in the area of maritime policymaking, interpretation, and implementation; its success, though, is spotty. In addition, most of the government agencies concerned with or affected by maritime policy have a congressional committee or subcommittee to look after each agency's interest and performance. The result is usually slow and ineffective decision making and compromise, which often hinders the achievement of the basic policy objective.

Considering the labor side, we note similar inconsistency with the established principle of manning U.S.-flag vessels only by U.S. citizens. Most maritime nations, including all western European nations, allow foreign manning of their national shipping to varying

---

[1] Peter N. Teighe, Commissioner, FMC, in remarks before Propeller Club of the United States, Los Angeles, May 1981.

degrees. In many cases foreign, low-cost, unlicensed personnel are used. The cost savings can be appreciable. For example, the manning cost of a ship crewed by low-cost, foreign seamen is only 25 percent of the cost of an equivalent U.S. citizen-manned vessel. European owners who maintain their own nationals as officers but who use low-cost, foreign crews usually save 50 percent of manning costs.

The main problem of our existing maritime policy has been the constraining effect on efficient shipping management, which needs operating flexibility and freedom to act with a minimum of government involvement. Furthermore, a consensus is growing that our present maritime policy represents a substantial deterrent to the growth and flexibility of U.S. shipping, particularly of the U.S.-flag sector. At the same time, much of our current maritime policy is not based on realistic premises. Shipbuilding subsidy laws and restrictions that require U.S. building of some U.S.-flag commercial shipping were based on the need to maintain sufficient U.S. shipbuilding capcity for emergencies. U.S. commercial shipbuilding, however, constitutes a very small fraction of U.S. shipbuilding business and therefore affects U.S. shipbuilding viability very little.

Congress is now debating approaches designed to allow U.S. liner operators to import foreign-built vessels and at the same time to qualify for operating subsidy and other government aids. Similarly, there are proposals for the elimination of the so-called "Essential Trade Route System" that assigns subsidized carriers to routes with no more than one such carrier per route.

In terms of participation in U.S. foreign and other international trade, U.S.-flag shipping is not significant. Over 95 percent of the U.S. foreign trade tonnage is carried by foreign-flag vessels. In fact less than 2 percent of bulk cargoes in U.S. foreign trade are shipped in U.S.-flag bottoms. While U.S.-flag liner shipping has been able to maintain a more reasonable share of U.S. liner trade (23 percent in 1970, 30 percent in 1975, and 26.5 percent in 1979), the industry is still far below the 40 percent participation rate that many cargo-sharing agreements stipulate, and that forms the basic premise of U.S. maritime policy.

The U.S.-flag liner fleet declined from 475 ships in 1970 to 263 ships in 1980. However, 153 of these vessels were containerships in 1980, with a much larger transport capacity than their 1970 equivalents. The main problem appears to be the U.S. bulk carrier fleet, which has hardly grown since bulk carriers in U.S. foreign trade qualified for government aids in 1970. The equivalent of 44 million DWT of foreign-flag shipping (or about 1,000 foreign-flag ships) were fully employed in serving U.S.-bulk foreign trades in 1980. At the same time, U.S.-owned foreign-flag (open registry) bulk carriers comprised a fleet with a capacity of over 50 million DWT, large enough to carry all of our bulk imports. The preferred use of that tonnage in U.S. foreign trade may offer many economic and political advantages to the United States.

The U.S. maritime industry, and particularly U.S. shipping, faces a crossroads now. Opportunities for revitalization of growth are unique. Unit costs, including those of U.S. labor, no longer exceed those of all countries. Many Western nations now pay as much or more for labor. There is similarly an increased acceptance of protectionism in shipping by the world's nations. While this trend conflicts with U.S. commitment to free enterprise on the one hand, it does provide an opportunity for the rebuilding of our merchant marine under the umbrella of internationally accepted practices.

1.1. Overview and Purpose

The objectives of this book are to present an overview of the organization of shipping and to discuss the framework under which shipping is managed and operated, with particular reference to U.S. shipping. It is designed to provide useful theories of shipping management and operation as well as methods of financial and cost analysis.

Chapter 2 continues with a discussion of the general organization of shipping. Here the foundation of shipping management and operations concepts is presented for those entering this exciting field. For those engaged in the profession, Chapter 2 is a basic reference. Chapter 3 provides a general review of the composition of international issues in shipping, and Chapter 4 presents a discussion of shipping operations. Chapter 5 presents a more detailed analysis of the effect of shipping management structure on operational effectiveness and an examination of management problems in liner and bulk shipping. The chapter concludes with a review of the requirements for and use of management information systems in shipping. Next, the cost of shipping operations is analyzed in Chapter 6, followed by a review of shipping finance and financial control in Chapter 7. This chapter evaluates different methods for cost and financial evaluation of current operations as well as planned uses of shipping, including acquisition of new tonnage, servicing new trades, and different methods of financing fleet expansion. Finally, Chapter 8 reviews the basics of shipping economics in terms of American shipping and discusses some of the opportunities and challenges facing the industry.

Chapter 2

THE ORGANIZATION OF SHIPPING

The character of shipping is becoming more complex. No longer primarily the transportation of finished goods, shipping has become a part of the process of manufacturing and distribution. This change is affecting the internal organization of companies more than the overall structure of the industry. The institutional setting of shipping is evolving very gradually, presided over by the same bodies and involving reactive changes in many ancillary industries. This chapter describes the principal operational categories of international shipping, liner and tramp, and the institutional arrangements under which tramp and independently owned bulk shipping (charter parties) operate. Also examined are the roles of the broker in ensuring the smooth functioning of the shipping markets, the classification society in ensuring the maintenance of shipbuilding and operational standards, and the marine insurer in providing the necessary financial security. Shipping regulation will form a separate chapter.

2.1. Categories of Shipping

Although shipping subsidiaries of manufacturing and heavy-industry companies own and operate significant fleets, these fleets seldom affect international shipping directly. In the first place, they are often built to supply transportation needs that are not adequately met by independent shipping. Second, they tend to be sized at, if not below, the company's minimum requirements, and they are frequently supplemented by chartered vessels. As their management is similar to but simpler than liner management, this category will not be considered separately.

Independently owned ships generally operate either as liner vessels or tramps. They are distinguished by the flexibility of their operations and the object/emphasis of their marketing efforts. Liners superficially resemble common carriers, but in fact they are not required to accept all cargoes or maintain specified schedules. Nor are they precluded from entry into the tramp market. However, it is instructive to consider liner shipping and tramp shipping separately in order to characterize their operations.

2.1.1. *Liner Shipping*

Liners follow published, relatively fixed routes and schedules, picking up interport cargo as well as line haul cargo. They tend to carry small consignments of individually packaged or containerized goods and require varied cargo-handling equipment to service the different kinds of cargo they may encounter. They are preeminent in carriage of high-value processed goods or manufactures. Liner companies are cartelized—that is, organized into conferences or consortia, which represent institutional responses to the economic problems of providing fixed-charge, scheduled service in the presence of tramp and other unregulated shipping. Liner operators are usually large, diversified companies serving the needs of regular and/or small shippers, as opposed to tramps, who characteristically voyage on behalf of single, or at least large, shippers of bulk cargoes. Under the conditions that favor liner operation, the shipowners can estimate how much the customer is prepared to pay and then fix a corresponding rate, as opposed to accepting a rate imposed by the interplay of market forces. Such liner rates, known as "tariffs," are relatively stable; this stability is regarded as a major justification for conference/consortium rate fixing.

Liner freight rates are quoted on the basis of weight or measurement, at the ship's option, since a ship's carrying capacity can be either weight or volume constrained. Light or bulky cargoes are charged on a volume basis, while dense, heavy cargoes are charged on a weight basis. Liner tariffs are often quoted for the commodities that move regularly on a given route through a given conference/consortium. These rates are based on (1) the stowage factor (reciprocal of density—relates measurement to weight), (2) the value of the cargo (representative of its elasticity of demand), and (3) the state of the market. Class rates are available for general cargo not otherwise specified. Some tariffs actually categorize general cargo for charging purposes. Goods moving in large quantities are susceptible to tramp competition when liners charge "open rates," which are whatever rates can be obtained on the market.

Liner conferences are semimonopolistic bodies, which set tariffs and schedules for the defined routes over which they operate. Conference membership imposes operational policies and obligations, and one admission requirement is the capacity and willingness to observe conference policies. These may include allocation of trade shares, restrictions on discounts and rebates, and pooling of earnings and sailings. Although chartered vessels may be used when necessary to fulfill conference obligations, the members require applicants to operate owned tonnage under normal conditions. The idea is to help suppress the competition from cross-traders and tramp operators. The above is most true of the "closed" conferences, where membership depends on consent of existing members. "Open" conferences, largely confined to U.S. trade, do not require consent but impose similar obligations. Applicants must satisfy the U.S. Federal Maritime Commission of their ability to maintain a regular service on the route. In both cases a conference tends to operate in only one direction; a different conference, frequently with a different membership, may cover the return route.

The prevalence of conferences in liner shipping is evident from the proliferation of their numbers—nearly four hundred worldwide. This form of operation, however, will undoubtedly be changed by the increasing number of consortia serving major routes and by the impending U.N. Convention requiring cargo sharing on a 40–40–20 basis (40 percent of the trade should be carried by the national lines of the origin country, 40 percent by the national lines of the destination country, and the remaining 20 percent by cross-traders). If large consortia dominate a route, the conferences may be displaced from their policymaking functions. In the event that major trading nations pass cargo-sharing legislation, the absolute scope of liner conference influence will be reduced and probably regulated in shippers' interests to some degree. The timetable for adoption of the convention would range from three years up, and studies are in progress to determine the potential economic impact and the most suitable form of legislation.

The overall legality of conferences is widely justified on the grounds that they are conducive to development of trade—by stabilization of freight rates and maintenance of services in time of recession. Other conference practices that assist trade, such as promotional tariffs, benefit developing nations in particular. However, this recognition is accompanied by a conviction that the conferences require regulation if their partial monopoly of transport services is not to be abused during conditions of high demand for shipping.

2.1.2. *Tramp Shipping*

The tramp ship has been the only type of commercial vessel serving ocean trades for most of human history. Having no fixed itinerary, the tramp ship picks up cargo where it is to be found and seeks new business for each voyage. Most tramp ship voyages nowadays are made on behalf of a single shipper and carry a full load of a bulk commodity such as coal or grain.

What the tramp shipowner offers, or in the language of the maritime industry, "charters," is an operating ship. This is done in two ways. First, the ship is made available for voyage charters—that is, to carry a full shipload from one port to another as the charterer wishes. It may be coal to West Italy, grain to Pakistan, phosphate rock to Japan, ores from India, Turkey, or South Africa, or lumber from British Columbia. The terms of hire are a fixed rate to pick up and deliver cargo.

Second, the tramp shipowner makes the ship available for time charters. Here the terms of hire are so many dollars per month for the use of a fully manned ship. The charterer may be another steamship company, generally a liner operator on a regularly scheduled route, or a government agency such as the Military Sealift Command, commonly abbreviated to MSC.

The time charterer may need the vessel for a variety of reasons. For example, there may be an unusual demand for additional shipping space too temporary in duration to justify purchase of an additional vessel. There may be peak movements on the route due to conditions, such as harvests, that create the need for additional vessels at certain periods of the year. Or, one of the charterer's vessels may temporarily be out of service for repairs at a time when the berth operator needs a vessel to maintain a sailing schedule. The tramp vessel is, therefore, the expansion valve of the steamship industry, available to move from job to job with the varying demands of world commerce and shipping or of government agencies for defense or national programs.

Prior to World War II, tramp shipping was frequently asserted to be on the decline. However, this statement was misleading, for the decline was only in relation to total seaborne cargo movements. With the growth of liner services in the period 1930–1960, the movement of tramp ships to a smaller proportion of the world's oceanborne commerce was axiomatic. Since 1960, though, there has been a sharp reversal even in this trend. For instance, before World War II liner vessels carried about two tons of cargo in U.S. foreign trade for every one ton carried by tramp vessels. Since 1960 the relationship has been reversed, and tramp vessels have carried nearly two tons for every one moved in liner vessels.

The major reasons for this shift undoubtedly are, first, relief and rehabilitation needs and, second, the demands created by the Korean hostilities and world tensions. However, the facts indicate that this shift is not a transitory condition. The rapid growth in world population and industrial capacity, the universal demand for higher living standards, and the resistance of people everywhere to the waste and high cost of "self-sufficiency" programs pursued by various governments have created a tremendous demand for worldwide movements of foodstuffs, fertilizers, and industrial raw materials, which can be handled more efficiently and cheaply by tramp vessels.

Just as it is less expensive for a church or social group to charter a bus for an outing rather than buy individual tickets, so too is it cheaper for a large shipper or importer of bulk commodities to charter a full ship rather than a ship at conference tariff rates based on parcel lots. These economies of scale have resulted in a drastic reduction in the cost of ocean transport of bulk commodities, which now move in larger quantities in world trade than ever before.

Unlike the liner vessel, which has published tariffs specifying the shipping charges and schedules for particular movements of cargo, the tramp vessel is hired in an auction market. Not that the charterers convene in a single room with the vessel owners and engage in open bidding, but the effect is the same. The charterer will generally place a request for a ship with a broker who will canvass the market for the lowest price of hire offered. In the case of a government agency such as the MSC, actual bids are requested and submitted.

Tramp ships do not follow regular routes but instead satisfy specific, transient needs as they appear. The tramp market is volatile. The shipper leases a major part, or the entire ship, generally for the purpose of shipping bulk commodities. Rates are negotiated for each individual contract on a long- or short-term basis. Tramp ships can be chartered under four types of agreements. The differences between these types revolve around the purpose of the charter, the basis for the rates, and the location of control of the ship, as discussed in the following section.

2.2. Chartering

Ships may be operated for an owner's account or leased out for variable periods of time (chartered). Charters, or fixtures, are categorized with respect to length of contract and locus of control. The major forms are voyage, time, and demise—and, of late, contracts of affreightment. Operation under charter means that a ship's commercial control, if not her operational control, passes from owner to charterer.

Standard charter parties (forms) are used, and though the contents and layout of a charter are specific to the particular contract, every charter has certain implied undertakings. Unless the contrary is expressed, the shipowner warrants that the vessel will be seaworthy at the beginning of each stage of the voyage and that the vessel will perform the voyage without deviation and with reasonable dispatch. Definitions of "seaworthy," "deviation," "dispatch," and so forth are the subject of a complex body of case law.

These implied undertakings can be expressly stated or excluded in the charter party. A *seaworthy* ship is one that is in every way able to meet the perils likely to be encountered on the voyage. The vessel must be stored, bunkered, and crewed, and hull/machinery must be in good order. This warranty of seaworthiness is absolute— that is, if the vessel is found to be unseaworthy, the shipowner is liable even though it can be shown that no amount of skill and care on the owner's part could have discovered or remedied the defect. A chartered vessel must also be fit to carry the intended cargo under appropriate conditions. This aspect of seaworthiness is called *cargo worthiness*.

Deviation is unjustified departure from the proper and usual route. Charter parties often contain clauses that define and circumscribe the liberty to deviate, and these clauses are always strictly construed by the courts. The shipowner also gives an implied warranty that reasonable dispatch in carrying out the contractual voyage will be exercised. This does not mean that there will be no delay, but rather that the shipowner will expedite the voyage.

2.2.1. *Voyage Charter*

Under a *voyage charter*, a vessel is leased for the transport of a specified cargo from one or more specified ports to one or more specified ports. Usually, but not always, the vessel is fully loaded. The rate is set according to such factors as the length of the voyage, the cargo, the expected port fees and charges, and the demand and available supply of suitable vessels. The actual gross revenue is determined by the amount (weight) of cargo loaded, unless the amount of cargo available to be loaded is less than the minimum originally agreed upon. In this case, the excess, unused capacity must be paid for by the charterer at the agreed-upon rate. If the vessel is to be part loaded by agreement, the rate will be adjusted accordingly.

The operating expenses on a voyage charter are borne by the shipowner, who is fully responsible for the operation of the vessel. Any cargo handling or other costs assigned to the charterers are reflected in the rate. If a voyage charter is for a fixed number of contiguous voyages, the charter arrangements are the same. The charterer is merely using the vessel more than once—the so-called *consecutive charter*. A vessel may be chartered for immediate employment—a *spot charter*—or for use at a specified date—a *future*. Voyage charters are usually negotiated three to twelve months in advance.

2.2.2.　Time Charter and Contract of Affreightment

Under a *time charter*, the charterer obtains the use of a ship for a set period of time. The cargo and itinerary are at the discretion of the charterer. Rates vary on time charters according to the standard speed and capacity of the vessel. Rates are set per deadweight ton per month. The shipowner pays the fixed costs of operating the ship, while the charterers pay for consumable and cargo-related items. Payment for the charter is made in advance, whether or not cargo is actually carried, since it constitutes a rental rather than a fee for a specific service.

Under the *bareboat* or *demise* form of time charter, the least common of the charter agreements, the charterer rents the vessel, without crew, for a given period of time. The charterers are responsible for all operations of the ship and for all operating costs. Rates are set, as for time charters, but they are lower, reflecting the length of the charter and the fact that only the physical vessel is supplied to the charterers. Demise charterers are usually liner companies that wish to add to their fleets on a temporary basis.

A *contract of affreightment*, though a contract for the supply of transportation services, does not follow the standard format of a charter party, which typically specifies the lease of a particular ship for a particular time. The contract of affreightment may be a long-term agreement with a ship-owning company to ship a certain amount of cargo between two ports, on vessels and at times of the shipowner's choice. Alternatively, the contract may specify a certain amount of shipping that must be completed within certain periods of time. The vessels employed need not belong to the shipowner, nor indeed, be under the shipowner's contract at the time of contracting.

2.2.3.　Charter Party Terms

Usually a standard contract is signed, which specifies:

- The two parties;
- The name and size (net, gross, and deadweight tonnage) of the vessel;
- A date by which the charterer may cancel the contract if the ship is not ready and possibly a specification of "readiness" (in general, a date is specified in the contract by which the ship must be ready to load and have arrived at the loading port; if the ship has not arrived by that date, the charterers may exercise the option to rescind the contract and claim damages);
- The type and approximate quantity of the cargo to be loaded;
- The freight rate and its basis for calculation, generally metric tons;

- The bearer of responsibility for loading and unloading;
- The number of days of, and method of calculating, allowed lay time: conditions under which the ship may be tendered for loading and unloading (when, how, where);
- Rates of demurrage and dispatch; and
- Other miscellaneous negotiated terms and certain standard clauses.

Some of these clauses require further explanation. *Financial responsibility for loading/discharging* may be borne by either the shipowners or the charterers. There are four arrangements for the allocation of these costs. Under "gross charter" terms, the shipowners pay all loading and unloading costs. Under "free-on-board" terms (FOB), the shipowners pay only the cost of unloading the cargo. Getting the cargo on board is "free" to them. Under "free-discharge" terms (FD), the shipowners pay only the cost of loading the cargo. Under "free-in-and-out" terms (FIO), all loading and discharge costs are borne by the charterers and are "free" to the shipowners.

"Lay-days" or *"lay-time"* is the amount of time allotted by the contract to charterers for loading and/or discharging the cargo. It may be expressed in any of several ways. For example, "hours," "running hours," "days," and "running days" refer to consecutive periods of time. "Working days" are days when work is normally done at the particular port, whether or not the work is actually carried out on the ship in question throughout the normal working time. "Lay-time" may be expressed as a rate of handling cargo when the approximate lay-time can be calculated from the cargo weight stated in the contract.

"Weather permitting" is generally added to denote that time lost when work is stopped due to bad weather is not discounted. "Weather-working days" adds this to the concept of working days. The more frequently used phrase "weather-working days of twenty-four hours" measures lay-days on a twenty-four-hour basis rather than just working hours. Saturdays, Sundays, and holidays can be included in or excluded from lay-time, depending on the agreement, but they are usually excluded. The term "unless used" is added to ensure that such days cannot be used for cargo handling without being counted as lay-time. In some contracts, excluded time counts toward lay-time at half time if it is used. Otherwise, the contract specifies that excluded time does not count "even if used."

In some contracts, lay-time is "reversible." This means that time lost in loading may be made up by quicker discharge, and time not used in loading may be allotted to discharge time. *Total time used* is compared to *total allotted time* in the calculation of demurrage and dispatch. These are charges and rebates that depend on whether or not lay-time is exceeded. In some cases, reversibility is implied by a phrase such as "cargo to be loaded or discharged . . . in a total of . . . ." And in some cases, the word "reversible" itself is used.

At the port of loading, the shipowner must give a valid "notice of readiness to load" to the charterer. Lay-time commences at a certain hour thereafter. In some contracts, lay-time begins twelve or twenty-four hours after notice is given, unless work can be started earlier. Alternatively, in some contracts, lay-time begins at a given time on the next working day.

When notice of readiness can be given is also a matter for negotiation. Naturally the ship must be physically ready to load, but whether or not it must actually be docked and waiting is open to agreement. In some contracts the ship must actually be at a berth, sometimes a specified berth, while in others the ship need only have "arrived" at the port, and lay-time begins whether or not the ship can find a berth right away. The same issues of tendering conditions apply to the discharge lay-time, though a notice of readiness is not usually given.

The issue of when "arrival" is considered to occur is naturally critical during periods of high shipping volume, for crowded ports may result in a delay between arrival at port and actual docking.

Demurrage is the penalty that charterers must pay to the shipowners when the lay-time is exceeded. The daily rate reflects the costs of detaining the vessel. Weekends and holidays always count once demurrage time has commenced, whether or not they count in lay-time. *"Dispatch"* is the opposite of demurrage. When lay-time is not used up, the difference is refunded to the charterers at a rate usually one third to one half of the rate for demurrage. Shipowners usually take care to specify that dispatch can only be given for lay-time saved, not for all time saved. The total saving may exceed lay-time savings, depending on the wording of the contract.

The *off-hire clause* states that in the event of the breakdown of vessel or cargo gear, or a deficiency of men hindering or preventing the working of the vessel for more than twenty-four hours, no hire is to be paid for the time during which the vessel is unable to perform the service immediately required. The calculation of the time loss for which hire is not to be paid can be very complicated, especially when strikes or port congestion takes place at the same time. However, the loss of time must be related to the service required immediately. Thus, an immobilized vessel still able to work cargo in port is not off-hire while cargo is being worked. Once cargo working is completed, she comes off-hire. However, the shipowner cannot be made responsible for loss of time experienced by the charterer in the employment of the vessel.

Dunnage, mats, and *separation cloths* are items that shipowners prefer charterers to pay for since the charterers would otherwise be overscrupulous in their requirements. The costs can be high if the cargo requires extensive protection and/or a separation of parcels.

Responsibility for damages, or indemnification for damage caused to the ship, is usually required by owners, though this must be specified. And *miscellaneous costs*, such as charges for wharf usage, use of barges for cargo handling, and other fees, must be allocated by the contract if they are anticipated.

2.2.4. Differences Between Voyage and Time Charter Parties

The differences between voyage charters and time charters revolve around responsibility for operation and the allocation of operating costs. Under a *voyage charter party*, the ship must be seaworthy at the beginning of each voyage and each segment of the voyage. Although the ship must be fit to receive her cargo at the commencement of loading, she need not be fit for sailing. Under a *time charter party*, the ship must be seaworthy at the beginning of each voyage under the charter. Otherwise the shipowner incurs a great loss of charter income as well as various costs. Similarly, an implied condition in every voyage charter party is that the vessel shall proceed on the voyage without delay or departure from her proper course. In a time charter, the charterer has full control of the vessel— thus deviation is not included in the contract.

In voyage charters it is usual to provide expressly that a ship will go to safe ports. In time charters it is an implied term of the contract that the vessel will only be used between good and safe ports. The basic rule regarding the shipowner's liability for cargo is that the cargo must be delivered to its destination in the same order and condition as it was when shipped, subject to certain stated exceptions. In relying on an exception, the shipowner assumes the burden of proving that the loss or damage was caused by an excepted peril, and the shipowner does not discharge this by merely showing that the loss or damage could have been so caused. Accordingly, in a voyage charter, the shipowner is responsible for all loss or damage to cargo, unless able to seek a defense afforded by the various exceptions. On the other hand, in a time charter, the responsibility between shipowner and charterer will be determined by the wording of the charter. Even if held responsible, the shipowner can usually claim indemnity from the charterer under the terms of charter.

If a vessel is damaged and the damage is caused by negligence in the navigation of the ship, the shipowner is always responsible. If the ship is damaged as a result of being ordered to an unsafe port, the charterer is liable under all charters, providing the master has exercised due diligence in entering the port. Under voyage charters, it is the shipowner's duty to ensure that damage caused to the vessel during loading and discharging is remedied by the person responsible (usually the stevedores). Under time charter parties, the vessel must be redelivered in the same good order and condition as received. The charterer is legally responsible for any damage, even when the charterer is not at fault in any way.

With respect to allocation of costs, although operating costs are clearly and usually for owner's or charterer's account, port costs and other expenses arising out of cargo operation are subject to negotiation. They are usually allocated under an arrangement described in the charter party. In a voyage charter, the following items are typically for the owner's account: fuel, wages, provisions, maintenance and repairs, stores and equipment, commission, insurance, depreciation, overheads, and claims for cargo damage. The owner may also pick up a negotiated proportion of port charges and cargo handling costs. In a time charter, under which the owner is not concerned with the commercial operation of the vessel, the owner does not pay for fuel, commission, cargo handling or claims for cargo damage. Nevertheless, the owner may be liable for cargo claims, depending on the charter wording.

2.3.   Brokerage

Three types of brokers are active in the maritime industry. The *tonnage broker* deals in the purchase and sale of ships. The *ship broker* represents a shipowner and obtains and arranges cargo commitments. The *cargo broker* represents the shipper and obtains the required space and service. Often one broker serves in different capacities for different owners.

A shipowner or charterer need not use a ship broker for transactions, but many routinely do so to take advantage of brokers' specialized knowledge and contacts and thereby improve their own operations. As certain branches of brokerage are highly specialized, choice is limited—as, for example, in the case of ship brokers of petroleum cargoes. Exclusive brokers may be used or business may be taken to an exchange. In either case a broker should be chosen on the basis of experience, reputation, and membership in a relevant national association of brokers.

The difference in the use of brokers by liner and tramp operators is distinct. The liner operator advertises and maintains fixed schedules, employs people to solicit freight, and maintains a large traffic department with representatives in many ports. The tramp owner or company maintains no corresponding staff. The particular type of cargoes carried by tramp companies normally requires intimate knowledge of local conditions and an abundance of contacts. The owners have found that the small commission a broker charges is negligible compared with the cost of setting up the required organization. Similarly, the shipper with a full load of cargo also profits by the specialized knowledge and counsel of the broker. Broker fees are universally fixed at 1.25 percent of the freight bill and are paid for by the shipowner only, although the cargo broker was selected by the shipper. The primary functions of the broker are:

- To determine the form of charter and special provisions that most nearly meet the needs of a particular transaction;
- To negotiate the terms and conclude the charter on behalf of the principals;
- To determine the vessel's position and availability for loading, to supervise notices of readiness, and to synchronize delivery of cargo to shipside;
- To mediate the choice of loading and discharging ports and berths;
- To supervise preparation of demurrage and lay-day statements, payment of dues, customs, settlements, and so forth;
- To procure certificates of freight invoices, arrange for surrender of bills of lading, facilitate collection of freight, and so forth; and
- To arrange for the appointment of outport agents and to issue appropriate instructions.

U.S.-flag shipping has traditionally not engaged in tramp shipping because of high first costs as well as high operating costs and, until 1970, the unavailability of government subsidies to nonscheduled operations. Even though both construction and operating cost differential subsidies were made available to U.S.-flag foreign-going bulk operators in 1970, there have been very few applicants for such aid and the U.S.-flag foreign-going tramp fleet remains very small.

2.4. Classification Societies

The stated aim of classification societies is to enforce reliable and uniform standards of ship construction and maintenance. Classification societies follow a ship from the builders to the breakers, and it is on their recommendation that insurance companies assume "risks." Compliance is recognized by the grant of a "class," which is meant to be a certification of the vessel's seaworthiness and overall character. Compliance is ensured by the classification society's close involvement in the vessel's design and construction, which includes not only approval of plans and specifications but also continual surveys of the vessel during the building process. The class is maintained during the life of the vessel by scheduled surveys that become more thorough as the vessel ages.

The societies were originally established around 1760 as a convenience to insurance underwriters to accumulate information and to compare and evaluate the merits of different ships. Today the functions of these societies are:

- To provide a register of ships, which contains essential particulars of the hull and machinery;
- To provide rules for the construction of new vessels and their machinery;
- To provide for testing and certification of materials; and
- To establish inspection services to report on the state of maintenance of ship and machinery.

Classification societies assign load lines, measure tonnage capacities, issue safety certificates, and so on, although these duties are usually subcontracted to them by one of the regulation agencies. A shipowner desiring insurance—a prerequisite in almost all cases to obtaining cargo for carriage—must provide each ship with a classification certificate from one of the recognized societies and then continue to keep the ship in class by following the rules the society provides. These rules prescribe repair and inspection schedules.

Unless the flag of registry insists, a shipowner is not actually compelled to classify the vessel. However, the commercial sanctions against nonclassification are so great, particularly in terms of hull insurance and any possible sale of a vessel, that compliance is virtually universal. The choice of a classification society (where choice is free) is usually made on the basis of shipowner's preference, broadly conditioned by nationality and the relative importance of detailed design.

Tables 2–1 and 2–2 summarize a recent year's classification activities of Lloyd's of London. The national breakdown of classed vessels indicates the supranational character of the society. In addition to Lloyd's, there are thirteen other societies:

- American Bureau of Shipping
- Bureau Veritas
- China Corporation Register (Taiwan)
- Deutsche Schiffs—Revision und Klassifikation
- Germanischer Lloyd
- Hellenic Register of Shipping
- Yugoslav Register
- Korean Register
- Nippon Kaiji Kyokai

- Norske Veritas
- Polski Regestr
- Registro Italiano Navale
- Register of Shipping of the U.S.S.R.

These societies are organized under different forms. For example, the French and German companies are joint stock companies. The Italian society is a state institution, with the right to register all Italian-flag vessels. The U.S., Norwegian, and British societies are private, nonprofit organizations, officially recognized by their respective governments. Normally government departments recognize the national society as their "agency" for classification purposes. The U.S. Government Merchant Marine Act of 1920 states:

> *That for the classification of vessels owned by the United States . . . all departments . . . of the Government are hereby directed to recognize the American Bureau of Shipping as their agency. . . .*

Unless the national classification society is prescribed, each government may delegate responsibility to any classification society throughout the world. Referring again to the American Bureau of Shipping, ABS has received authority to issue Load Line Certificates and Safety of Life at Sea Certificates, either wholly or in part from seventy countries.

Lately the societies have played an increasingly important role in ship research, in particular concerning application of modern technological development to maritime transport. Although all societies have their own precepts and building regulations with regard to construction and maintenance, it should be mentioned that they were all influenced by the rules of the oldest and largest regulating body, *Lloyd's Register of Shipping*.

Table 2–1   Classification with Lloyd's Register

| | World Total | | | |
| | Steam and Motor | | Non-Propelled | |
Class	No.	Tons Gross	No.	Tons Gross
100 A	10,061	107,218,063	610	667,638
A	181	110,646	135	253,217
A (for a period of years)	12	635	—	—
BS	109	394,646	1	1,686
Class contemplated	597	5,408,236	276	279,424
Total	10,960	113,132,226	1,022	1,201,965

Note: The total classed, or to be classed, with Lloyd's Register was 11,982 ships of 114,334,191 tons gross in 1979.

**Table 2-2   Number, Tonnage, and Flags of Vessels Classed with Lloyd's
Register in 1979**

Flag	No.	Tons Gross
Commonwealth		
United Kingdom	2,580	25,148,055
Australia	206	1,167,876
Bahamas	12	30,746
Bangladesh	86	153,190
Bermuda	81	1,697,668
Canada	403	2,187,275
Cayman Islands	22	56,148
Cyprus	272	1,238,962
Ghana	47	162,275
Hong Kong	62	435,314
India	294	3,069,009
Malaysia	71	262,394
Malta	11	15,640
Mauritius	7	26,992
Nauru	5	48,353
New Zealand	39	156,282
Nigeria	62	152,735
Seychelles	5	40,752
Singapore	266	1,550,485
Sri Lanka	15	42,860
Tanzania	7	12,609
Other Commonwealth countries	81	66,510
Algeria	16	533,817
Argentina	54	406,898
Belgium	61	881,722
Brazil	142	1,333,019
Bulgaria	3	107,129
Burma	33	50,898
Cameroon	2	15,378
Chile	29	265,240
China, People's Rep. of Taiwan, Province of	} 29	265,534
Colombia	12	82,158
Cuba	97	404,255
Czechoslovakia	5	102,589
Denmark	250	3,683,620
Ecuador	13	82,250
Egypt	140	212,072
Ethiopia	2	10,364
Finland	141	989,911
France	67	703,163
Germany, Federal Rep. of	272	1,614,390

Table 2–2   (continued)

Flag	No.	Tons Gross
Greece	1,197	12,004,738
Guinea	2	10,787
Honduras	8	38,644
Iceland	77	73,745
Indonesia	54	156,081
Iran	195	587,133
Iraq	119	764,580
Irish Republic	46	182,170
Israel	46	305,475
Italy	111	2,051,040
Japan	13	199,907
Korea (South)	16	859,490
Kuwait	101	1,386,559
Lebanon	52	105,376
Liberia	692	18,634,718
Libya	48	574,327
Maldive Is.	27	70,847
Mexico	61	470,556
Morocco	13	108,142
Mozambique, People's Rep. of	11	14,733
Netherlands	521	2,912,782
Nicaragua	8	18,720
Norway	176	4,117,170
Pakistan	61	357,032
Panama	550	3,854,603
Peru	93	247,877
Philippines	34	193,009
Poland	7	50,276
Portugal	110	580,949
Qatar	8	82,788
Romania	2	62,745
Saudi Arabia	61	538,981
Somali Republic	3	13,298
South Africa	52	157,833
Spain	646	5,161,943
Sudan	22	44,519
Sweden	321	5,012,884
Switzerland	7	73,614
Thailand	14	117,240
Turkey	107	365,779
U.S.S.R.	16	332,492
United Arab Emirates	50	105,092
United States of America	20	175,582

Table 2–2   (continued)

Flag	No.	Tons Gross
Uruguay	6	30,956
Venezuela	40	263,300
Vietnam	4	27,234
Yugoslavia	154	1,294,200
Zaire	2	16,333
Other countries	96	59,575
World Total	11,982	114,334,191

Note: Included above are 34 floating docks and 16 off-shore drilling rigs.

SOURCE: *Lloyd's Register of Shipping.*

2.5.   Marine Insurance

The insurance of property afloat is of interest not only to the ship-owner but also to exporters, importers, bankers, shipbuilders, ship operators, and so on. The number of risks involved in marine insurance is larger, and the subject is much more complicated than in any other form of insurance.

Insurance can be defined as protection against financial losses due to circumstances beyond normal expectation or control. Some large operators self-insure these risks, but normally insurance is carried with outside companies. In the description of classification societies, Lloyd's of London was mentioned. While the society only acts as a register and classification body, and does not issue or assume liability under policies, individual members of the society transact underwriting business. All members are legally liable in respect to their engagements under Lloyd's policies, to the full extent of their means. Over half of the marine insurance business in the world is handled by Lloyd's underwriters, although insurance brokers in other countries also handle marine insurance, usually under the same rules. Marine insurance is not based on any tariffs, as in other insurance coverage; each policy is obtained by negotiation. Competition among brokers and various risk estimates, as aspects determined from experience or as matters of expediency, affect insurance rates offered for similar coverage. The underwriter will consider the quality and quantity of equipment on board (radar, navigation aids, etc.), the reputation and the qualifications of its responsible officers, the operating practices of the company, and other facts that may influence the risks involved. These considerations do not mean that an underwriter will assume greater risks than a competitor. They reflect, rather, various underwriters' estimates of risk.

To guard themselves from unknown factors, and to ensure that the ship on which a policy is issued is maintained, operated, and navigated properly, all underwriters rely on classification. Apart from assuring the seaworthiness of the vessel and the reliability of its machinery, the classification society also provides the insurer with information about the master, the operator, shipper, and loading and discharging hazards, as well as navigational risks involved on a particular trade route.

Marine insurance is the oldest type of insurance. Some of the language used is archaic, but retained despite the modern conditions prevailing in the industry because the old terms have very definite and still useful meanings. The following wording is used in all policies issued in English-speaking countries concerning the hazards against which protection is granted:

> *Touching the adventures and perils which we the Assurers are contented to bear and do take upon us in this voyage, they are, of the Seas, Men of War, Fire, Enemies, Pirates, Rovers, Thieves, Jettisons, Letters of Mart and Countermart, Surprisals, Takings at Sea, Arrests, Restraints and Detainments of all Kings, Princes and People, of what Nation, Condition or Quality soever, Barratry of the Master and Mariners, and of all other perils, Losses and Misfortunes that have or shall come to the Hurt, Detriment or Damage of the said Goods and Merchandise and Ship and or any part thereof.*

The following list of definitions will aid in translating and understanding this archaic wording:

- *Perils of the Sea:* damage due to action of wind, waves, lightning, stranding, collisions, damage from salt water, ice, fog, etc., but excluding damage in the course of navigation.
- *Thieves:* robbery by force; pilferage, etc., is not covered.
- *Jettison:* voluntary disposal of cargo, fittings, fuel, etc. for lightening ship, for the common good.
- *Men of War and Enemies:* includes any and all actions of belligerency resulting in loss.
- *Letters of Mart and Countermart:* permission of belligerent governments to their citizenry authorizing confiscation of property.
- *Takings at Sea and Arrests:* capture with view of retaining possession.
- *Restraints and Detainment:* applies to any and all restrictions to the lawful movements of the vessel, resulting in loss.
- *Barratry:* loss due to sabotage, negligence, or willful damage by members of the crew.
- *Others:* misfortunes, losses, damage to goods, etc.

Marine insurance can be subdivided into the following categories: cargo, hull, freight, builders risk, and marine loss insurance. An operator will normally carry all but builders risk insurance, but negotiating each risk separately, even with different underwriters, can often be advantageous. This is especially true in the common case where a deductible clause is included, as the underwriter will quote lower premiums for the policy if total evaluation of risk is lower (for example, the cost of separate insurance for hull and machinery, each of $1,000,000 value with $5,000 deductible, will be cheaper than an equivalent policy written on the complete ship valued at $2,000,000).

Keeping the vessel's senior operating personnel fully informed about coverage and procedure for all possible claims is of prime importance. Records, signed testimony, list of witnesses, condition of equipment before and after incidents, and so forth must all be recorded using a standard procedure. Records of even the smallest irregularities must be forwarded to the technical department of the company and incorporated into the records of the vessel. Surveyors should always be called in for large material damages.

2.5.1. Cargo Insurance

Cargo insurance is usually negotiated for a single voyage and a particular cargo (a single vessel may have hundreds of cargo interests), and the underwriter is liable as soon as goods are loaded and remains so until they are safely landed. The definition of "loaded" and "landed" is complex and interpreted in light of legal precedents. Some cargoes have liability limitations and are covered under what is termed the "sweeping memorandum" (explosives, dangerous cargoes, cargoes in advanced state of spoilage, etc.).

2.5.2. Hull Insurance

Hull insurance is usually issued for one year but may be made out per voyage or other time period. Although voyage policies define the trip to be covered and limit deviations, time policies impose no specific limitations unless they specify, for example, that the vessel may not exceed a stated latitude or a similar general restriction. Hull insurance can be issued for part risks only, at a much reduced rate for vessels laid up or undergoing repair. Hull insurance premiums can also be substantially reduced by covering "total loss only." The insurer always assumes certain implied warranties, such as the seaworthiness of the vessel and the legality of the venture, and prohibits "unnecessary deviations."

The valuation of a vessel for insurance purposes presents complications. Manifestly, the insured should be fully protected, but valuation should not be such as to induce willful destruction of the vessel. Also, the actual value of a vessel is difficult to establish. With varying building costs and estimates of depreciation, improvements, and damages, generally no single "objective" determination can be made. The shipowner will quote the replacement cost plus a loss-of-opportunity value, while the insurer will evaluate the vessel by first cost minus reasonable depreciation. The result is normally a compromise between the conflicting viewpoints. (Hull and cargo policies contain a variety of clauses too numerous to mention here and are normally based on precedents.)

2.5.3. Freight Insurance

Freight is money payable for the hire of a vessel or for the conveyance of cargo or passengers from one port to another. The operator insures himself against nonpayment, delays, devaluation, and so forth. Freight insurance is also issued for "dead freight," where ship space was engaged by a merchant but subsequently shipment was not made. "Future freight insurance" is another form in which a definite contract has been entered into for conveyance of cargo at a future date, which at the time is not forthcoming. Similarly, at higher premiums, policies are also issued for "anticipated freight," in which case a ship merely expects a cargo.

2.5.4. Builders Risk Insurance

Builders risk insurance relates to risk in construction and often to repairing of hulls. Marine losses are divided into total and partial. Total loss (actual or constructive) renders a ship irretrievably useless. Partial loss can be divided into general average, particular average, and salvage. Another kind of loss is "abandonment." This complicated legal situation is of little consequence, as it occurs very rarely.

2.5.5. General Average

General average covers losses and expenditures that result from sacrifice of an interest voluntarily made by the vessel's master for the safety of the vessel and cargo in time of real distress and which must be repaid proportionately by each.

2.5.6. Particular Average

Particular average refers to partial losses due to accident and is paid only by the insurer of part damage and is not regarded as a general average loss. This may be damage to certain cargo, a part of the vessel, or its machinery. A particular average claim may also arise from loss of freight, profit, or commissions.

2.5.7. Salvage

Salvage has several meanings; it may refer to an underwriter's value of property that has been saved or to the size of award granted under maritime law to a salvager for services rendered in saving property or life at sea. The value of "salvage" varies with respect to the employ of salvors. (A ship owned by the same company will be awarded a much smaller salvage premium than an unrelated vessel.)

2.5.8. Membership Associations

Marine insurance protects shipowners primarily against partial or total loss of their own vessels and seldom covers all "second party" claims. Protection against the balance of such claims, and other liabilities arising from operations, is usually provided by membership associations of shipowners. Contractual and/or third-party liabilities may be covered in this way, depending on the rules of the association. Contractual liabilities are those arising out of the contract of affreightment; third-party liabilities are primarily those arising out of negligent operation of the vessel. Early associations were, accordingly, called "Protecting and Indemnity Clubs"—protection against claims for negligent operation, indemnity against cargo claims.

The mutual associations are composed of owners who insure the commercially uninsurable portion of their vessels and liabilities by contributing to meet the losses, as they arise. Sufficient charges are levied to cover management costs and claims. Mutual associations do not generally have reserves. Where originally the claims were merely prorated on tonnage, now they are carefully allocated to reflect owner's standards of operation and exposure to risk. Clubs may reinsure their risks, in accordance with their regulations.

Marine insurance encompasses a vast field on which libraries have been written. An attempt has only been made to emphasize and define the most common terms and to explain the general theory underlying these terms.

2.6. Physical Factors in Sea Transport

The International Load Line Convention, to which over eighty nations subscribe, is a voluntary international agreement with respect to safe loading restrictions. The convention divides the oceans into summer, winter, and tropical zones and accordingly prescribes the load line and freeboard of all vessels above 150 tons gross. Periods of validity for the freeboard lines in the different zones are fixed and have a marked influence on trading. A ship legally loaded in one zone may inadvertently contravene the rules when entering another zone unless its draft has changed sufficiently to be in compliance with the load lines of that zone. Maximum revenue is obtained by arranging loading, sequences, and schedules in such a way that the final port of loading is in a summer or tropical zone. Bunkers and stores will be consumed en route to a more restricted zone to give a legal arrival draft. Legal considerations apart, loading is constrained by the ship's stability requirements and capacity to resist stresses. Generally, appropriate reserves of both are designed into a vessel, and the legal requirements are paramount. If, however, a ship is converted for another trade, or chartered into a trade widely different from that for which it was designed, its loading may be dictated primarily by considerations of strength and stability. It may be advantageous in such a case to apply for "alternative tonnage" or modified gross and net tonnage measurements. These are calculated in the same manner. The alternative tonnage applies only when the tonnage mark (see Figure 2–1) is submerged.

The United States Coast Guard defines "Zones and Seasonal Areas," to which certain load lines apply during specified periods or seasons. In the Atlantic Ocean, the Tropical Zone (T), for example, is generally defined as an area between the Tropic of Capricorn and Latitutde 10° North, while the Summer Zone (S) in the Atlantic Ocean extends south of the Tropical Zone to Latitude 34° South and north to Latitude 36°. Other zones are similarly defined. The zones usually extend to different latitudes in the various oceans. Similarly, the timing and duration of the seasons are different for the various locations.

2.6.1.　*Tides*

Tides generally constrain shipping schedules because they condition the times of approach or entry and the maximum drafts for ports, estuaries, and canals. They can increase or reduce ships' speed and maneuverability, and schedules must take into account the strength and direction of tidal currents, as well as the times of high and low water and resultant drafts. Tides also restrict the service that can be obtained in shallow ports. Hull insurance normally requires that the vessel be "AA" (always afloat), even though many vessels can ground with no ill effects and continue operations throughout the tidal cycle.

2.6.2.　*The Effects of Seasons on Shipping*

The seasonal influence on sea transport is appreciable. The transport of agricultural crops, such as rice, sugar, grain, and fruit, must take place during the relatively short harvest times. As the storage capacity of most producing countries is limited, immediate shipment to consumer countries is essential. Even activities like whaling, trading of frozen meat, and lumbering are seasonal. Sea transport in some areas depends on the navigability of the waters and ports. All these factors cause large fluctuations in the amounts of cargoes carried. Taking an average of world shipping demand, it is found that January to April are the months of the lightest shipping requirements, while June to October are the months of maximum demand.

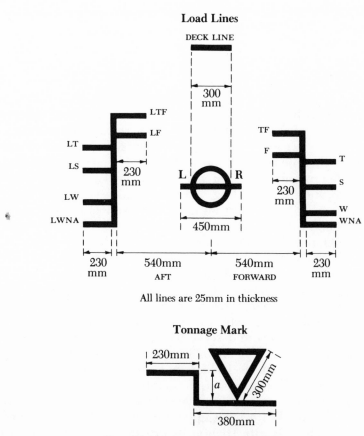

Load Lines

All lines are 25mm in thickness

Tonnage Mark

Note: Distance *a* is 1/48 molded draft to tonnage mark. All lines are 25mm in thickness.

Figure 2-1 Load Lines and Tonnage Mark. Utilized in conjunction with defined zones and seasonal areas, initials on either side of the plimsoll line are those of the classification society, such as Lloyd's Register or the American Bureau of Shipping. The other initials indicate the depth to which a ship may be loaded in salt and freshwater during different times of the year and in different zones of the globe. (*Source:* Lloyd's Register of Shipping, *"Rules for the Construction of Ships."*)

2.6.3. *Weather Routing*

Today winds are of minor importance. The exploitation of ocean currents, which run at up to five knots, and avoidance of bad weather are the primary physical determinants of ships' routes. Individually adapted routes (tracks), based on current meteorological and oceanographic data and the ship's operational characteristics are available from private and government organizations. The initial course is modified at intervals, as the ship's own reports and further physical data reach the routing center via radio telegraph. The service is highly cost effective in many cases, and trade-offs can be arranged, for example, between fuel economy and schedule considerations, to suit the operator's requirements.

2.7. Trade Routes and Trades

Once loading and discharging terminals are set, routing considerations are determined. They include fixed and variable costs, mileage, load line restraints, weather, navigational hazards, fueling and supply facilities, and schedule considerations. The final decision will reflect these and other requirements of the immediate situation. Nevertheless, the location of exporting or producing areas in relation to the overseas market is the most important determinant of the route a commodity takes when it moves in oceangoing trade. Other physical factors that influence the routes are normally secondary (for example, navigational hazards such as ice, currents, winds, and coastal passages). In most countries industrial centers or the natural outlets of industrial regions have become shipping terminals, but strategic location or good access to natural resources and internal transport routes may be a deciding factor. A port may also be located at a crossroads of trade routes and serve as an important transit area. Fueling facilities and costs are another important factor. Also, during wars strategic ports, such as Halifax or Gibraltar, will disrupt accepted routes to satisfy tactical requirements.

Ocean trade routes converge on geographic points that are fairly well defined. The world's major shipping lanes are often designated by adjectives such as North Atlantic, North Pacific, South African, South American, South Pacific, or Indian. The Federal Maritime Commission has officially recognized thirty-one trade routes as being essential to the economy of the United States. U.S.-flag vessels maintaining scheduled services on these lanes are eligible for operating subsidies. With one exception the government has followed a policy of limiting operating subsidies to a single line on each of the thirty-one routes to prevent competition among U.S.-flag services. Recently, however, the recommendation has been made that several operators be aided on parallel lines, particularly if the operators maintain multiple services on several routes concurrently.

2.7.1. Trade Patterns

For the past two decades seaborne trade has reflected the primary importance of oil, followed by iron ore, grain, and coal. Though the value of these trades lags behind the value of general cargo, oil, iron, grain, and coal account for the bulk of the ton-mileage and therefore determine the volume of shipping requirements. Interestingly, the amount of dry cargo carried has remained practically constant for about thirty years, while liquid cargoes have increased from negligible quantities to comprise over half the tonnage carried, and dry bulk cargo has become a specialized trade. Another important point is that the average distance cargo is carried has increased substantially, indicating a decrease in importance of inter-European and coastal trade. With the development of modern technology, production centers of commodities have become more concentrated at places of minimum marginal production costs—a tendency that reduces final costs appreciably. Development of output and export volumes between 1963 and 1978 is shown in Table 2–3 for agriculture, mining, and manufacturing.

2.7.2. The Oil Trade

The main oil-producing centers are North America, the Middle East, South America, Europe, and the Far East. The picture changes considerably when export tonnages are considered—the Middle East and Africa are the main exporting areas. Lately, China has discovered further reserves, and the future may show a production shift to Mexico, Brazil, and Canada.

Since 1973, the growth of world consumption of oil has slowed to about 1 percent per year, as a result of slowed economic growth, increased oil prices, and deliberate conservation attempts. This growth has derived largely from continued expansion of oil consumption in the developing countries (including the oil-exporting countries themselves). Increased seaborne movements of oil occurred during the period 1973–1977, reflecting annual growth rates (Table 2–4) of more than 20 percent in U.S. crude imports, which began to decline in 1978.

Table 2–3   Development of World Exports and Production, 1963, 1973–1978

	1963	1973	1974	1975	1976	1977	1978
World Exports							
Volume (1963 = 100)							
Total	100	231	239	232	258	269	284
Agricultural products	100	147	142	149	163	166	179
Minerals[a]	100	195	190	176	184	188	190
Manufactures	100	280	304	290	328	344	363
World Commodity Output							
Volume (1963 = 100)							
All commodities	100	180	185	183	196	205	214
Agriculture	100	128	130	134	137	139	144
Mining	100	171	174	171	181	191	195
Manufacturing	100	197	203	200	216	217	238

SOURCE: *International Trade 1978/79*, "General Agreement on Tariffs and Trade," Geneva, 1979.

[a] Including fuels and nonferrous metals.

Table 2–4   Imports of Crude Petroleum into Industrial Countries, 1973–1977

	Million Tons			Annual Rate of Growth (percent)					
	1973	1977	1978	1973–1974	1974	1975	1976	1977	1978
United States	161	362	348	22.4	6.2	19.2	46.0	21.4	−6.9
Canada	46	34	31	−7.3	−13.1	2.5	−12.2	−5.6	−8.0
Japan	245	237	230	−0.8	−2.9	−5.9	2.2	3.4	−2.7
EC	607	491	501	−5.2	−6.3	−17.1	7.4	−3.2	0.0
EFTA	42	50	46	4.4	4.7	0.0	13.6	0.0	−9.8
Total	1101	1174	1156	1.6	−3.6	−7.3	13.7	4.8	−3.4

SOURCES: *International Trade 1978/1979, International Trade 1977/1978*, "General Agreement on Tariffs and Trade," UNCTAD, Geneva, 1978 and 1979.

2.7.3.   The Coal Trade

The trade in all types of coal was once the most important of the tramp trades, accounting for over 30 percent of all cargoes carried. Today the trade in "hard" coal for coking and steam coal for power generation appears to be receiving fresh impetus from increased oil prices. The size of the hard coal trade correlates with the level of European Economic Community (EEC) and Japanese steelmaking. The United States, once the major exporter, is now joined by Australia, South Africa, Canada, and Poland, among others.

2.7.4.　The Iron Ore Trade

Iron ore is generally transported in large, long-haul ore carriers or oil/bulk/ore carriers (OBOs), which carry oil or bulk commodities on the return leg. This trade is generally governed by long-term freighting agreements, although there is a small spot tonnage market. The major exporting countries are Africa, India, the Philippines, Chile, and Brazil, while the main importers are the United States, Germany, England, Japan, Ialy, and France. The iron ore and coal trades comprise nearly 40 percent of all dry cargo (by weight) and are highly significant in generating bulk-carrier demand.

2.7.5.　The Grain Trade

Although some grain-exporting countries would like to reduce their involvement with agricultural exports, the growth of world population and the increased demand for meat and poultry feedstuff will probably sustain the grain trades at the high levels of the seventies. World wheat trade is principally from the United States, Argentina, Australia, Canada, and the EEC to the developing countries. The United States also dominates the coarse grain trade. The world trade in rice represents a mere 2 to 3 percent of world production, and the pattern is variable. Only comparatively small tonnages are transported, and these mainly in the Far Eastern zone. Importers are China, Japan, India, and Malaysia. Exporters are Burma, Thailand, and China.

Other important trades include coffee and tropical beverages, sugar, oil seeds, pulp and wood, and other foodstuffs, but these will not be discussed here. Table 2–5 shows the growth of output and export volumes of the three gross categories of goods and conveys the overall development of world trade.

2.7.6.　The Passenger Trade

Contrary to popular belief, the passenger trade plays a very minor role in shipping. Most passenger trade routes are not self-supporting and are usually maintained only for reasons of prestige, national pride, or as an essential service. On the North Atlantic (the most significant of the passenger routes), nearly all the larger operators were directly or indirectly subsidized. From World War I to 1950, traffic decreased from 1.5 million to 0.5 million passengers carried. The decline has continued, precipitated by airline competition.

Passenger traffic on routes other than the North Atlantic was always of lesser importance and normally was maintained in combination

Table 2–5   Percentage Growth of World Exports and Production, 1963–1978

	1963–1973	1973–1978	1975	1976	1977	1978
World Commodity Output						
All commodities	6	3.5	−1	7	4.5	4
Agriculture	2.5	2.5	3	2	2	3
Mining	5.5	2.5	−1.5	6	5.5	2
Manufacturing	7	4	−1.5	8	5	5
World Exports						
Total	8.5	4	−3	11	4.5	6
Agricultural products	4	4	5	9.5	2	8
Minerals[a]	7	−.5	−7.5	4.5	2	1
Manufacturers	11	5.5	−4.5	13	5	6

SOURCE: *International Trade 1978/79*, "General Agreement on Tariffs and Trade," UNCTAD, Geneva, 1979.

[a] Including fuels and nonferrous metals.

with mail or express cargo liner service. These passenger services are also being phased out. Immigrant and pilgrim ships have almost entirely disappeared. However, amenity travel may increase or at least sustain itself during the coming decade, as leisure and personal affluence increase absolutely.

2.8.   Ship Types and Uses

The number of ship types in existence is as large as the number of different trades. In a specific trade, the kind of cargo carried usually determines the most desirable type of vessel, although other factors are considered, such as:

- The route of the vessel;
- The draft available at loading and discharging ports;
- The passages to be navigated;
- Average voyage distance;
- Quality and availability of personnel, port facilities available; and
- Maintenance and docking services accessible, etc.

Nearly every vessel eventually undergoes some alterations in hull construction and form, loading equipment, crew/passenger accommodation, and propulsion plant. Although shipbuilding does not lend itself easily to "mass production" methods, limited (structural) standardization is being attempted with success.

Notable exceptions occurred during World Wars I and II, when a standard system of shipbuilding was evolved to produce large numbers of ships by "prefabrication" methods. The only important criterion was to build vessels as speedily as possible for the conveyance of cargoes necessary for the war effort. These vessels were not constructed to meet requirements of any specific trades, and consequently they were not popular for permanent replacement of commercial tonnage. Shipowners everywhere have their own ideas, based on long experience, convention, and even prejudice, as to what is best suited for the work to be undertaken. They specify accordingly. The prefabrication system was a necessity during the war and definitely helped to win it, thus attaining its objective. From the shipowners' point of view, however, the utility of these vessels is very limited.

Space considerations limit a detailed presentation and analysis of ship types, but some of the definitions and terms will be restated for reasons of completeness. By and large all merchant ships can be grouped under the following three headings:

- *Full scantling ships*—designed to carry heavy, dense cargoes, and therefore constructed with heavier plating and framing. Freeboard is measured from uppermost continuous deck, and the freeboard assigned is the minimum possible. Many variations of this basic type are possible; for example, raised quarter vessels, or raised poop deck vessels. Representative ships include bulk carriers, tankers, coal carriers, wood pulp, and heavy machinery ships.
- *Shelter deck ships*—can be either closed or open shelter deckers. Open types are specially designed for volume cargo and do not include the tween or shelter deck in freeboard requirements. They require a well or a tonnage opening and can actually be considered ships with a continuous superstructure. Shelter deck space is therefore excluded from "gross tonnage" as the uppermost deck is technically not watertight. Closed shelter deckers do not have tonnage openings, and the uppermost deck is therefore used for freeboard measurements. However, this ship is built with relatively light scantlings and is assigned a load draft somewhat less than maximum. The shelter deck is not exempted from gross tonnage.
- *Special ships*—a multitude of types, including passenger, combination passenger-cargo, liquid, gas, container, ferry boats, fish factories, wood carriers, refrigerated ships, tankers, and fruit carriers. Most special design ships are a variation of the basic full scantling or shelter-deck vessel, and can be categorized as in Table 2–6.

Ship construction is a large-scale, highly concentrated international industry. Competition for contracts often acquires nonmonetary di-

Table 2–6　Summary of Ship Functions

Type of Cargo	Type of Ship
Dry general	Refrigerated carrier
	Cargo liner
	Dry cargo tramp
	Multipurpose general cargo
	Roll-on/roll-off
	Cellular containership
	Trailer—containership
	Trailership
	Fruit (ventilated-refrigerated) carrier
	Universal cargo ship
	Automobile (car) ships
	Barge carrier (cellular)
	Barge carrier (horizontal shelf)
	Pallet ship
Specialized dry	Lumber carrier
	Car ferry
	Paper carrier
Dry bulk	Gypsum carrier
	Cement carrier
	Coal carrier
	Oil/bulk/ore (OBO) carrier
	Grain carrier
	Ore carrier
	Sugar carrier
Liquid bulk	Crude oil tanker
	Products tanker
	Slurry tanker
	Oil/bulk/ore (OBO) tanker
	Wine tanker
	Milk tanker
	Chemical tanker
	Liquefied petroleum gas (LPG) tanker
	Liquefied natural gas (LNG) tanker

mensions, such as availability of berth space and terms of payment. Governments frequently support national shipbuilding industries by providing financial support or mortgage guarantees. The United States guarantees 75 percent to 87.5 percent of the loans taken out by U.S. firms to purchase ships from U.S. yards. Italy, Japan, Sweden, Germany, and the United Kingdom also provide some form of financial support for national and foreign purchasers of ships built in their respective yards. The United States provides construction differential subsidies for vessels built in U.S. shipyards for U.S.-flag operations. These subsidies are based on the estimated cost differences between producing ships in foreign and U.S. yards. As such, they reduce, but do not eliminate, the incentive for producing ships in foreign yards. For example, a vessel built with a construction differential subsidy must remain a U.S.-flag vessel. If, on a cost basis, the potential ship buyer is indifferent to purchasing a vessel constructed in the United States or abroad, this restriction might be an inducement to buy abroad.

2.9. The International Organization and Management of Shipping Companies

Until the first quarter of this century, shipping was concentrated in the hands of owner/managers, family concerns, and small partnerships. Today, corporate ownership of shipping companies predominates, a trend brought about by the rapid increase in the size of vessels, technological advancements, the increased complication of management, and last, but not least, the greatly increased capital required per ship.

Although the prevailing form of organization in the shipping industry is the corporation, other significant forms also exist. The private management companies and industrially owned companies control appreciable fleets. Management companies may be private firms operating public companies (often the case where the original firm has gone public but the old proprietors retain close connections), or they may be public companies managing single vessels or whole fleets for shipowners. Industrially owned companies are generally susidiaries established expressly to provide specialized shipping services to the parent. These are becoming more popular as independent sources of transport manifest disinterest in contracts of affreightment.

In some countries, particularly the newly independent or newly industrializing nations, shipping companies are government owned and/or controlled. This form of management also applies to countries with strong nationalistic leanings. Although modern economic factors have tended to force sole proprietorship off the shipping horizon, interestingly the very small, often single-ship, owner and the very large sole-owner-controlled concern have gained great influence in the shipping industry lately. This applies particularly to the foremost maritime nations, Norway and Holland on the one hand, and Greece and the "Flags of Convenience" on the other. The influence of these companies is especially noticeable in tramp shipping and the charter market and is probably explained by their operational flexibility. The functions of the shipping company management comprise policy, legal, engineering, commercial, operating, research, development, and accounting activities. The bureaucratic form of company structure reflects these functions by providing for directors, company officers, and functional departmentalization. Smaller companies often delegate functions such as legal duties and research and development by using independent law firms and subscribing to ship research organizations. A firm operating worldwide liner services, which carries cargo and passengers in subsidized and nonsubsidized services, has been chosen to exemplify typical liner company organization. The operation of a fleet of one-commodity cargo carriers (tankers, tramps, or heavily time-chartered vessels, ore/bulk/oil, and so on), requires a less complex organizational structure.

2.9.1. *Traditional Shipping Management Structures*

The firm is organized as a corporation; stockholders elect directors, who in turn elect company officers. Though it is not the case in the exemplary firm, in many shipping companies the directors are also executive heads of departments. The directors are in charge of corporate planning and strategy, including ship acquisition and scrapping. They also deal with matters that cannot be delegated to any one department—for example, diversification into activities connected with offshore energy supplies and cooperation with other shipowners in consortia and cargo pools.

There are nine departments, reflecting a distinction between "line" and "staff" functions, each of which is presided over by an executive. The freight and passenger traffic departments are the revenue-producing departments. The operating department is the production or "line" department. Finance, public relations, service and supply, research, claims, and the general department "staff" are designed to service all others. As most expenditures will be made by the operating department, its degree of efficiency will directly affect the profitability of the company.

The geographical scope of operations has a profound effect on the organizational structure of traditional liner companies. Adequate representation has to be assured in all areas of operation. In addition to company headquarters, offices are maintained in all the major ports of call. It is also advisable to maintain a liaison staff, headed by a high executive, in the capital of each country served. In our example, a large company with a worldwide operation, small replicas of company headquarters are established on each continent. These Far Eastern, European, South Pacific, and so on head offices will

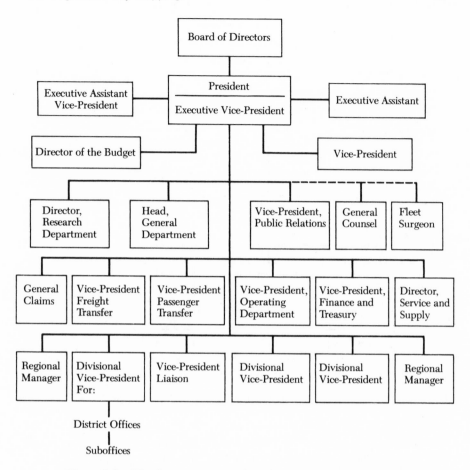

Figure 2–2 The Organization of Shipping Company Management.

be under a vice-president of the company who coordinates operations in the area and formulates overall policies. Throughout the company, functional organization is maintained, and each department exercises line authority within the scope of its activity.

Executives who administer the company's policies and activities in a particular division are delegated line authority, and personnel report to them administratively. Functionally, personnel may also report to the head office. For instance, a key person dealing with passenger traffic in the European division reports administratively to the executive in charge of that division, but functionally to the vice-president in charge of passenger traffic. The formal organization chart in Figure 2–2 depicts the arrangement. A brief description of the functions of individual departments follows.

The subdivisions of the freight traffic department (Figure 2–3) are

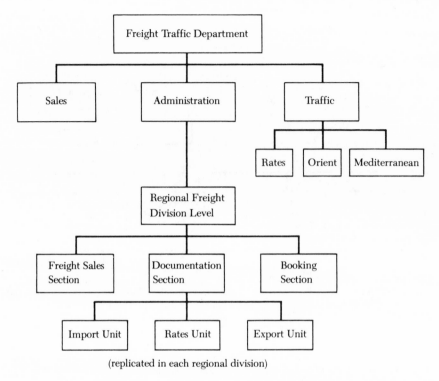

(replicated in each regional division)

Figure 2-3 Organization of Traffic Department.

freight, sales, traffic, and traffic administration. Freight personnel are located at all the company offices; in addition, agents are appointed in all places of interest to provide freight service to all prospective shippers. Rates, changes in schedules, handling procedures, booking, quotas, freight sales programs, terminus operation, and similar items are handled by this department. Records of tariffs, formulation, conference procedures, and masters' reports are kept and analyzed.

The subdivisions of the passenger traffic department are passenger administration, sales promotion, and service department division. Responsibilities include passenger traffic, analysis of competition, computation (of fares, agency commissions, and revenues), utilization of vessels, budgetary matters pertaining to passengers, clearance (health, customs, and immigration), booking, and refunding of claims. In addition, the passenger department supervises services and maintains offices or agents in all the ports of call of passenger vessels. This department also deals directly with travel agents and other organizations interested in travel arrangements.

The divisions of the operating department include marine engineering, cargo handling, and terminal and port stewards divisions. This department is responsible for all phases of ship and terminal operation. Each division is headed by a superintendent with a staff of assistants, some of whom may be delegated to suboffices. Operating, sailing, and maintenance instructions are issued by this department. Personnel are selected, expenditures approved, and reports (and logs) checked by the staff. Coordination of new construction, decisions on laying up, obsolescence, improvements, and changes are all handled by this department.

The finance department takes charge of matters pertaining to insurance, accounting and banking, and all phases of finance, including operating and construction differential subsidies, credits, mortgages, premiums, pay, and so forth. The public relations department has charge of all advertising, promotion, and publicity. The claims department coordinates and administers all claim activities, both domestic and foreign. The service and supply department coordinates procurement of all stores, equipment, and supplies.

The general department is the service department, whose functions include training, grievances, collective bargaining, mail room, switchboard operation, working conditions, office facilities, etc. The research department works in general improvement of procedures, construction, operation analysis, efficiency analysis, and any other field that may yield reduction in expenditure or increase in revenue.

2.9.2. Contrasting Management Systems

The organization of a company may reflect external factors, such as government regulation, which are independent of other factors, such as the company's trade and geographic sphere of operations. Or, companies attempting to meet the demands of rapidly changing markets or evolving technologies may decentralize and create independent divisions. This is an "organismic" form of organization. The biological analogy is based on a simple view of specialization.

A company frequently adopts, either consciously or unconsciously, an "organismic" structure when it intends to exploit an unpredictably developing opportunity. There is no "right" hierarchy; rather, managerial roles and functions adapt to the requirements of the situation, an approach that involves the constant upgrading of management skills. Managers stay focused on company goals and are more aware of the factors that affect the company's shipping operations and commercial success. Where a shipping company is active in traditional, as well as technologically developing, enterprises, managerial conflict may arise between the proponents of the traditional approach and those of the evolving approach. A conflict not resolved through mediation may persist until the company grows to the extent that divisions can be established to serve the changing market/technology. The adoption of divisions as the solution to problems of organization is complemented by the organismic management structure.

Traditional and organismic management structures both represent rational forms of organization but are appropriate for different conditions. A traditional management system is appropriate for fully known, slowly changing conditions. It develops specialized tasks by which the problems and activities of the shipping company are broken down. Each activity exhibits techniques and purposes distinct from those of the company as a whole. The rights, obligations, and technical methods used by each role and department are precisely specified. These rights, obligations, and methods translate into the responsibilities of a position and are ossified in the job description.

A complex hierarchy of control, authority, and communication is reinforced by the concentration of information at the higher levels of management. Interaction between members of the company, therefore, tends to be vertical—that is, between superior and subordinate. Consequently, instructions and decisions issued by superiors tend to govern operations and working behavior. The superiors may also insist on loyalty to the company and emphasize obedience to superiors. More importance and prestige may be attached to internal (local) than to general (cosmopolitan) knowledge, experience, and skill.

The organismic management structure (Figure 2–4) is appropriate to changing conditions that constantly give rise to unforeseen requirements. These requirements cannot be broken down or distributed automatically by using the functional roles of the traditional structure. The organismic structure is characterized by the employees' contribution of special knowledge and experience to the common task of the company. The individual task appears "realistic," as defined by the total situation of the company, though adjusted and continually redefined through interaction with others. Responsibility is no longer a limited field of rights, obligations, and methods. Individuals do not pass responsibility for problems upward, downward, or sideways to another person. There is often a commitment to the company beyond the technical definition.

Control, authority, and communication form a network. The rules that govern the individual's work derive more from the person's community interest in the working organization than from a contractual relationship with an impersonal corporation, represented by the immediate superior. Knowledge about the technical or commercial nature of the present task may be located anywhere in the network. Concentrations of knowledge become centers of control, authority, and communication as circumstances prescribe. Communication through the organization is lateral rather than vertical:

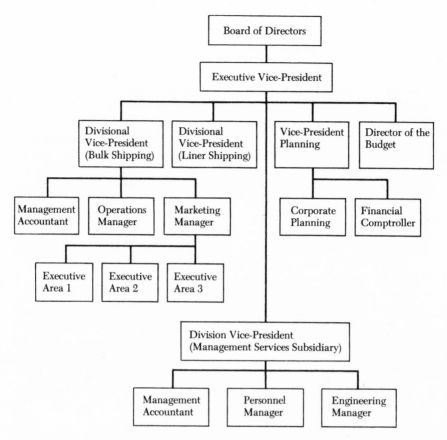

Figure 2-4 Decentralized Organization.

the communication typically consists of information and consultation rather than instructions and decisions.

Commitment to the company's goals and tasks and to the "technological ethos" is more highly valued than loyalty and obedience. Importance and prestige attach to affiliations and expertise in the industrial, technical, and commercial milieux outside the firm. Positions are differentiated according to degree of expertise. The lead in joint decisions is frequently taken by seniors, but it is presumed that the lead will be taken by whoever demonstrates the greatest knowledge and capabilities. Authority is conferred by consensus.

As the two forms of systems represent a polarity, not a dichotomy, there are intermediate stages. The relation of one form to the other is elastic, so that a shipping company oscillating between relative stability and relative change may also oscillate between the two forms. A company may (and frequently does) operate with a management system that includes features of both types.

2.10.   Seafaring Labor

Up to the middle of the nineteenth century, the seafarer's contract of employment was by law and, in fact, with the master of the vessel. The master was often owner or part-owner, with full authority to fix wages and regulate conditions aboard. If the master proved intractable, legal provisions prevented crew members from improving their lot, intolerable though conditions might be. The introduction of steamships in the 1850s, by necessitating a new order of capital investment, replaced "personal" ownership with government or institutional ownership. While the master remained the *legal* employer of the seamen, in fact responsibility for wages and conditions moved ashore to managements largely ignorant of the seafaring profession and greatly enamored of laissez-faire economic concepts. The need for protection against the effects of unregulated labor markets and operational practices led to union formation by the 1870s.

Despite the advent of maritime trade unions, the first significant changes in the seafarer's conditions came through government legislation. In some respects, shipping is an extraordinarily circumscribed industry. Seafarers are virtually wards of the state in many nations. Merchant shipping legislation tends to treat them as childlike and ignorant outside their profession and suitable objects for the anachronistic paternalism of legislators. Seafarers and ships also pose a public health problem, and as such attract considerable regulation. However, parallel with this legislative concern is a proscription on many forms of industrial action.

At the present time, a large proportion of the world's seafarers are represented by unions or associations. Their control over the supply of labor has invested them with a degree of "countervailing power," still further increased by solidarity with unions of ancillary industries. Most seafarers' unions are affiliated with the International Transport Workers Federation (ITWF) and are represented at the Maritime Sessions of the International Labor Organization. However, this control is tempered by two factors: the existence of a long-term trend to automation (presently impeded by legal considerations and job protection agreements) and the owners' power to contract for labor in a free international market. The latter usually implies recourse to a less developed country where the supply of seafarers (especially ratings) is greater. The ITWF can, of course, "black" offending ships and owners, and in many countries seamen risk personal sanctions if they desire to return to their national merchant marine after service aboard a "flag-of-convenience" ship.

Despite the troubled history of labor relations in the shipping of some countries, the benefits of collective bargaining are widely recognized. The present temper of industrial relations in shipping is conservative. Law, which still regulates large areas of maritime employment and practice, is a slow institution of social change.

2.10.1. Seafarers' Unions

Ship crews and officers are organized in unions of unlicensed and licensed personnel. Even masters, who represent the owners or operators and manage the ship, are generally members of a union.

2.10.1.1. Unlicensed Personnel

The main U.S. unions for deck personnel are the National Maritime Union (NMU), the Seafarers' International Union of North America (SIU), and the Sailors' Union of the Pacific (SUP). The first two unions were founded in 1937, following the disintegration of the old International Seafarers' Union. As in many industries, the two unions grew up independently due to the separation of the "industrial" (CIO) from the "craft" (AFL) unions. The NMU belonged to the CIO and the SIU to the AFL. Other distinctions, however, have kept the two unions at loggerheads even after the AFL-CIO merger in 1957. The NMU represents most of the crews of the subsidized part of the U.S. Merchant Fleet, while the SIU, in general, represents the unsubsidized sector. This split has caused a major divergence in policy. The main object of the NMU is to obtain large increases and fringe benefits—an objective made easier by the fact that a very large part of such increases is paid for by the federal government through increased subsidies. The SIU is much more concerned with the size of the nonsubsidized fleet. An objective of the SIU is to hold the flight of American shipowners to "flags of convenience." With this in mind, an attempt was made by both unions to extend the power of the NLRB. The U.S. Supreme Court in February 1963 ruled that the NLRB does not have control over American-owned ships under a foreign flag. This decision was, understandably, strongly supported by all foreign maritime countries who saw implications of control over all foreign-flag ships calling at U.S. ports. Unable to organize foreign crews directly, the American unions can only encourage their unionization by support of international union organizations such as the ITWF.

That so many American shipowners transfer their ships to foreign flags is not hard to understand; it can be summed up by lower costs and greater management freedom. A ship flying a flag of convenience will have lower wage and fringe benefit costs, tighter manning scales, less strict safety requirements and accommodation standards, lower taxation rates, probably a smaller initial construction cost, and certainly lower repair costs over her life.

There is good reason to feel that seafaring unions, encouraged by ship-operating subsidies, have had a considerable effect on wages and conditions in the U.S. shipping industry. After comparing today's wages and working conditions with those prevalent in the 1930s, this change can only be welcomed; however, many people think that seafaring unions are now too powerful. They point as an example to union rationing of job opportunities, which, although made illegal by the Taft-Hartley Act (1947), in practice still exists. Unions ration jobs by restricting membership and operating an effective preferential hiring procedure. Although union preferential hiring was outlawed in 1947, the unlicensed unions got around the act by enforcing preference to those having seniority on vessels under contract with the union. The unions argue that restriction of membership is necessary since the number of employment opportunities is falling.

2.10.1.2. *Licensed Personnel*

The main unions representing licensed personnel are the International Organization of Masters, Mates and Pilots (MMP—AFL), representing about 5,000 deck officers, and the National Marine Engineers' Beneficial Association (NMEBA—CIO), representing about 5,500 engineers). Other smaller unions are the Brotherhood of Marine Officers (BMO), representing 600 engineer officers; the American Radio Association (ARA—CIO), representing 600 radio officers; and Radio Officers Union (ROU—AFL), representing 400 radio officers. The affiliations of the unions of licensed personnel also tend to be divided between the AFL and the CIO. The unions of licensed personnel, like other seafaring unions, restrict membership and enforce preferential hiring, but since they represent supervisory personnel, they are exempt from various restrictions of the Taft-Hartley Act.

All unions permit owners to select masters, first mates, chief engineers, and first assistant engineers freely, as these officers directly represent the company. Licenses for officers and engineers are issued by the Coast Guard in the United States.

2.10.2. *Collective Bargaining*

The individual shipowner, economically much weaker than the union, will normally negotiate through one of the following two large employer associations:

- *The American Merchant Marine Institute, Inc.* The AMMI represents the majority of the shipping companies on the Atlantic and Gulf coasts in their negotiations with maritime labor unions. Several committees have been established with the AMMI to represent various employer groups around the bargaining table. They are not, however, empowered to bind a represented company to a contract. Each company must concur and sign a final agreement individually. Any company may refuse to ratify a final settlement and is not legally bound to accept a contract agreed to by groups with the AMMI.
- *The Pacific Maritime Association.* The PMA represents American-flag companies on the West Coast in collective bargaining with various seafaring unions. Unlike the AMMI, the agreements negotiated by PMA are binding on all companies authorizing the PMA to bargain in their behalf; contracts are executed by PMA officials rather than by each authorizing company.

A third group, an informal association of Atlantic and Gulf operators, also exists to negotiate with the Seafarers' International Union, Atlantic and Gulf District. Originally, the companies in this group were members of the AMMI, but bargaining difficulties caused the companies under contract with SIU to withdraw from the AMMI. These companies then bargained individually with the SIU until the end of World War II.

In 1945, ten of the companies having contracts with the SIU organized the Atlantic and Gulf Ship Operators Association to bargain with the SIU. The association dissolved in 1948, although group bargaining with the SIU has continued on an informal basis. When a union contract reopens, the SIU invites all companies to join in the negotiations. Most companies send representatives for consideration of union demands and selection of a subcommittee to carry on negotiations. After the negotiating committee has met with the union, the full committee reconvenes to develop bargaining strategy. The negotiating subcommittee then resumes bargaining with the union, although this committee has no power to bind any company to settlement. After the group agreement, the union concludes negotiations with each company separately.

Generally, current collective bargaining agreements in the industry stipulate (1) that, on request, unions dispatch qualified and competent men from the top of the rotary hiring list; (2) that these employees must be satisfactory to the operators, who may turn down or discharge them, provided bona fide reasons are given for the action taken; and (3) that neither the operators nor the unions may discriminate against anyone for union or nonunion affiliation.

The collective bargaining agreements entered into by the different unions are closely related for all practical purposes, stipulating approximately the same wage scales, hours of labor, and other working conditions for the respective licensed and unlicensed seamen covered by the contracts. The basic differences among the various agreements relate to types of ships—cargo, passenger, or tanker. Benefits gained by any one union are often incorporated in the other union agreements.

One important exception to the standardization of terms is found in the current Sailors Union of the Pacific (SUP) contract, affecting hours of work and certain premium pay practices. In the 1955 negotiations, the SUP established a wage pattern unique in maritime history, which incorporated certain premium payments in the basic monthly wages. The previously established working hours at sea and in port were maintained, based on 56 hours a week at sea and 40 hours a week for dayworkers both at sea and in port—hours that are similar in all union contracts. Until this time, watchstanders were paid a premium rate for all hours worked on Saturday and Sunday.

The new contract eliminated the premium pay for Saturday and Sunday as such and incorporated the average amount earned by watchstanders and dayworkers in a month into the basic monthly wage scale. The result was the elimination of the special pay rate from the agreement, and this pay was reflected in the new wage rates. This new wage pattern did not actually affect the workweek, since all the watchstanders work 56 hours at sea. What it did was eliminate the extra-pay premium provision for Saturdays and Sundays while retaining the extra pay. This agreement, however, still contains provisions for a special rate for certain specified items. Other agreements in the seafaring industry still provide premium pay for all hours over 40 per week, and all unions stipulate that watchstanders at sea work 56 hours per week.

2.10.3. *Determinants of Industrial Relations on Board Ship*

The ship is a small, physically isolated, occupational community. Communication, replenishment, indeed *any* recourse to shore-based services are difficult and often subject to the elements. Interchanges between owners and ship are often delayed and usually terse. Consequently, the employer's part in industrial relations is played by the master—also an employee—while the vessel is away. The master's role in shipboard industrial relations is circumscribed by tradition, the owner's management patterns, and the ship's social climate.

The seafarer's working community is also a social community, and for the duration of the voyage, there are few contacts with others.

Even supportive communication with the seafarer's family or native community is circumscribed by expense and schedules. These restrictions mean that the vessel's peace and efficiency depend on the success of various tension-relieving techniques, particularly those regulating interpersonal relations. Privacy becomes sought after, and is often a prerogative of rank, or a medium of exchange in the community. Recreation and routine alike are integrated or collectivized.

The physical limits to movement aboard ship are difficult to conceive. Access to many areas is restricted for safety or status reasons, thus further reducing the common areas. Release of physical tension after days of confinement may be explosive. Mixing of work and leisure areas also contributes to a low-key, uncritical social ethos.

The social structure of the ship is fragmented. Crew members are differentiated by rank, department, and distinctions such as age, class, and place of origin. The officer-rating distinction is particularly harmful: it counters the egalitarian trend of the supporting society and has some damaging operational effects. One effect is to further stratify the small social community aboard.

Turnover is extremely high among seafarers. Many entrants to the profession leave promptly, in the first throes of culture shock, and a majority leave within a few years, although a portion reenter. Seafarer career patterns show wide variation; some intersperse seafaring episodes with shore employment, while others work steadily and progress to command. The pattern depends on the shipboard group to which the individual belongs. The problem of discontinuity in manning is partly solved by the process of role formalization. Minimal, circumscribing job and behavior specifications are widely known and

> make it possible for a seaman to man a ship without developing personally balanced relationships with work comrades. Explicit formalization . . . must have developed as an answer to the demand that a ship must be able to emerge as a cooperative unit at one stroke without previous preparation. . . . A ship's community is an empty structure of roles, ready to be filled at short notice by a group of highly different and individualistic men.[1]

Role formalization ensures at least minimal effectiveness of operations. It also encourages rigid organization and a "sufficing" frame of mind, for ship members tend to identify occupants with their roles. The overemphasis of the occupational identity, together with the "stimulus paucity" of the seafarer's environment, exposes the seafarer to a risk of alienation from self.

---

[1] V. Aubert and O. Arner, "Work and its structural setting," *Acta Sociologica* 3 (1959):200–19.

2.11. Ship Maintenance and Repair

Except for crew wages, maintenance, repair, and stores, costs can be assumed to be fairly equal for all operators on similar runs. Under a cost equalization clause, amortization and insurance payable by the U.S. operator is only due for a fair market value of the vessel. The operator's financial expenses are not in excess of those paid by a foreign operator. Cargo handling and fuel costs will be the same for all, and little can be done about reducing the pay differential of the operating personnel. The only major area in which an improvement in the competitive position of the U.S. Merchant Fleet can be achieved is in the field of maintenance, repair, and technical stores. The cost for these items varies among operators with respect to their runs, the condition of their fleet, and their different maintenance philosophies.

Maintenance and repair (M&R) and stores account for 12 to 15 percent of operating costs. Given our technological advance in all fields, it is astonishing to witness how archaic the maintenance and repair function is in some companies. Advances in M&R operations must be based on the superior skill, know-how, and organizational ability of this country, and the maritime industry is probably the last to take advantage of these achievements. Apparently, this situation has arisen through the comparatively sheltered economic conditions under which operators and shipyards were functioning until the early 1970s.

Disregarding the old make-and-mend method, M&R philosophies can be roughly divided into two main schools of thought. Most European operators tend to do all maintenance and routine repairs during the voyage. The ship's staff does most of the work, thus avoiding lengthy yard lay-ups and spending the minimum of time required by surveys. Efforts are mainly directed toward the continuous maintenance and survey required by the main diesel engines. The majority of U.S. operators tend to lay up their ships for general M&R once a year, during which time they attend to everything. The comparatively high speed with which U.S. repair yards operate, union rules, and the fact that most U.S. ships are steam-turbine driven are the main reasons for yearly lay-up. Either method, carried to an extreme, is probably suboptimal, and the most advantageous results will require a combination of both, together with changes in routine, usage, abolition of prejudices, instigation of cooperation, added incentive from insurance and regulatory bodies, and, most of all, taking proper advantage of all technological advances soon after they are made. The tempo of our time has increased, and, although proper caution with respect to safety and reliability must be exercised, the courageous adoption of new methods must not be delayed.

2.11.1. *The Importance of Planning*

Since most shipowners' operations are planned using statistics and experience, that the M&R phase is undertaken erratically is surprising. Planned M&R provides reliability, economy, and information for managerial guidance. Repairs can be done at the most economical places, and specialized facilities can be used. Planning also includes preventative maintenance. Although no enginemaker or shipbuilder could be expected to suggest all the things that could go wrong with the product, many problems can be anticipated and preventive routines devised. Spares can be bought well in advance. In "olden days," marine engineers prided themselves in never using a spare part as long as the worn or broken part could be repaired (by hook or by crook). Many an old ship was scrapped after thirty years' service with a complete set of spares in their original condition on the bulkhead. Now, planning allows proper weighing of the most efficient and cheapest way to counter wear. Today's engines are built to use spares, as neither shipboard nor yard facilities have the proper machining abilities; these parts are, therefore, prefitted. Services ordered well in advance can be placed on competitive bidding.

Stores and supplies, especially chemicals, paints, greases, lubricating oils, packing, jointing, hardware, ropes, tallow, boiler tubes, sanitary fittings, filters, electrical parts, and so forth, can be ordered in bulk with proper planning, thereby saving the profits of wholesalers, middlemen, and ship handlers and getting direct service and advice from the manufacturer at a probable cost reduction of over 50 percent. A well-planned M&R assures the owner of always being ready for classification and government (Coast Guard) surveys, and prevents holdup of vessels. The documentation of planned M&R provides guides to future planning of ship's machinery and services. The advantages of planning M&R are so numerous that it is surprising how little it is practiced.

2.11.2. *Planning During New Construction of Ships*

Planning of M&R starts with the construction (or actually the design) of a new vessel. Much money, labor, and time can be saved by incorporating certain features into the ship. Some of these designs may mean additional initial expense, which the design staff will have to justify, but in most instances the cost can be recovered within a short time. The following are examples that can be designed with M&R in mind.

Inaccessible spaces like cofferdams, tailshaft wells, chainlocker wells, spaces under refrigerating insulation, and so forth should be well coated with epoxy resin or other permanent corrosion preventatives. The number of inaccessible places must be kept to an absolute minimum. Main cooling water lines should be made of good copper nickel alloy or rubberized. Particular care must be taken in places like antirolling fin recesses and seachests. Spare parts should be accessible and well protected against damage and corrosion. Parts prone to corrosion, such as injection pipe bends and condenser and cooler headers, must be properly coated.

One of the major items will always be the proper inspection of all electrical contacts, insulation, switchgear, and instrumentation. No circuit should be too small to be tested. Also, all valves should be properly marked with complete and accurate data manuals, and the latest corrected plans should be supplied to the vessel. Care should be taken to ensure that all the individual manufacturer's standard spare parts and special tool chests are handed over by the shipyard for every piece of machinery onboard.

2.11.3.   *Takeover of Old or New Vessels*

The most important phase of any organized M&R schedule is the proper taking over of the vessel. Most of the above points apply only to a new vessel built to the owner's specifications, but the condition and performance of all pieces of machinery and equipment should be checked and properly noted on any ship joining the fleet. The data so obtained will form the basis of the planning for M&R. Inventory spare parts and supplies, including a record of their condition, should be taken, properly filed, and deficiencies made good. Tank spaces and other containers should be properly calibrated, and all safety equipment tested. Dates of previous government and classification inspections of all pieces of equipment must be recorded. Condition of hull, deck, hold, and tankplating should be properly investigated and noted. In the case of new vessels, application of specified coatings should be verified. If the takeover is not done properly, this basic information is lost forever.

2.11.4.   *Supplying of Vessels*

One of the most important phases of properly organized M&R is a well-organized chain of delivery of stores, tools, parts, and equipment. Well over 70 percent of all deck and engine consumable stores are standard. Estimating the normal consumption of a vessel is quite simple. Consequently, savings can be gained by ordering in bulk from wholesalers or manufacturers, thereby cutting the middleman's profits. By ensuring constant replenishment of stores, rush orders can be prevented. Technical stores are best obtained from specialized firms and electrical equipment from an electrical wholesaler or marine electrical workshop. The same applies to air conditioning, carpentry, and other technical requirements. By ordering chemicals, as well as packings, and so on, directly from the manufacturer, better consulting services for related technical problems are also assured.

Proper tools should be available for all necessary work. Much time and labor can be saved by items such as industrial vacuum cleaners, proper boiler cleaning tools, and compressed air and vacuum outlets at different positions in the engine room, and possibly over the whole vessel. The supply of spare parts requires special attention. Although most manufacturers will recommend a greater renewal rate than is actually required, ensuring that a full set of recommended spare parts is always at hand is good practice. The latest catalogs and spare part lists should always be available, and a complete reference of manufacturers' depots and addresses of representatives should be provided for every piece of equipment on the ship. The money spent to fabricate special parts, actually readily available at nominal cost, is often staggering.

An established wear rate will allow a proper ordering schedule to be devised, which requires a minimum of transportation charges for heavy spare parts. Although little standardization can be done on old vessels, great savings in spare part stock, as well as supply terms, can be achieved in new buildings. Installing some service equipment that does not exactly fulfill requirements may even pay under certain conditions if standardization is thereby maintained.

Most manufacturers maintain a large technical and service staff; surprisingly operators make little use of these services, normally free or inexpensive. Manufacturers are very interested to see their equipment in operation and may pass on or even install improvements discovered for their products by comparing service experiences.

2.11.5. *Initial M&R Routines*

Until sufficient experience with equipment is acquired, makers' recommendations should be adhered to strictly, especially in regard to new ships under guarantee. Individual repair and maintenance schedules can be planned after experience has been accumulated. To organize prevention properly, a complete checklist must be worked out, which the chief engineer must sign weekly to assure that all tasks have been performed. A complete data card, with main operating requirements, number and location of spare parts onboard, and quality and makeup of materials to be used should be displayed in a conspicuous place near every piece of machinery. A complete list with checkoff spaces must be provided; all items should be tested at regular intervals and serviced as required. The duties of all watches must be defined and routine maintenance assured for all watch-keeping operations. Scheduling operations performed at definite times and by the same personnel if schedule permits makes good sense, as only then will changes in operation and performance be noticed and equipment get the best possible care.

All of these routines, which may be termed operational mainte-nance and prevention, can normally be done by the watch-keeping staff, with the addition of "dayworkers" such as the ship's electrician or reefer engineer. The same people are also able to perform running or emergency repairs, cope with small breakdowns, or even under-take refitting. A permanent skilled fitter or mechanic can be added to the crew to be in charge of workshop operation. The availability of gas as well as electric welding onboard can also be a great money saver.

With proper planning, the ship's staff, with the addition of only one or two dayworking engineers and/or fitters, can easily do the annual overhaul of all auxiliaries. Standby auxiliaries not required for the main propulsion unit can be dismantled and refitted at sea, while others can be normally repaired during port time. The quality of the work and adjustments obtained are normally superior to those of shipyard jobs. The ship's staff tends to make sure that the work is as perfect as possible, knowing only too well that the results of bad workmanship will entail "consequent overhaul under duress."

2.11.6.   *Repairs by Shipyards*

Main propulsion unit repairs, boiler and refractory maintenance, as well as all hull and superstructure defects, should be handed over to a yard. These repairs should all be timed to coincide with the annual or special survey dates, and the ship's schedule arranged accordingly. Although the cost and availability of a dry dock is a major factor, workmanship, experience of the yard, machining fa-cilities, and location have to be considered as well. Cheap dry-dock-ing with insufficient machine shops will be a very costly proposition if essential work has to be handed to a competitor.

By informing the chosen yard of all the ship's particulars and history, as well as supplying the yard with all the important dimen-sions, much time and money can be saved. The repair can be done at a fixed-price arrangement, and specialists, as well as makers' rep-resentatives, called in with ample notice. Paint and other major material requirements can be obtained by competitive bid. Proper keelblock spacing to prevent "dead spaces" can be ascertained.

On vessels trading overseas, cleaning and other unskilled work is most economically scheduled in low-cost ports of call. Owing to the tremendous overheads of shipyards (150 to 300 percent), minor voyage repairs should always be handed to small repair firms or specialized outfits. It is well to contract a small electrical and re-frigerating repair firm to do all voyage repairs not done by shipstaff. Their overheads seldom exceed 60 to 100 percent, and a full eight hours' work is obtained per working day. (As shipyard workers report and sign out of the yard, one to three hours are lost if the ship is at her berth). Chemical cleaning, coating, or descaling should be handed to a specialized concern of repute; otherwise much damage and little positive effect can result from improper use of the harsh detergents and acids.

2.11.7. Work Order Procedure

Work handed to outside concerns should be properly defined. De-sired limitations and tolerances, as well as preferred or recommended materials, should be given. Unless the item is essential for vessel operation, a cost limit should be applied; in every case a firm estimate with detailed prices should be demanded. A complete record of work orders, removal orders, and procedure should be kept and, if pos-sible, countersigned by the repairer. The operator can thus keep a record of everything that has been done to a particular piece of machinery.

As a result of competition, many yards will give an unrealistic estimate for one essential phase of work and highly overcharge on other items. Care should be taken to always get completely itemized bids, as "packages" are nearly always to the detriment of the operator. As handling of heavy machinery parts is extremely expensive in some areas, machining should always be investigated.

2.11.8. Record Keeping

Clearly, careful documentation is the prerequisite of successful M&R, as it is for successful ship operation on the whole. Every machinery item onboard must have a data sheet, histogram, and record file. The data sheet contains all pertinent data about the item, including dimensions, manufacturers' recommendations, spare part lists, location, operating data, tolerances, and so forth. The histogram gives details of the operation, defects, breakdowns, and repairs done to the unit. The record file contains all bills and other records per-taining to this particular part of machinery. Required maintenance is also recorded on the histogram, and movements of spare parts can be entered in the data sheet. All the above information can be handled quite simply by normal IBM or similar cards and modern computing machinery and the actual accounting and bookkeeping kept to an absolute minimum.

Cards must be arranged so that insufficient maintenance, faults, excessive wear, or unduly costly repair bills are immediately conspicuous. Copies of these cards should be supplied to the operator's technical department. Manufacturers of machinery should also introduce the system, which will give them a permanent up-to-date-record of the performance of their product and indicate possible remedies and improvements to it. Sheets of operating procedures, and above all, maintenance and routine inspection checklists, should be worked out and their use be made compulsory. Data for the IBM cards are taken from the information of these lists.

By proper arrangements of the records, the efficiency, performance, reliability, and cost of proper maintenance of every piece of equipment can be judged on sight. Using a punchcard system will permit these records to be traced out electronically. Excessive wear, repair costs, or consumption of any item can be shown immediately, and preventative action can then be taken. By using statistics and correlating all the different data, costs, availability, efficiency, and degree of obsolescence can all be calculated. Timely action can be taken at minimum cost, and at the convenience of the operator.

The maritime industry would benefit if some standard of record keeping could be agreed on and if experience data were universally available. A consequent improvement of performance and design and a reduction in operating as well as construction costs would probably result.

The foregoing pages are actually an introduction to the problems involved in ship maintenance and repair. M&R problems can be handled in many different ways, and since no two ships are alike, no universal set rules can be given. Of course, with the advent of modern machinery, as well as the high cost of repairs, M&R of ships cannot be left to arbitrary decisions of the operating personnel. Preventative maintenance and proper record keeping, with the resulting possibility of proper M&R planning, are essential, not only for cost reduction but also for reliability, managerial guidance, and the overall progress of the maritime industry.

New machinery is normally evolved from experience with the old, and in the past, records of operations have always been scanty. Thus an operator would do well to hire the most proficient staff available, as well as to add to the essential operating crew at least one or two technical personnel for maintenance and repairs of auxiliaries. With a proper preventative maintenance schedule, all running repairs and overhauls of auxiliary machinery can be done by a ship's staff, while the main propulsion units, as well as boiler and hull repairs, are handed to a competent shipyard. Voyage repairs, to be done at the berth between voyages and not concerned with the main propulsion plant, are best handled by smaller repair shops. Specialized electrical, air conditioning, electronic, and other repairs should be handed to specialized firms.

Manufacturers' technical consultants should be fully utilized, as well as advice available from chemical and other suppliers. Finally, badly worn parts and machinery whose repair cost reaches 50 percent of the price of a new unit should be replaced.

Chapter 3

FRAMEWORK OF SHIPPING

International shipping is the cheapest and most widely used means of transport in international trade; well over 90 percent of all goods so traded are transported by sea. Even so, transport costs have assumed an increasing percentage of landed value of goods in international trade—a fact of major concern to developing countries that are largely dependent on export of raw or semifinished goods for foreign exchange earnings. An attempt is usually made to achieve trade flows that minimize transport requirements, although success is not often achieved. By and large, demand for international shipping is mainly a function of demand for international trade in fuel and raw materials on the one hand and manufactured goods on the other hand. Demand for shipping, as a result, is not necessarily a direct function of economic activity in terms of traditional macroeconomic factors, though an indirect link exists with an 80 to 90 percent correlation to factors such as overall production and GNP of trading partners. Time lags play an important role and must be analyzed in any study that attempts to project future demand for shipping.

Many other economic factors, such as substitution of goods or raw materials, affect shipping demand. Political and various artificial factors such as regulatory constraints also affect shipping demand. Contrary to often heard assumptions, there is significant elasticity of demand for shipping transport. Similarly, price elasticity is quite significant, reflected by wide freight and charter rate fluctuations.

Freight and charter rates depend on the interaction of a number of complex factors as shown in Figure 3–1. The most important factor is obviously the balance of shipping capacity demand and supply, which in turn depends on transport demand and ship acquisition costs. Transport demand again depends on the supply and demand for goods, as well as the imposition of trade restrictions, both of which are controlled by economic activity. In recent years an increasingly important factor in determining freight rates has been the cost of bunkers, which in many cases assumes as much as 50

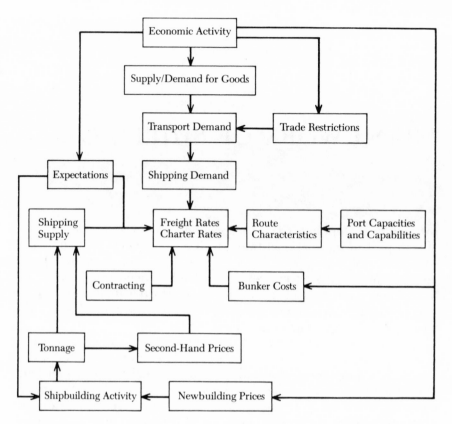

Figure 3-1 Global Economic Factors Determining Terms of Affreightment or Charter.

percent or more of ship operating costs. To reimburse operators for large increases in bunker, port delay, and similar costs, surcharges are often added to the basic freight rates.

Another major consideration is the characteristic of the route, with special concern to port capacity and capability, which may result in secondary surcharges to the basic rate. Factors influencing surcharges now play an increasingly important role in setting the rate as well.

Shipping supply and, as a result, supply/demand balance are largely affected by entry into and exit from the shipping market (which is quite easy) as well as by operation/supply factors such as tonnage lay-up and slow steaming, which have a major impact on ton-mile capacity of shipping available for transport. In fact in recent years, with increasing bunker prices, slow steaming and similar operational approaches have become increasingly popular in adjusting the supply/demand balance.

3.1. Free Trade and Shipping

Freedom of the seas is a concept developed during the mercantilist period and defined later by Grotius. It is a doctrine that confers a right to all commercial vessels to engage in peaceful use of the sea in a lawful manner, including use of territorial waters and safe harbor in case of need in the pursuance of their enterprise. The freedom-of-the-seas doctrine, long considered to be a fundamental right, is an extension of the laissez-faire principle of world trade.

World trade has long been assumed to be fostered by relative competitive advantages in raw material, labor and capital availability, and cost. These factors of production are not mobile, in a real sense, and differences will therefore persist. Recent trends, however, show a move toward a diminishing differential in the cost factors of production. This trend increasingly affects routes and volumes of traditional seaborne trade.

The cost and effectiveness of transport is a major factor in determining magnitude of international seaborne trade, particularly in low-value commodities, which comprise well over 80 percent of all the goods traded. Many nations use shipping as a means for increasing their participation in international trade and its transport by offering their own shipping various forms of government aid. Shipping offers employment to nationals and foreign exchange saving and/or earnings, as well as the important impact of presence. Many countries use shipping companies as trading companies, or at least have shipping companies form part of trading companies. Today, showing the flag not only conveys military or strategic importance but also serves an important commercial function as well.

The growing nationalism in shipping has also led to increasing protectionism. This development, however, is not really new. As long ago as 1660, the British Navigation Acts stipulated what imports and exports must go in British ships. They also stipulated that goods arriving in England on foreign ships from Europe had to pay double duty, that all commodities for trade with colonies were to go in British ships, and that cabotage was reserved for British ships. In addition, British ships were to be built in England or its colonies and have both a British captain and a crew composed of a majority of British citizens. Even trade between the colonies was restricted, and all intercolonial trades had to have British nationality. These acts probably represented the most protectionist maritime legislation passed. Britain only relaxed its protectionist approach to shipping when its fleet comprised in excess of half the world's total tonnage.

Freedom of the seas and free trade laissez-faire doctrines became the ideals of the nineteenth century, but after over one hundred years of trying to introduce liberal, nonprotectionist rules to shipping, we find today that protectionism is stronger than ever. It differs, however, in that modern protectionism in shipping relies less on national than bi- and multinational or even international protectionism, as formulated in the recent UNCTAD (United Nation Conference on Trade and Development) agreements. In a way this is a response to the fact that the major "liberal" OECD nations that stand for free trade principles control well over 72 percent of the world's shipping.

Ultimately, we must accept the fact that neither pure liberalism nor rigid protectionism is an effective approach to shipping. Both are unable to accommodate the range of complex issues involved in shipping and international trade. More flexible approaches that consider the realities of modern economic needs and aspirations must be adopted if we are to achieve a more orderly development of trade and shipping.

3.2. The International Shipping Industry

The world shipping industry comprised at the beginning of 1978 a fleet of 24,096 oceangoing vessels of 1,000 gross registered tonnage (GRT) and over, with a combined deadweight capacity of 641.3 million tons (375.8 million GRT), as shown in Table 3–1. This is a decline of over 30 percent in the number of oceangoing ships since 1960, with a corresponding increase in total GRT of over 100 percent over the same eighteen-year period. (The deadweight capacity increased by about 116 percent over this period.) This increase is due to the large increase in the average size of ships.

Over the same period of time, world waterborne trade increased by a factor of 3.2, as shown in Figure 3–2. World trade, after suffering a decline to 3.1 billion metric tons in 1975, is now approaching four billion metric tons, according to U.N. figures. Exports of developed market economies were only about 40 percent of the volume of imports between 1970 and 1975 (Table 3–2), while the value of developed country exports was well above the value of their imports. While only a small amount of developed country exports are destined to developing market economies, practically all the exports of developing countries are destined to developed market economies.

Total dry cargo in international waterborne trade was about 300 million metric tons in 1950 when it constituted over 60 percent of world shipping tonnage. By 1975 dry cargo had increased to about 1,438 million tons but constituted less than 45 percent of world oceangoing trade. Considering the growth of world oceangoing trade in comparison with the increase in world population between 1950

Table 3–1   Major Merchant Fleets of the World, December 31, 1977

Country	No. of Ships[a]	Rank by No. Ships[b]	DWT	Rank by DWT
Liberia	2,627	1	157,788,300	1
Japan	1,846	5	62,455,300	2
Norway	978	7	52,568,600	3
United Kingdom	1,377	6	51,105,500	4
Greece	2,379	3	49,825,000	5
Panama	2,041	4	31,250,500	6
France	415	—	20,815,100	7
U.S.S.R.	2,456	2	20,480,500	8
Italy	603	8	17,858,100	9
United States (privately owned)	571	11	17,321,400	10
Germany (West)	592	9	14,664,400	11
Spain	479	13	12,195,200	12
Sweden	286	—	11,965,000	13
Singapore	574	10	11,889,800	14
India	363	—	8,890,600	15
All others[c]	6,509	—	100,235,200	—
Total	24,096	—	641,308,500	—

SOURCE: Office of Subsidy Administration, Maritime Administration.

[a] Oceangoing merchant ships of 1,000 gross tons and over.
[b] By number of ships, Cyprus ranks 12th with 502 vessels aggregating 3,638,300 DWT, the People's Republic of China ranks 14th with 462 vessels aggregating 6,476,600 DWT, and the Netherlands ranks 15th with 443 vessels aggregating 7,686,500 DWT.
[c] Includes 269 U.S. government-owned vessels of 2,650,300 DWT.

and 1979, the dependency on shipping has increased manifold, as shown in Table 3–3. In fact, the average amount of trade carried per capita increased by a factor of 4.2 between 1950 and 1970. Beginning in the early 1980s, this ratio is expected to level off, due largely to the decreasing rate of growth of per capita energy consumption and the increasing development of domestic energy sources throughout the world.

Table 3–4 indicates the growing importance of liquid bulk tanker cargo in world oceanborne trade. Tables 3–5 through 3–9 show the breakdown of seaborne trade by major groupings of countries. The growing dependence of developed country economies on oil imports is shown in Tables 3–5 and 3–6. Table 3–5 also indicates the decrease of U.S. dry cargo exports, compared with an increase of Japanese dry cargo exports, since 1970. Tables 3–7 and 3–8 show the rapid increase in oil exports by OPEC countries. Centrally planned econ-

Table 3–2 International Seaborne Shipping, 1950–1979 (millions of metric tons)

Year	Export			Import		
	Total	Tanker	Dry	Total	Tanker	Dry
World						
1950	550	225	325	549	216	333
1970	2,605	1,440	1,165	2,530	1,403	1,127
1972	2,901	1,654	1,247	2,866	1,643	1,223
1973	3,276	1,873	1,403	3,238	1,862	1,376
1974	3,313	1,837	1,476	3,261	1,784	1,477
1975	3,082	1,644	1,438	3,056	1,660	1,396
1976	3,346	1,823	1,523	3,332	1,814	1,518
1977	3,475	1,897	1,578	3,441	1,905	1,536
1978	3,550	1,899	1,651	3,523	1,954	1,569
1979	3,778	2,003	1,775	3,781	2,039	1,742
Developed Market Economies						
1950	215	16	199	380	134	246
1970	812	113	699	2,013	1,122	891
1972	907	149	758	2,267	1,321	946
1973	1,048	164	884	2,553	1,482	1,071
1974	1,071	149	922	2,563	1,429	1,134
1975	1,034	143	891	2,358	1,333	1,025
1976	1,081	137	944	2,546	1,435	1,110
1977	1,120	140	980	2,595	1,497	1,098
1978	1,199	138	1,061	2,548	1,474	1,074
1979	1,349	203	1,146	2,738	1,547	1,191

Developing Market Economies						
1950	308	208	100	154	81	73
1970	1,628	1,262	366	442	262	180
1972	1,808	1,437	371	496	291	205
1973	2,061	1,636	425	574	344	230
1974	2,059	1,611	448	593	327	266
1975	1,850	1,416	434	576	296	280
1976	2,047	1,576	471	637	340	297
1977	2,118	1,628	490	700	365	335
1978	2,117	1,624	493	817	439	378
1979	2,194	1,666	528	873	451	422
Centrally Planned Economies						
1950	27	1	26	15	1	14
1970	155	65	90	75	19	56
1972	159	67	92	97	27	70
1973	167	73	94	111	36	75
1974	183	77	106	105	28	77
1975	188	85	103	122	31	91
1976	218	110	108	149	38	111
1977	237	128	109	145	42	103
1978	234	137	97	158	41	117
1979	235	134	101	170	41	129

SOURCE: United Nations, *Monthly Bulletin of Statistics*, March 1981 (Vol. 35).

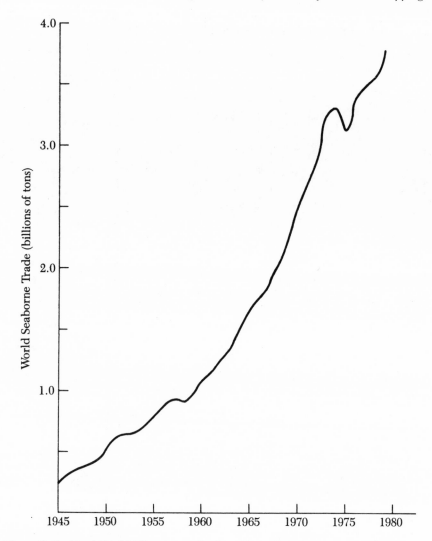

Figure 3-2   Total World Waterborne Trades, 1945–1979. (*Source: United Nations, Monthly Bulletin of Statistics, January to December 1978 (Vol. 32) and March 1981 (Vol. 35).*

omies, however, show little growth in any major segment of seaborne trade (Table 3–9).

3.3.   Shipping in Developing Countries

Growth of shipping in developing countries is related to their economic history, which has fostered agrarian societies with raw material

Table 3–3   World Waterborne Trade and Population Growth

Year	World Population (millions)	Total Dry Cargo (MM tons)	Total Tanker Cargo (MM tons)	Total Trade (MM tons)	Trade/ Population
1950	2520	330	130	433	0.17
1955	2760	450	492	932	0.33
1960	3010	540	744	1284	0.43
1965	3300	812	1092	1804	0.55
1970	3600	1165	1440	2605	0.72
1975	4033	1438	1644	3082	0.76
1979	4336	1775	2003	3778	0.87

SOURCE: United Nations, *Monthly Bulletin of Statistics*, March 1981 (Vo. 35) and January to December 1978 (Vol. 32).

or primary product exports and manufactured goods imports. With the price of manufactured goods increasing at a faster rate than that of primary products, with the exception of petroleum, the income gap between developed and developing trading partners has widened. The exceptions, obviously, are some developing petroleum-exporting countries. As a consequence, the gap between per capita GNP has also continued to widen and is today larger than ever before in relative terms. Some claim that shipping has played a dominant role in widening this gap because the producer of the primary products, often a developing country, usually pays the cost of shipping. The effect on the producer's economy is detrimental, despite who owns the shipping, as a rise in shipping costs usually lowers the returns to the producers and does not affect the price to consumers. Another important factor is the increasing impact of economies of scale in bulk shipping on the location of primary product processing plants. As shipping costs decrease in the aggregate in relation to the value of the commodity, locating finishing or processing plants closer to the consumer becomes economically more attractive. This is particularly the case where processing results in the production of multiple products from a single raw material. The same basic rationale also applies to primary materials shipped on liners, as conferences traditionally charge freight rates based on some relation to value of cargo and not on long-term costs of service. This again encourages most of the "added value" to be introduced by process plants located near the consumer.

One major problem affecting the growth of shipping in developing countries has been the lack of accountability of operator/owner associations, such as conferences, to shippers as well as governments or international agencies. A typical example is the claim that levels of shippers' discounts, pool, and share earnings are often discriminatory. These issues have recently been addressed by the "Code of

Table 3–4 World Oceanborne Trade

Year	Dry Cargo		Tankers		Total	
	Metric Tons (millions)	Increase/Decrease over Previous Year (percentage)	Metric Tons (millions)	Increase/Decrease over Previous Year (percentage)	Metric Tons (millions)	Increase/Decrease over Previous Year (percentage)
1950	300	—	225	—	525	—
1951	360	20	255	13	615	17
1952	350	−3	285	12	635	3
1953	360	3	295	4	655	3
1954	390	8	320	8	710	8
1955	450	15	350	9	800	13
1956	490	9	390	11	880	10
1957	510	4	420	8	930	6
1958	480	−6	440	5	920	−1
1959	490	2	480	9	970	5
1960	540	10	540	13	1,080	11
1961	570	6	580	7	1,150	6
1962	600	5	650	12	1,250	9
1963	640	7	710	9	1,350	8
1964	720	13	790	11	1,510	12
1965	780	8	860	9	1,640	9

Year						
1966	830	6	940	9	1,760	7
1967	860	4	1,010	7	1,870	6
1968	930	8	1,130	12	2,060	10
1969	990	6	1,260	11	2,250	9
1970	1,165	17	1,440	14	2,605	16
1972	1,247	—	1,654	—	2,901	—
1973	1,403	12	1,873	13	3,276	13
1974	1,476	5	1,837	−2	3,313	1
1975	1,438	−3	1,644	−11	3,072	−7
1976	1,523	6	1,823	11	3,346	9
1977	1,578	4	1,897	4	3,475	4
1978	1,651	5	1,899	0	3,550	2
1979	1,775	8	2,003	5	3,778	6

SOURCE: United Nations, *Monthly Bulletin of Statistics*, March 1981 (for 1970–1979) and January to December, 1978 (for 1950–1969).

Table 3-5 World Seaborne Export Trade by Major Developed Countries, 1950–1979 (millions of metric tons)

	Total						Tanker						Dry					
	E	C	U	S	J	A	E	C	U	S	J	A	E	C	U	S	J	A
1950	124	19	57	3	4	8	7	—	9	—	—	—	117	19	48	3	4	8
1970	339	96	218	15	42	94	100	1	5	—	—	1	239	95	213	15	42	93
1972	380	99	210	18	54	123	115	5	3	—	2	2	265	94	207	18	52	121
1973	431	112	250	19	56	152	123	7	3	—	1	3	308	105	247	19	55	149
1974	435	106	242	19	67	169	109	7	2	—	2	3	326	99	240	19	65	166
1975	393	102	246	21	70	173	105	6	2	—	1	3	288	96	244	21	69	170
1976	431	115	258	26	76	166	122	4	2	—	—	3	309	111	256	26	76	163
1977	456	120	250	30	79	175	125	4	1	—	—	3	331	116	249	30	79	172
1978	489	117	274	52	81	180	120	5	9	—	—	2	369	112	265	52	81	178
1979	550	135	326	60	83	189	178	5	16	—	—	3	372	130	310	60	83	186

E = Europe   U = USA   J = Japan
C = Canada   S = South Africa   A = Australia and New Zealand

SOURCE: United Nations, *Monthly Bulletin of Statistics*, March 1981 (Vol. 35).

Table 3-6 World Seaborne Import Trade by Major Developed Countries, 1950–1979 (millions of metric tons)

	Total						Tanker						Dry					
	E	C	U	S	J	A	E	C	U	S	J	A	E	C	U	S	J	A
1950	226	33	88	6	12	14	69	11	45	2	2	5	157	22	43	4	10	9
1970	1165	54	293	18	436	37	705	15	162	12	201	22	460	38	131	6	235	15
1972	1265	62	341	21	522	32	796	24	206	14	245	16	469	38	135	7	277	16
1973	1387	66	422	22	588	37	853	25	275	15	273	16	534	41	147	7	315	21
1974	1381	61	425	25	597	41	810	22	272	14	267	17	571	39	153	11	330	24
1975	1232	64	416	27	549	39	727	21	279	16	247	15	505	43	137	11	302	24
1976	1351	56	488	25	576	35	765	18	360	17	254	15	586	38	128	8	322	20
1977	1307	59	568	25	582	36	743	18	431	17	264	16	564	41	137	8	318	20
1978	1306	62	546	25	558	37	728	18	424	18	262	16	578	44	122	7	296	21
1979	1438	67	547	22	608	41	784	18	432	14	274	17	654	49	115	8	334	24

E = Europe   U = USA   J = Japan
C = Canada   S = South Africa   A = Australia and New Zealand

SOURCE: United Nations, *Monthly Bulletin of Statistics*, March 1981 (Vol. 35).

Table 3–7 World Seaborne Export Trade by Developing Countries, 1950–1979 (millions of metric tons)

	Total						Tanker						Dry					
	AF	NA	AM	VC	ME	OA	AF	NA	AM	VC	ME	OA	AF	NA	AM	VC	ME	OA
1950	35	21	165	126	78	30	—	—	121	114	75	12	35	21	44	12	3	18
1970	395	254	415	299	668	153	289	226	255	244	659	59	103	28	160	55	9	94
1972	370	194	382	268	868	181	268	165	234	223	855	79	102	29	148	45	13	102
1973	394	195	436	291	1010	213	184	166	258	238	1001	92	110	29	178	53	9	121
1974	370	161	430	272	1043	205	257	127	227	213	1033	94	113	34	203	59	10	111
1975	338	149	373	206	935	196	230	124	177	158	921	88	108	35	196	48	14	108
1976	360	172	380	210	1053	242	266	145	178	161	1033	98	194	27	202	49	22	144
1977	401	182	380	205	1057	268	302	153	173	151	1041	112	99	29	207	54	16	156
1978	438	268	379	190	1012	279	346	232	179	149	982	116	92	36	200	41	30	163
1979	468	276	421	211	1007	290	377	244	198	154	981	110	91	32	223	57	26	180

AF = Africa   VC = Venezuela and Caribbean
NA = North Africa   ME = Middle East
AM = America   OA = Other Asia

SOURCE: United Nations, *Monthly Bulletin of Statistics*, March 1981 (Vol. 35).

Table 3–8 World Seaborne Import Trade by Developing Countries, 1950–1979 (millions of metric tons)

	Total						Tanker						Dry					
	AF	NA	AM	VC	ME	OA	AF	NA	AM	VC	ME	OA	AF	NA	AM	VC	ME	OA
1950	24	16	90	57	6	34	8	5	60	48	3	10	16	11	30	9	3	24
1970	72	35	182	110	32	152	32	18	133	93	13	83	40	17	49	17	19	69
1972	66	28	206	118	28	180	23	8	149	99	15	100	43	20	57	19	23	80
1973	72	32	245	138	44	207	26	9	181	119	16	118	44	23	64	19	28	89
1974	80	40	245	132	53	209	26	9	174	113	17	106	54	31	71	19	36	103
1975	84	42	225	113	58	203	25	9	153	91	15	99	59	33	72	22	43	104
1976	90	47	236	121	77	227	26	10	169	103	26	113	64	37	67	18	51	114
1977	116	52	239	117	85	254	46	11	160	93	28	125	70	41	79	24	57	129
1978	177	127	250	124	90	293	105	88	161	94	25	144	72	39	89	30	65	149
1979	185	133	263	127	96	323	103	87	171	95	30	144	82	46	92	32	66	179

AF = Africa   VC = Venezuela and Caribbean
NA = North Africa   ME = Middle East
AM = America   OA = Other Asia

SOURCE: United Nations, *Monthly Bulletin of Statistics*, March 1981 (vol. 35).

Table 3–9 World Seaborne Trade by Centrally Planned Countries, 1950–1979 (millions of metric tons)

	Year	Exports			Imports		
		Total	Tanker	Dry	Total	Tanker	Dry
Europe	1950	—	—	—	—	—	—
and	1970	145	64	81	57	17	40
USSR	1972	150	67	83	82	27	55
	1973	155	72	83	95	35	60
	1974	167	73	94	87	27	60
	1975	168	76	92	102	29	73
	1976	197	97	100	115	37	78
	1977	213	112	101	105	40	65
	1978	215	126	89	117	39	78
	1979	214	123	91	129	39	90
USSR	1950	—	—	—	—	—	—
	1970	107	61	46	14	3	11
	1972	109	63	46	30	8	22
	1973	113	69	44	37	13	24
	1974	118	70	48	22	4	18
	1975	120	73	47	35	6	29
	1976	144	92	52	41	8	33
	1977	154	104	50	33	7	26
	1978	151	115	36	43	7	36
	1979	150	112	38	52	8	44

SOURCE: United Nations, *Monthly Bulletin of Statistics*, March 1981 (Vol. 35).

Conduct for Liner Conferences," which, when ratified, will stipulate owner-shipper consultation, cargo sharing, and other principles.

The cargo-sharing principle of the code was proposed to be extended to bulk shipping. Under proposals submitted at UNCTAD V in Manila (1978), developing countries would be accorded a share of bulk cargoes. The same proposal also suggests the gradual phasing out of flags of open registry or flags of convenience as they are sometimes called. The reason for this demand is that, although developing countries export well over 60 percent of the world's commodities carried by shipping, only 8.5 percent of the world shipping tonnage is owned or controlled by them (as noted in Tables 3–10 and 3–11). The growth of developing country shipping capacity, while impressive, still falls well below their ambition. It more than doubled between 1970 and 1977 at a compound growth rate of just over 10 percent.

The largest participation of the developing countries is in general cargo shipping, in line with the traditional requirements of their nonbulk trades. The labor intensity and relative capital extensity of

Table 3–10 **Cargo Shipping Capacity by Developing Countries (in millions of GRT, 1977)**

	Tankers	Dry Bulk	General Cargo	Container	Total
Developing countries	24.3	6.0	11.7	0.2	33.1
Total world	173.8	97.9	75.4	7.5	388.5
Percentage of total world	14.0	6.2	15.5	3.0	8.5

SOURCE: *UNCTAD Review of Maritime Transport*, 1977.

Note: Flag-of-convenience fleets, such as Liberia, Singapore, etc., are excluded.

this segment is also of benefit. Oil-tanker ownership is largely concentrated in the hands of oil-exporting developing countries. It is in the dry bulk trades, though, that most developing countries are looking for expansion. This trend could also revitalize American dry bulk shipping by introduction of bilateral agreements, capacity sharing, and other arrangements of mutual advantage. Developing countries have tended toward development of national shipping, which is often government owned, controlled, or financed. This approach is justified for any or all of the following reasons:

- Generation of employment opportunities
- Enhancement of trade through involvement of shipping to marketing
- Balance of payment effects
- National income effects
- Increased commercial and strategic security
- Increased leverage on shipping company organizations such as conferences
- Price stability and predictability
- Prestige and visibility
- Transfer of technology and training
- Shippers' consultation in service pricing

Although some of these factors do contribute to the economic growth of a developing country, the economic contribution of national shipping is often overestimated, as the majority of costs, such as vessel acquisition, fuel, foreign port stevedoring, and repair and manning costs as well, often are paid in foreign exchange.

Increased participation in liner conferences has often been found to be of doubtful national advantage because of the inherent conflict between the shippers' interest in low freight rates versus national-flag liner shipping interest in maximizing company profitability. As

Table 3–11 Shipping of Developing Countries by Flag

Developing Countries	GRT	Developing Countries	GRT
Algeria	1,055,962	Honduras	104,903
Angola	22,043	Jamaica	7,075
Benin	912	Mexico	673,964
Cameroon	78,180	Montserrat	1,248
Congo	4,172	Nicaragua	34,588
Egypt	407,818	Paraguay	21,930
Eq. Guinea	3,070	Peru	555,419
Ethiopia	23,989	Uruguay	192,792
Gabon	98,645	Venezuela	639,396
Gambia	1,608	Bahrain	6,409
Ghana	182,696	Bangladesh	244,314
Guinea Bissau	219	Brunei	899
Ivory Coast	115,717	Burma	67,502
Kenya	15,192	Hong Kong	609,679
Madagascar	39,850	India	5,482,176
Libya	673,969	Indonesia	1,163,173
Mauritius	37,288	Iran	1,002,061
Morocco	270,295	Iraq	1,135,245
Mozambique	27,618	Israel	404,651
Nigeria	335,540	Jordan	696
Senegal	28,004	Kampuchea	3,558
Seychelles	59,140	Korea	2,494,724
Sierra Leone	7,298	Kuwait	1,831,194
Sudan	43,375	Lebanon	227,009
Tanzania	35,613	Malaysia	563,666
Togo	134	Maldives	110,681
Tunisia	100,128	Pakistan	475,600
Uganda	5,510	Qatar	84,710
Zaire	109,785	Philippines	1,146,529
Zambia	5,513	Saudi Arabia	1,018,713
Argentina	1,677,169	Sri Lanka	92,581
Anguilla	399	Syria	20,679
Antigua	149	Thailand	260,664
Barbados	4,448	UAE	152,100
Belize	620	Yemen	1,436
Bermuda	1,751,515	Malta	100,420
Brazil	3,329,951		
Chile	405,971	Fiji	10,879
Colombia	247,240	Nauru	48,353
Cuba	667,518	New Hebrides	12,189
Ecuador	197,244	Gilbert Is.	1,333
El Salvador	1,987	Papua New Guinea	16,217
Faulkland Is.	6,937	Solomon Is.	1,746
Guatemala	11,854	Tonga	14,180
Guyana	16,274	Total	33,145,909

SOURCE: UNCTAD Review of Maritime Transport, 1977.

a result, clearly determining the benefit of national shipping to developing countries is difficult, particularly when measured against benefits achievable through investment of scarce resources into other segments of the developing country's economy. As a result, many developing countries have put a rather low priority on shipping; they consider the use of alternate shipping arrangements such as joint ventures, chartering, and share licensing to be more effective approaches for a greater role in and economic control of shipping in their foreign trade. This trend should enhance the opportunities for American shipping.

3.4. Bulk Shipping

Dry and liquid bulk shipping have dominated the volume of international seaborne trade. As noted in Table 3–4, dry cargo increased from 1,165 million to 1,775 million tons between 1970 and 1979, of which dry bulk cargo composed 580 million and 1,117 million tons, respectively. Ton-mile transport of dry bulk cargo increased at an even faster rate, as shown in Table 3–12. Liquid bulk transport, which is mainly oil, increased from 225 million tons in 1950 to over 1,400 million tons by 1970, reached one peak of 1,868 million tons in 1973, then declined to 1,690 million tons by 1975, then rose once again to just over 2 billion tons in 1979. It has since declined at an annual rate of about 2.7 percent. Average distances over which petroleum is carried have declined at an even larger rate, and total ton-mile tanker demand in 1980 was only 84 percent of the average distance in 1976. (See Table 3–13.)

Bulk trade continues to dominate U.S. international trade. U.S. crude oil imports declined by 23 percent in the two years between 1978 and 1980, while U.S. coal exports more than doubled during the same period. The volume of U.S. bulk trade has remained relatively constant in recent years, as seen in Table 3–14.

Table 3–12   World Dry Bulk Shipping Demand Index (1970 demand = 100)

Year	Tons Carried	Ton-Miles Produced	Average Distance
1970	100	100	100
1971	101	102	100
1972	119	120	100
1973	137	138	100
1974	150	152	101
1975	149	155	102
1976	162	168	103
1977	170	175	103
1978	181	187	103
1979	202	209	103
1980	213	225	105
1981*	226	242	107

SOURCE: *World Bulk Trades 1980*, Fearnleys, Oslo 1, Norway.
* Estimate.

**Table 3–13   World Crude Oil Petroleum Tanker Demand Index
(1970 demand = 100)**

Year	Tons Carried	Ton-Miles Produced	Average Distance
1970	100	100	100
1971	108	114	110
1972	118	140	116
1973	136	162	120
1974	136	169	125
1975	125	155	124
1976	141	176	126
1977	147	184	125
1978	145	172	115
1979	142	170	107
1980	140	152	106
1981*	136	146	102

SOURCE: *World Bulk Trades 1980*, Fearnleys, Oslo 1, Norway.
* Estimate.

Table 3–14   Major U.S. Bulk Trades (millions of tons)

	1978	1979	1980
Crude oil (import)	369.42	358.30	293.20
Iron ore (import)	20.91	22.68	16.67
Coal (export)	36.38	56.04	81.62
Grain (export)	110.25	120.23	128.33
Bauxite and alumina (import)	21.71	21.35	23.19
Phosphate rock (export)	13.32	14.42	14.64
Other bulk	36.12	36.82	36.34
Total bulk trades	598.13	629.84	593.99

SOURCE: *World Bulk Trades 1980*, Fearnleys, Oslo 1, Norway.

Chapter 4

ISSUES IN SHIP OPERATIONS

Ship operations are usually considered in the broad categories of technological issues, ship management issues, and ship logistics issues. Technological issues deal with the planning, design, and physical operations of ships; management issues with the running of a ship as a production unit; and logistics issues with the supply and maintenance operations. Chapter 4 discusses the challenge of technological issues, reviews modern concepts of ship management, and considers the issue of ship bunker supply—the most pressing and important issue in ship logistics.

4.1. Technological Issues

Ship technology has advanced in many diverse directions in recent years, a trend that can be expected to continue. The large increase in the average size of recently built ships, however, will not continue, as economies of size are replaced by economies of systems costs. While average and maximum ship size continue to increase in some trades, such as coal, tanker and other bulk carrier sizes have started to decline as the average trading distance has declined. In fact, the market for very large and ultra-large tankers (VLCCs and ULCCs) has all but evaporated. The reason is declining ton-mile demand, lack of adequate deep draft terminals, and smaller shipment sizes. On the other hand, container, RoRo, and specialized carriers continue to be built with very gradual increases in carrying capacity but lower speeds. As a result, these vessels are usually of similar size as the vessels of their type built a few years ago.

The following major technological issues presently confront international shipping:

- Energy conservation by use of energy-efficient hulls, effective hull maintenance, efficient energy conversion levels (power plant, transmission, and thruster), and effective ship condition and routing. Also under study are unattended engine rooms with energy-saving plants and adaptable ambient conditions.

- New ship designs and arrangements that are both energy-efficient and also efficient carriers of specialized cargo or cargo in specific physical form. Some examples are high-volume containerships and RoRo vessels, dry and liquid bulk-parcel carriers, and warehouse ships. Specialized tug-barge and ship-train concepts are also of increasing interest, as are multiple hull displacement and semisubmerged vessels, not only to reduce ship motions (for example, in offshore supply) but also to increase efficiency in carrying high-volume, low-density cargoes.
- To take advantage of the availability of modern communications, monitoring, information storage and retrieval, and computing technology. Optimizing of ship routing to weather and economic conditions, ship condition monitoring and control, cargo and tank planning including loading, stowage and unloading, and sequence planning and control are just a few of the areas where tremendous advances can be made in attaining more efficient and reliable ship operations.

Many new technological issues and opportunities will affect ship operations in the future. One important issue is the changing role, operation, and technology of ports, port approaches, cargo transfer methods, and interfacing transport needs. We must expect increasing control of ships navigating in port approaches, greater control of ship effluents, particularly those considered pollutants, changes in ship handling, changes in cargo transfer, and more. Ports are increasingly involved in the physical form change of cargoes, from break bulk to unitized, gas to liquids, and so forth. Many ports or their tenants engage in processing, assembly, or manufacturing activities. Ports are also increasingly concerned with continuity of cargo flow between transport modes interfacing at the port to reduce both port turnaround times as well as goods in storage in port.

Ship handling by ports and terminals will be improved and may ultimately lead to automated or mechanized ship docking and mooring to improve berth utilization and also to accommodate future ships with minimum manning. Automation is making major inroads into ship operations, and although unmanned ships may not become feasible, practical, or realistic concepts, ships with a minimum of skeleton manning are already being planned. Such designs will not only reduce ship capital and operating costs but may ultimately allow ships to be controlled more effectively.

4.2. Ship Management

Ship management could be defined as the set of decisions required
to assure effective operation and performance of a ship, either as a
unit, part of a fleet of ships, or part of a transportation system.
Although many aspects of ship management, such as ship navigation,
ship condition (trim, stability, etc.), crewing, and supplies, are
largely based on a long history, many recent developments may
make traditional methods and procedures obsolete. Ship technology
has changed radically in recent years. The increasing cost of fuel will
undoubtedly result in additional technological changes in ship design,
propulsion, and arrangement during the next decade. Communications, information handling and data processing, control, cargo
handling and storage, and other relevant technologies are changing
so rapidly that few achieve expiration of their supposed economic
life before a new generation is developed. Ship technology has also
changed as a result of differences in the physical form of cargoes,
integration of transport modes and services, and novel methods of
operation of ships, such as a combined containership/bulk carrier.

The organization of shipping companies has also changed and, in
turn, affected the way ships are managed. Ships have become extremely capital intensive, and operations often require short-run
decisions or plans that are difficult to make at a faraway office.
Shipboard management is therefore assuming more and often different responsibilities than in the past. The following factors also
influence the role of ship management and affect the division of
responsibility and consequently the decision-making function between ship and shoreside management:

- Modern approaches to ship maintenance management;
- Vessel traffic control and congestion in ship traffic lanes;
- Changes in jurisdiction of shipping lanes and coastal and open
  waters;
- Effect of rules on environmental impact and control;
- Division of ownership and operating representatives.

In earlier times, particularly in the tramp trades, the shipboard
management had to obtain the cargo, purchase supplies, route and
schedule the ship, collect freight, and pay the crew. During the last
century these conditions changed, and shoreside management assumed ever larger responsibilities until the shipmaster's functions
were confined essentially to just "running" the ship. This trend is
now increasingly being reversed, with onboard performance of in-

ventory and maintenance control, optimum ship weather routing and cargo planning, as well as numerous financial management functions being taken over by microprocessors, other electronic aids to ship management, and efficient satellite communication systems.

There is an increasing trend toward more delegation of authority to ship management. The major issue in deciding on the degree of delegation, though, is control. In other words, shipping companies try to delegate authority without losing control. The following are major reasons for the delay in transferring more authority to ship management:

- Inability to provide the ship with, or store on the ship, all the information required to make decisions.
- Updated knowledge of the management objectives of the company, including continuously varying competitive factors.
- Access of interacting decisionmakers.
- Comprehension by ship management of the financial implications of decisions.

Decisions directly affecting the ship but usually made by shoreside management concern bunker purchase, ship repair and docking, crew exchange, cargo planning (including shutting out of cargo), financing of or payment for supplies, use of agents, and more. These decisions are made on shore because shipboard management has little information or understanding of contracts of affreightment, charter parties, cost of ship's time, cost of ship inventory holding, or future commitments or trading opportunities. Of course, one might speculate that shipboard management's participation in or assumption of decision-making in such problem areas might greatly improve the quality and timeliness of the decision—a role that would require more extensive communication and information transfer to the ship and more feedback from the ship. Telex, satellite communications, facsimile, radio telephone, and even more advanced communication and information transfer systems offer future opportunities of tying ship management closely into the decision-making loop.

A major factor in increased shipboard responsibility is the availability of microprocessors or computers for shipboard use, which may be dedicated, or special function, machines or general purpose machines. Shipboard computers can be used to perform or assist in the following functions:

- Operations Planning
    Loading—cargo planning
    Ship conditions planning
    Inventory and supplies

      Maintenance and repair planning
      Routing
      Scheduling
      Allocations
- Operations Control
      Weather routing
      Ship docking
      Precision steering
      Collision prevention
      Ship motions control
      Hull surveillance, machinery surveillance
      Navigation control
      Propulsion machinery
      Monitoring of ship (machinery conditions)
      Cargo systems control (condition)
      Cargo-handling control
      Communications—MIS
      Ship traffic control
      Ship accounts, personnel, and finance

4.3. Emerging Impact of Bunkers on Shipping Operations

Marine bunkers comprise fuel for main engines, auxiliary and ancillary equipment, and the galley. These fuels consist mainly of heavy or residual petroleum fractions and marine diesel fuel, which is a middle distillate. The heavy fuels vary in chemical qualities according to the type or blend of crude from which they are made. They also vary considerably from area to area (and from month to month as the crude runs change) and are sold according to viscosity.

Bunkering costs now represent the largest single factor in a vessel's operating costs—over 60 percent for some ship types. With price differentials of up to 80 percent between residual and distillate fuels, many owners have been forced to burn heavy fuels that are, in essence, simply the by-product of crude oil refining. Over 80 percent of all bunkers now purchased comprise heavy residual fuel. Because of soaring bunker prices and insufficient supply, quality in some areas is deteriorating to a point that effects on main and auxiliary engines, ship types, and sizes are expected to be critical. Prior to 1970, bunker prices tended to move little and infrequently. Then followed three years of minor changes. Since 1973, the volatility of oil prices and markets has made the planning of oil purchases very difficult and has eroded all traditional reference points to a stage where they have little meaning.

Price changes for different grades of bunker fuels now occur frequently; they are large and geographically irregular. The Iranian crisis, for example, caused bunker prices in many ports to double within a few months. Oil suppliers were encouraged to adopt a distinct sellers' market attitude toward marine bunkers, with contracts and fixed prices for regular customers replaced by spot deliveries and posted prices at time of delivery.

The following questions raise issues that must be addressed in the evaluation of bunker purchasing and its problems:

- *How did the present predicament of higher bunker price and low quality come about?* Is it only the result of seller monopoly-driven market forces or did buyers play a role in these developments? Have the changes in the market come to a halt and will it now become increasingly a buyer's market?
- *Does fuel consumption—choice and cost—receive the required attention in planning, design, and operation of shipping?* Do shipowners really plan ahead in the acquisition of tonnage and the planning of its use? How many old concepts are carried over from times when bunkers cost $15 per ton?
- *What are the options?* Can buyers really affect the market, the price, the quality, the delivery reliability, and other factors in bunker purchasing?
- *What is the present situation?* We continuously hear about shortages, gluts, OPEC resolutions, available supplies, recoverable reserves, refinery capacity, and utilization, all of which are supposed to explain the trend in bunker prices, quality, and availability. Yet, many of these factors in fact seem to indicate trends that ought to go counter to actual bunker developments. Why is that so?
- *What is the future outlook?* The economic and technological outlook offers many new and some not so new options. These vary from re-engining to change of fuel and slow or rationalized steaming for existing vessels. There are similarly many options in the design or acquisition of new vessels (see Table 4–1).

Owners are affected by and are often dependent on many players and uncontrollable variables in their selection of options (see Table 4–2). What can owners or, for that matter, oil suppliers, bunker brokers, ship agents, or oil companies do? How can they cooperate to resolve the difficulties in bunker supplies? Some options, such as slow steaming, are only owner/operator dependent, while others affect many of the players. To work, they require cooperation. Coal, as an example, is again seriously considered as marine fuel; yet limited availability at traditional bunkering locations, as well as reluctance in investing in coal-bunkering facilities, makes conversion

Table 4–1 **Fuel-Related Options in Design, Operation, and Modification of Vessels**

OWNER OPTIONS

Ship Design Alternatives
  Hull form, size
  Arrangement
  Choice of power plant
  Single or multiple fuel use
  Choice of RPM/thruster

OWNER/OPERATOR/CHARTERER OPTIONS

Ship Operating Alternatives
  Bunker strategies
  Slow steaming
  Fuel quality change
  Fuel type use
  Optimal routing
  Maintenance (hull and engine) program

Ship Modification Alternatives
  Re-engining
  Propeller-shaft-duct-gear
  Fuel treatment plant installation
  Combustion equipment change
  Bunker fuel handling arrangements

Table 4–2 **Options to Counter Problems of Bunker Supply and Cost**

The Players
  Shipowner/operator/charterer   Ship agent
  Oil supplier   Oil operating company
  Bunker broker

The Variables
  Price
  Availability: quantity
  Quality: cost of fuel treatment and added plant maintenance

The Alternatives
  Fuel oil
    Characteristics: viscosity, density, pour point, carbon residue, asphaltenes,
      sulphur, metals, ash, calorific value, cetane number
  Alternative fuels
    Coal, oil-coal slurries, coal liquids, syncrude, direct coal distillates, etc.
  Alternate power source
    Nuclear, wind

to coal difficult, quite apart from technological and operational problems.

4.3.1. *Market Factors*

Bunker fuel accounts for some 5 to 10 percent of all petroleum products sold. The percentage is declining. More serious is the fact that it comprises an ever smaller percentage of oil company sales. As a result, oil companies are increasingly unwilling to make concessions to the heavy fuel bunker market, although it does play a significant role in balancing refinery output. Refineries used to be concentrated in developed or industrialized countries, with output aimed largely toward the lighter, more expensive products. Middle distillates such as gas, oil, and diesel are in demand for space heating and heavy transport, while residual, heavy fuels are used for electricity generation, steel making, and marine use—considered a declining market. The light distillates include products such as gasoline.

Market demands for particular products such as heating oil and gasoline vary with the season in most countries. Similarly, a downturn in a country's economy as a whole, when electricity-generation demand is decreased, less petrochemical feedstock is processed, and fewer miles are covered by diesel transport, has a similar effect. Refinery underutilization can also generate its own product imbalance. A marketing imbalance can produce a surplus of heavy fuels which, in turn, could mean low prices and eager selling attitudes. Under these circumstances, heavy fuel could be shipped by tanker to other parts of the world where demand and prices are high enough to justify freight costs.

The price of petroleum has increased more than fifteenfold in a span of barely eight years. After a very gradual increase to about $2 per barrel of crude by 1972–1973, it increased five- to sixfold to a level of $10 to $13 per barrel in the 1974–1978 period. From 1979–1981 another rapid run took it up to over $35 per barrel—the current level (see Figure 4–1). Currently, however, there is a glut, and world petroleum consumption is actually declining. It appears that conservation and the use of alternative sources of energy will result in a continued decline of world petroleum consumption, which, in turn, should lead to a stabilization or actual decline of prices. Yet this is true only in a free market environment, which the petroleum market is definitely not. Considering world bunker consumption, we similarly find a gradual reduction since 1972–1973 in both real terms (Figure 4–2) as well as in terms of bunkers used per ton or per ton-mile (Figure 4–3).

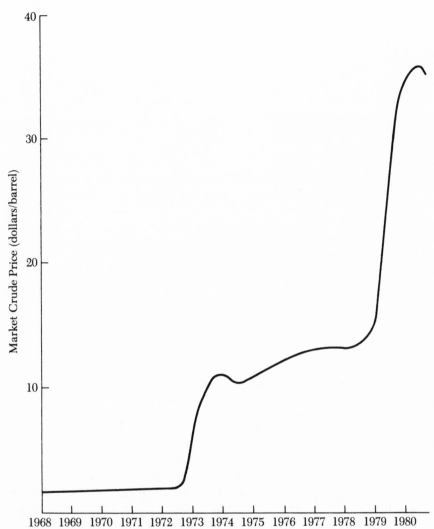

Figure 4-1 Rise of Petroleum Prices. *(Source: American Petroleum Institute, Annual Reports 1973-1981.)*

4.3.2. *Impact on Ship Operating Costs and Revenues*

The cost of bunkers has assumed an ever larger percentage of total vessel operating costs, as seen in Figure 4–4. It now averages 43.2 percent of tanker and 60.4 percent of liner operating costs. In containership operating costs, bunkers may assume a value of 64 percent.

Considering revenues, one measure may be the shipping freight

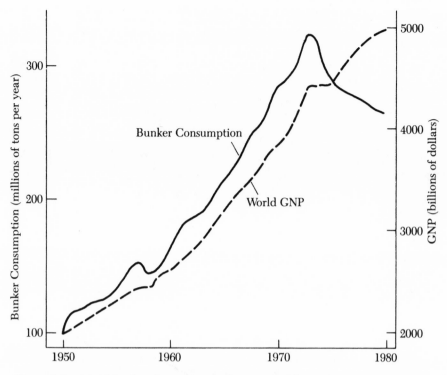

Figure 4-2   World Bunker Consumption. (*Source:* World Petroleum *Annual Statistical Survey, Dec. 1981.*)

index, which, as seen in Figure 4–5, does not follow bunker price. In fact, if we divide the shipping freight index by bunker or operating costs (Figure 4–6), we note a continued and serious erosion and resulting decline in profitability of shipping. The fuel consumption and cost of typical merchant vessels are shown in Table 4–3, which shows dramatically why few containership operators run their ships at speeds exceeding 21 knots.

4.3.3.   *Bunker Price Variations and Surcharges*

In shipping, effective planning is essential to success. Until recently, effective planning meant operational and fleet planning; now, however, it must also include bunker purchase planning, which involves strategy formulation for timing, location, quantity, and quality of bunker purchases. Bunker costs today may vary by as much as 40 percent among two ports, or fluctuate by more than 50 percent within a short period of time such as a month. Similarly, bunker availability and quality change rapidly.

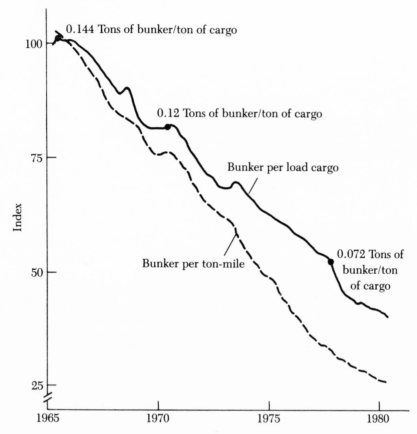

Figure 4–3 Bunkers Used Per Ton of Cargo Carried and Per Ton-Mile of Sea Transport Produced. (*Source: Data from* World Petroleum *Annual Statistical Survey, Dec. 1975–Dec. 1981.*)

Owners are now forced to add surcharges to account for fuel cost escalations. The computation of surcharges has become not only difficult but also a subject of justification and credibility. Many shippers using conference services, for example, feel that fuel cost fluctuations should be considered part of operating cost variations and be included in periodic increases of freight rates, subject to negotiation and review by shippers' councils or other arbitration bodies. Some have claimed, for instance, that conference surcharges are based on added fuel costs of the least efficient conference operator or ship. Similarly, there appears to be little standardization in the derivation of surcharges, with each conference using its own method of calculating surcharges.

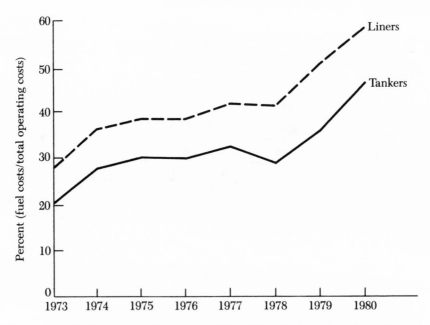

Figure 4–4   Fuel Cost as a Percentage of Total Vessel Operating Costs. (*Source:*
Data from World Petroleum *Annual Statistical Survey, Dec. 1973–Dec. 1981.*)

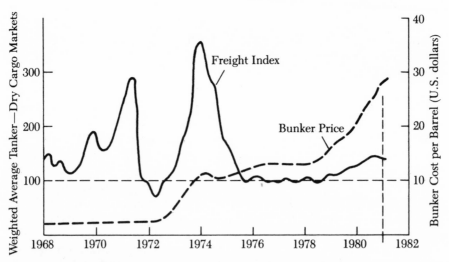

Figure 4–5   Shipping Freight Index. (*Source: Data from* World Petroleum *Annual*
Statistical Survey, Dec. 1973–Dec. 1981, and Fairplay.)

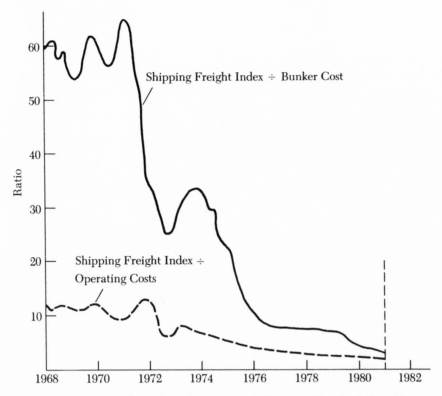

Figure 4-6 Relationship of Bunker Cost and Shipping Freight Index. (*Source: Data from* World Petroleum *Annual Statistical Survey, Dec. 1973–Dec. 1981, and* Fairplay.)

4.3.4. *Refining Developments*

New fluid catalytic cracking and vis-breaking processes used in modern refineries now take more from the lighter end of the crude oil. A heavy residue is left, with a high proportion of carbons that also include catalytic fines in the form of aluminum silicate. A vis-breaking or thermocracking process is then used to reduce the viscosity of this heavy, dirty residue. In the past such reductions would be achieved by cutting back with gas, oil, or other distillates, and as much as 25 to 30 percent of the crude processed ended up as residual fuel. With the new cracking processes, only 6 to 7 percent is currently produced. This, then, is our new bunker C—the basic marine fuel.

Table 4–3 Typical Fuel Consumptions

Vessel	Engine	DWT	Knots	Tons/ Day	$/Day
Tanker	Diesel	70,000	16	55	15,400
Tanker	Steam turbine	275,000	16.3	170	28,900
Tanker	Steam turbine	330,800	15	183	31,100
Container	Steam turbine	48,000	26	390	66,300
Container	Steam turbine	48,000	22	200	34,000
Bulker	Diesel	25,082	15	32	8,900
Ferry	Diesel	15,000	26	163	45,000
Cargo	Diesel	23,800	16	36	10,080
Cargo	Diesel	13,656	16	25	7,000
Cargo	Diesel	9,100	14	16	4,480

Typical Lubricating Oil Cost
(Average cost $960/ton)

	Tons/Year		$/Year	
Annual Consumption for:	12,000 BHP	40,000 BHP	12,000 BHP	40,000 BHP
Motor vessel	30	150	28,800	144,000
Steam turbine	15	25	14,400	24,000

SOURCE: Operator data, private communications.

4.3.5. *Impact on Ship Operation*

Increased concentration of solids leads to higher specific gravities, which in turn makes the separation of water more difficult for centrifugal fuel purification plants. Some of the fuels currently coming from cracking plants are reaching viscosities of 460 CSF at 50°C (see Table 4–4). Asphaltene and carbon residues, however, are more difficult to cope with, as they affect ignition quality. When burned, high carbon fuels produce a large ignition lag, longer burning life, and lower combustibility. High levels of vanadium cause high-temperature corrosion leading to piston and exhaust valve damage, while sulphur causes low-temperature corrosion through the formation of sulphuric acid. High levels of nickel, iron, and magnesium are also hazardous.

Generally, beyond a specific gravity of 0.985, purifying fuel by the use of centrifuges is practically impossible. As a result, treating many of the heavier fuels now received as bunkers for safe, effective combustion in diesel engines has become exceedingly difficult. Steam-turbine plants can burn these heavy, dirty oils without much trouble in their boilers, but with plant consumption about 35 percent

Table 4–4   Typical Current and Future Marine Fuel Oil Technical Specifications

	Typical Current Straight Run Residual Fuel	Possible Future Straight Run Residual Fuel
Specific gravity	0.96–0.98	0.96–0.98
Viscosity CST at 50°C	230–370	250–400
Pour point °C	10–15	10–40
Carbon residue % weight	8	10
Asphaltenes % weight	4	6

Typical Characteristics of 180 CST Marine Fuel Oil

	Iran	Kuwait	Saudi Arabia	Libya	Venezuela
Specific gravity	0.949	0.949	0.952	0.904	0.959
Pour point °C	16	7	−4	38	−12.
Carbon residue % weight	8.4	8.5	9.4	5.7	9.6
Sulphur % weight	2.3	3.8	3.9	0.25	2.3
Vanadium ppm	170	43	100	2	335

Typical U.S. West Coast Fuel Oils (Alaskan Crude)

	Current	Future
Specific gravity	0.988	0.988
Viscosity CST at 50°C	420	480
Pour point °C max.	24	27
Sulphur % weight max.	4.3	5

SOURCE: *Alternative Fuels for Maritime Use*, MTRB, U.S. National Academy of Sciences, 1980.

higher than those of a comparable diesel plant and the prevailing high costs for fuel of appropriate quality, steam propulsion is becoming less popular. Similarly, while a diesel has the advantage that efficiency does not dramatically change with a reduction in output, the same is not true of the steam turbine. Its efficiency in terms of fuel consumption drops considerably during conditions of a slow steaming or partial load. For a diesel, a reduction of one knot of a fifteen-knot speed implies a considerable reduction of output and consequently also of fuel consumption. Advantage is gained in both normal operating conditions and when the ship's speed is lower than the rated speed, as the specific consumption of a diesel varies comparatively little over a reasonable range of outputs.

4.3.6.   New Types of Fuel

There are many new developments in the quality and types of fuel used in marine machinery. Implementation of these developments will depend on their acceptance by a conservative industry. In the short to medium term, ship types and prime movers can be expected to undergo only slight modification in adapting to changing fuel qualities and different economic parameters.

Adapting for coal as a marine fuel is probably the most commonly accepted short-term development. Coal can be burned in pulverized or lumpy form, or injected as a coal-oil or coal-water or steam slurry. Unlike the diesel engine, steam boilers can be readily adapted to burn coal. Coal is now used in hundreds of coal-fired stoker boilers built for industrial use in the United States. There are many problems, though, such as the danger of fire, compacting, and slow heat buildup, even under inert conditions. Coal-oil slurry is supposedly an alternative, and slurry burners have already been fully developed and directly applied to shipboard use, but bunkering would be a major problem, as on-shore processing would have to be arranged. Modern automated coal-handling devices are available for the transfer of the coal from the ship's bunkers to the day hoppers at the stoker on the boiler front. Traveling grates and conventional ash sluices are available for ash removal.

4.3.6.1.   Synthetic Fuels

The technology to develop synthetic fuels, such as oil from oil shale, coal tar, and coal, as well as plants and wastes, is still in its infancy but growing as the pressure mounts to find alternatives. "Synthetic" is a misnomer, however, for it implies something artificial or manufactured. In fact, it denotes basic fuels that have been transformed by an industrial process into a more usable form such as oil or gas.

4.3.6.2.   Nuclear Power

Nuclear power has for many years now represented the way of the future in power generation and as a substitute fuel. Although some nuclear-powered merchant vessels and a significant number of nuclear-propelled naval vessels have been built and have operated relatively trouble-free for millions of miles (the USNS Savannah alone, for example, sailed some 500,000 miles), the cost of nuclear vessels has skyrocketed to such a level that nuclear power is no longer an economically viable alternative. Nor is it environmentally acceptable. Of course, this may change in the future, although the problems with Japan's first nuclear cargo ships have probably caused a lot of damage to the cause of nuclear merchant ship propulsion.

4.3.7. *Alternatives to Petroleum*

There are many alternatives to petroleum as a fuel for ship propulsion. Some of the most important ones are listed in Table 4–5, compiled as part of a recent U.S. National Academy of Science study (1980), which shows that overall efficiency of coal and coal-oil slurry is among the highest achievable. Considering the cost of alternative fuels per million BTU, coal leads with an average cost of $1.25, followed by coal-oil slurries with $2.60 and petroleum with $2.20. Shale oil, coal liquids (syncrude), and shale syncrude are all in the $4.20 to $4.40 range, or twice as expensive. Methane, methanol, and direct coal distillates are all in the $6.10 to $11.50 range and therefore three to five times as expensive as heavy petroleum-based fuels. The costs above include only fuel costs. Maintenance, financial, and plant nonfuel operating costs are excluded. But even taking these into account, coal and coal slurries or coal-derivative fuels appear to offer the best near-term opportunities for fuel economy and diversification.

4.3.8. *Where Are Bunker Prices Headed?*

Until recently this question had only one answer—up. OPEC countries that have sent fuel prices rocketing since 1973 have met periodically to adjust the price upward or tighten the screws. Now the screws seem to have been tightened so far that the trend of consistent worldwide increase in petroleum consumption appears to have been reversed.

Petroleum consumption is down everywhere, and stocks are high. The demand for petroleum, which started to decline in 1979, is declining at an ever greater rate. West German and U.S. imports fell by about 20 percent during the first quarter of 1981. Western oil demand is down to 45 million barrels per day from 52 million barrels per day in 1979. Recession, conversion to alternate energy sources or fuel, and determined energy consumption are all affecting petroleum consumption. These factors may lead to a lowering of prices and more competition in the petroleum markets to foster consumption or to a drastic cutback of production.

OPEC, at a meeting held in late May 1981, mapped out plans to counter these new and unaccustomed trends. What OPEC is countering is a general feeling that prices are too high and that a further increase in prices would weaken OPEC's influence and hold on the

Table 4-5 Overall Thermal Efficiencies (mine to shaft horsepower, percentage)

Fuel	Steam	Diesel*	Otto (IC)	Free Piston	Gas Turbine		Fuel Cell	
					Simple	Regenerator	PO$_4$	CO$_3$
Coal-derived								
Coal	24–34	—	—	—	—	—	—	—
Coal/oil slurry	21–29	29–34	—	—	—	—	—	—
Coal liquids	13–18	18–20	11–15	13–15	13–17	15–19	—	26–31
Methanol	11–16	16–18	10–13	11–13	11–14	13–16	18	22–26
Hydrogen—gas	11–16	16–18	11–18	11–13	11–14	13–16	18	22–26
—liquid	6–8	8–9	6–10	6–7	6–8	7–9	9	12–14
Methane—gas	14–19	19–22	12–16	14–16	14–18	16–20	22	28–34
—liquid	12–16	16–19	10–14	12–14	12–15	14–17	19	24–29
Shale								
Liquids	14–20	20–23	13–17	14–17	14–18	16–20	22	28–34
Biomass								
Ethanol	7–10	10–11	6–8	7–8	7–9	8–10	11	14–16
Methanol	8–10	11–12	7–9	8–9	8–10	9–11	12	15–18

SOURCE: *Alternative Fuels for Maritime Use*, MTRB, U.S. National Academy of Sciences, 1980.

* Assumes dual feed.

market and its own members. Recent months have seen many un-usual developments such as the following:

- Oil companies who refuse to renew contracts with producers;
- Surcharges that suddenly vanish;
- Posted prices that are not maintained;
- Production agreements that are modified before expiration.

It will be interesting to see how the maritime industry is affected by these developments in the bunker market and how it can operate effectively in this world of changing bunker prices, availability, and quality.

One important consideration is the relation between OPEC crude oil sales price and oil consumption in the Western World as shown in Figure 4–7. Among factors that must also be considered is the amount of oil in storage at any one time. Western World oil stocks have risen from 4.3 billion barrels in 1979 to over 5.5 billion barrels at the end of 1980. It may be too early to predict whether the downward trend in Western demand is accelerating and whether much of it is solely a factor of price (conservation or improved ef-ficiency) or changeover to alternate fuels. Energy consumption in the Western World has leveled off since 1979 and has started to decline at about half the rate as the reduction in Western oil con-sumption. A new pattern of consumption seems to be emerging. It is difficult to assess whether this new pattern implies that oil con-sumption will continue to fall, as so much depends on the (1) cost and availability of alternative sources of energy, (2) cost and avail-ability of oil, (3) political, strategic, and world economic consider-ations, and (4) technological developments.

Although many OPEC countries would like the price of oil to increase so as to at least maintain their purchasing power from oil income in real terms, others feel that the limit has been reached and that any further near-term increase would be counterproductive. For shipping operations, the problem is that bunker costs and avail-ability can no longer be projected with any degree of certainty. Thus selecting ship types and propulsion systems and planning shipping operations are becoming increasingly difficult.

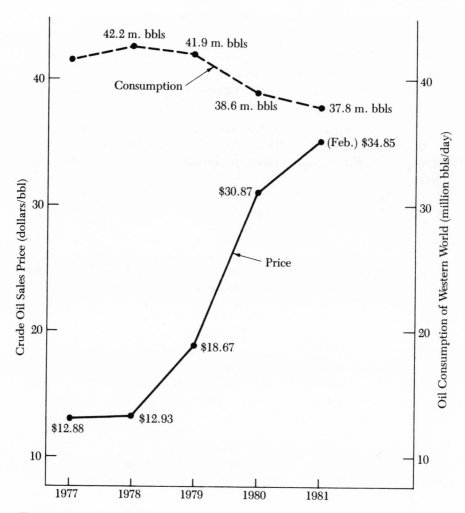

Figure 4-7   Crude Oil Price and Western Consumption. *(Source: U.S. government and International Energy Agency.)*

Appendix 4A

EQUATIONS FOR ESTIMATING VESSEL DAILY FUEL CONSUMPTION AND VARIABLE VOYAGE COSTS

Fuel consumption (C) in tons per day is given by

$$C \approx 0.0042 \, (\%)^{\, 0.92} \, (SHP_D)^{\, 0.996} \quad \text{Diesel,}$$
$$C \approx 0.0055 \, (\%)^{\, 0.90} \, (SHP_D)^{\, 0.99} \quad \text{Steam,}$$

where SHP_D = function of (speed, displacement, ship form, power plant, etc.).

SHP_D = design shaft horsepower
$\%$ = percent of SHP_D used

Total Variable Voyage Costs (VC) excluding cost of lost revenue are

$$(VC) = \left[\left(\frac{D}{V + 24} \times C \times FC \right) + \left(LF - \frac{D \times C}{V \times 24 \times 2} \right) FC \right.$$

$$\left. \times i \times \frac{D}{V \times 24 \times 365} \right]$$

$$= \frac{D \times FC}{V \times 24} \left[C + \left(LF - \frac{D \times C}{V \times 48} \right) \frac{FC \times i}{365} \right]$$

101

where

V	=	speed in knots of vessel
C	=	fuel consumption in tons per day
i	=	opportunity cost of capital
FC	=	fuel (bunker) cost per ton
D	=	voyage distance in miles
BC	=	bunker capacity of vessel $BC \leq LF$
LF	=	bunkers onboard vessel
LR	=	loss in voyage revenues

If the amount of bunkers loaded, LF, reduces the amount of freight offered and not accepted, then the loss in revenues (LR) must also be considered.

Chapter 5

MANAGEMENT OF SHIPPING

The management of shipping is complex because it involves the administration of large capital units (ships), distributed or operating over large and distant regions of the world where management has little ability to control the day-to-day operations. Furthermore, ship operations are affected by variations in national or international trade as well as complex financial and management relations, and are thus subject to wide fluctuations in demand for and price of services. The responsibility for shipboard management is usually delegated to the ship's master. Shipping management is largely involved in financial planning, investment control, fleet management, marketing of shipping services, and planning, as well as the accounting affairs of the shipping enterprise.

A large number of diverse organizational structures are used in shipping management. These depend on such factors as:

- the type of services rendered (liner, bulk, tramp, etc.);
- the degree of ownership, if any, the shipping company has in the vessels it operates;
- its relationships with users (shippers, consignees, etc.);
- its method or proposed method of operation;
- technology used;
- external or environmental factors that impose certain requirements and constraints.

Because of the large geographical dispersal of shipping operations, management information and related communications systems play a major role in the functions of shipping management.

5.1. Organization of a Shipping Company

The organization of a shipping company is viewed from two perspectives—a traditional functional form of organization and a modern

103

viewpoint where the key principle is no longer separation of line and staff functions. Functional and divisional forms of organizations are introduced to relate to the objective of a ship's manager—to carry cargoes safely and efficiently while maintaining the hull and machinery of the vessel within statutory, classification, and company standards and within an authorized budget. Reference will be made to the industry's manning problems to show how this affects organization design and ship management policies.

In developing the organization for a ship management operation, identifying all the organizational tasks is imperative. Such design may also show how a "matrix" organization evolves from a divisionalized organization. In this context the roles and responsibilities of specialists would be highlighted, and the roles of line and functional responsibilities properly defined. The effective operation of shipping involves the choice of a fleet of ships, the routing of ships, determination of the frequency of service, and scheduling. Many factors enter into the multitude of decisions that must be made by both the operator and the shipmaster.

The role of planning is complicated by the fact that investment and other capital decisions are usually long-term, while many operational decisions are short-term. Because of the risks involved in shipping, it is important to formulate and reevaluate operational strategy in terms of investment and operational planning. Planning involves demand forecasting, route studies, technology forecasting, analysis of economic development planning, and determination of the potential impact of the proposed or contemplated services. Only after the impact information is obtained can the operational planning be performed.

The selection of desired ship or fleet characteristics and development of routing and scheduling schemes to satisfy a given criteria form a proposed operational strategy or plan. Planning in shipping must consider all the physical, social, economic, and regulatory/jurisdictional constraints imposed by the environment of the proposed services or operations.

An issue that must be resolved by shipping management of privately or publicly owned shipping companies is the selection of the objective or criteria of the enterprise. Criteria may be to (1) maximize profit, (2) maximize utilization of fleet of vessels or revenue from the operations of these vessels, or (3) attract the maximum or a given level of demand to undercut competition or gain a foothold in a market at least cost. Since these and other criteria may be conflicting, assuring that the applicable criteria are explicitly defined is important. Too little, if any, effort is usually devoted to criteria definition. This must be done before vessel allocation and scheduling are performed because, as was pointed out, different criteria will result in different optimum vessel allocation and scheduling solutions.

Any effective vessel scheduling and allocation exercise, therefore, must start with a demand analysis and explicit determination of the applicable criteria or objective. Like demand, the criteria may be time varying. For example, the criteria may be to capture a certain market share for a number of years, independent of profitability (though at least cost), and to maximize profitability thereafter.

These inputs provide the requirements and measures for vessel allocation and scheduling methods. A number of formal mathematical, as well as heuristic, methods are available for vessel allocation and scheduling. As will be noted in our discussions, all the formal methods require the adoption of a set of simplifying assumptions. However, they usually permit the derivation of an optimum solution to the problem for both the deterministic case, where all inputs are assumed known, as well as for the probabilistic case, where some inputs (such as demand or physical form of cargo) are only known in terms of some probability distribution. Heuristic methods, as well as simulation models, generally permit use of a realistic set of inputs with few, if any, simplifying assumptions. The methods, though, permit only an analysis of the allocation or scheduling problem without any guarantee of achieving or converging onto an optimum solution. Various approaches have been developed, however, some of which permit effective evaluation of results and convergence on increasingly better solutions until a satisfactory, although not necessarily optimum, solution to the problem is found.

5.1.1. *Structure of Shipping Company Management*

In seeking to understand the complex decision process involved in managing a shipping firm, analysis can proceed along two complementary lines. In one we interpret how decisions are made by shipping executives. Conversely, we can study the structure of shipping decisions. Considering the latter approach first, we would start by constructing a model of the shipping firm; then we would define the principal classes of business decisions, with particular reference to strategic decisions. Shipping firms can usually be distinguished by their economic purpose or objective, in which the measure of success is profit. The basic premise is that the problem in shipping management is to structure decisions regarding resource application or use so as to optimize attainment of the business objective—in other words, to maximize profit.

Just as in any business, decisions can conveniently be divided into strategic, tactical, administrative, and operating decisions. Strategic decisions relate to or are affected by external or longer-range planning problems of the firm, such as financing and fleet expansion. Tactical decisions are concerned with competitive decisions, such as routing and scheduling. Operating decisions relate to resource application, and administrative decisions are concerned with the structure, including its organization and internal lines of authority. All these classes of decisions interact, while distinct decisions within these classes are interdependent and complementary. Strategic and tactical problems are the most difficult to recognize, and, as a result, strategic and tactical decisions are the most likely to be ignored or often are made belatedly. Any proper management environment and administrative structure must provide a good balance of management attention to the different decision classes and decision requirements.

The decision-making process in a shipping company is usually more intense, complex, and far-reaching than in most types of businesses. On the one hand, bulk shipping management is usually concerned with few, but crucial, decisions affected by short-term considerations. The exceptions are obviously bulk carrier owners who space charter their vessels—a small minority. Liner shipping management, on the other hand, is concerned with many, but less critical, decisions based primarily on longer-term considerations. Although some systematic approaches and analytical techniques have been successfully used, judgment, experience, and the right mix of aggressive caution are usually the ingredients required for effective shipping management decision making. Management of even a small shipping company requires international contacts, access to international financing, and an ability to accept risks. As a result, shipping managers must not only be knowledgeable but also astute businessmen. Important, successful shipping management decisions are made quickly, and usually by individuals. Lengthy reviews, committee meetings, and studies have seldom been part of tactical or operational shipping management decisions, although some operators have recently introduced these elements into strategic decision making. Because the decision-making process is so complex and immediate, the structure of shipping management organizations is usually quite dynamic, with decision responsibilities often assumed on an "as needed" basis.

Bulk and liner company management differs not only by decision-making function but also by the range of decisions made. Bulk operator organizations are usually small and highly technical; they consist largely of financial and ship-operating managers. Decisions are usually strategic and operational. Liner operators, on the other hand, usually have a much larger management organization concerned with tactical, operational, and administrative decisions. Strategic decisions play a comparatively minor role in most liner company management.

Liner companies are concerned with marketing, customer relations, cargo booking, cargo planning, and a myriad of other activities of little concern to the bulk carrier operator.

Both centralized and decentralized organizational structures are used in shipping management. In the first a pyramidal organization structure is used, with each manager assuming some line function in a tree-type hierarchy. A centralized structure is organized by specialized functions, relies on rules, and depends on the decisions of a few. In the second a decentralized organizational structure assigns to each manager largely independent decision functions, so that top management deals only with strategic problems; all operational decisions are made at a defined technical manager level. A much greater level of skill is required at all levels in the decentralized organizational structure, which today is increasingly being used in shipping management. An alternative is a matrix-type of management organization, which is discussed in the next section. Centralized organizations are useful where rules can be made and a degree of certainty exists. But in the everchanging environment under which modern shipping management operates, a decentralized organization is usually found to be more effective.

The factors influencing the organizational forms and management styles of shipping companies are summarized in Table 5–1.

If a shipping company is organized by liner function, its structure will be centralized. This is usually the case when there is a degree of certainty in decision-making function by content and timing. For

Table 5–1   Factors Influencing Shipping Company Organization and Management

Ownership	Organizational Forms
Private	Publicly owned, closely held
	Subsidiary of trading firm
	Subsidiary of transport firm
	Subsidiary of large commodity-using firm
	Joint venture
Public	Government corporation
	Government company
	Government department
Function	Liner
	Tramp
	Bulk shipping proprietary
	Bulk shipping contract
	Bulk shipping charter

the company that operates in a constantly changing environment, a divisional, decentralized structure is often adopted.

An increasing number of shipping companies find it necessary today to use a hybrid management approach that combines a centralized vertical line and decentralized functional structure of management and decisionmaking. This is often the result of requirements of changing operations—for example, when a traditional liner company finds itself operating charter or tramp vessels.

5.1.2. *Matrix-Type Organizations*

Shipping management often requires both a centralized and a decentralized organization because it needs both specialized decisions in highly technical areas such as ship design, marine engineering, cargo planning, ship scheduling, etc., as well as a high degree of integration of all these specialized decisions into a coherent whole. The traditional line type of organization is ineffective under such conditions because it lumps people of similar specialization effectively together into a vertical hierarchy, but there is no mechanism for integration at any but the top level in such an organization. In shipping management some of the most crucial decisions revolve around the effectiveness of cooperation among people of different skills at various lower levels of the hierarchy of the organization. In other words, port engineers, ship schedulers, cargo planners, and others must all work together to assure effective operation of the company.

In a shipping organization it is imperative that individual line managers at various levels have a high degree of responsibility and freedom to consult and coordinate decisions with lateral counterparts in the organization. "Lateral" here should not be taken too literally, as titles or positions representing levels in the organization do not necessarily reflect the desirable level of cooperation under a particular situation. This may require coordination or consultation between managers at one level in one organizational line with managers or technicians at a different level in other organizational lines—for example, a port captain coordinating decisions with a senior cargo booking clerk. Therefore, matrix-type organization is designed to permit both line and functional coordination in management decision making.

The matrix structure is essential in shipping, as decisions from ship cargo planning, ship dispatch, and tonnage assignment to complex fleet or new acquisition financing all require both line and functional coordination to converge on a good, valid, timely, and implementable decision. Even though the final decision may be the responsibility of a financial or accounting professional, the advice, as well as consent and decision, of such technical professionals as port captains, engineers, and ship officers will be required to assure the effectiveness of the decision.

There are various types of matrix structures, and organizational theory differentiates among five matrix formats. The selection depends largely on the formality of the matrix that is set up and management strategy in the use of the real or implied matrix structure in furthering its objectives. In formal matrix structures of management a system of approvals and agreements in bipolar or matrix-type decisions is set up. It is a system that requires coordination among system or line and functional managers concerned with a problem, or who can make a contribution to the resolution of the problem.

In an informal type of matrix organization, cross-coordination is achieved by using the advice of professionals in parallel line structures. These are "internal consultants" who are brought into the decision-making process and whose advice is sought and used but who do not share in the final decison-making power. Authority and responsibility are linked in many organizations, and line organizations are usually set up to control a specific set of resources. In an informal matrix structure this remains the case, with the exception of an implied requirement that other laterally involved or interested managers be consulted before the decision is made.

5.2. Management of Personnel

The management of personnel is an important, yet not often recognized, function of shipping management. The skills needed for the shoreside operation of a shipping company are in many ways unique, but seafaring, and all its various jobs, requires long years of specialized training. Although personnel in many manufacturing or service industries require skills that are transferable among industries, skills in shipping must usually be acquired by specialized training. For example, chartering, cargo booking, stowage planning, and many shore jobs require special skill, as do most seafaring jobs. In addition, a major part of a shipping company's personnel is afloat or abroad at any one time—circumstances that require continuous dispatch, repatriation, and other arrangements for shipping personnel. Also required are more extensive and complex approaches to manpower planning, recruitment, and training. Figure 5–1 depicts some of the major issues and activities involved in shipping personnel management for a large shipping company.

Obviously, a much less formal approach would be taken by a small shipping company where personnel management might be in the

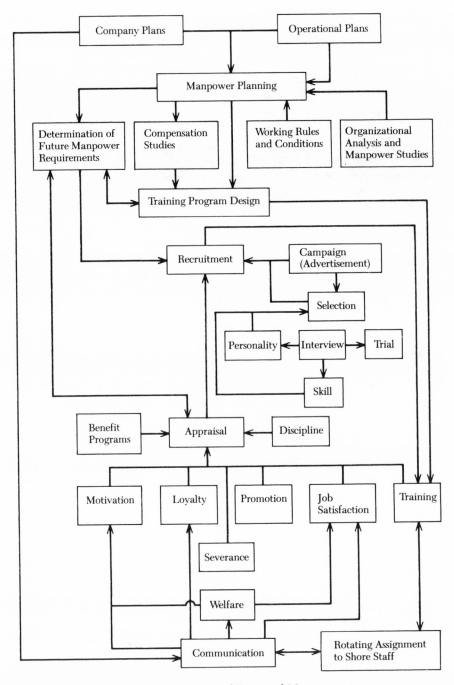

Figure 5–1   Structure of Personnel Management.

hands of a single manager. Regardless of the size of the personnel department, however, some planning to determine future manpower requirements is necessary, as the demand for staff or crew may be thousands of miles away and may require unique skills and qualifications. Holding up a vessel because of the inability to replace a ship's officer would cost thousands or tens of thousands of dollars per day.

Manpower planning requires assessment of a company's plans and objectives as well as its operational plans in terms of schedules, routings, ship assignment, and fleet expansion plans. Using compensation studies, existing or contemplated work rules, and the results of organizational analysis and manpower studies, future manpower requirements can be determined and recruitment can be planned. Another important input into the determination of future manpower requirements is the appraisal of the current manpower level, service times, motivation, loyalty, job satisfaction, training, and promotion or advancement opportunities perceived by personnel.

Communication plays an important role in manpower appraisal. Misrepresentation of company policy or intent or misunderstanding of company benefits and opportunities may result in lowering morale and increasing turnover. Turnover is especially expensive, as replacement of overseas and seafaring personnel often entails heavy relocation and repatriation costs in travel, wages, and other expenses. In 1980 replacement costs at a foreign port of a U.S. crew member averaged $6,200.

Training is another continuous requirement. Ships' officers have the responsibility for the safe operation of a tremendously expensive asset, which can cause large damage to itself, other ships, and its environment if improperly operated. With ship design and operating technology changing all the time, ships' officers require periodic upgrading of skills, long after passing their highest license examination.

The assurance of minimum standard skills of seafarers worldwide has long been of concern to maritime nations. A special IMCO conference was held in June 1978, with ILO participation, to establish such basic seafarers' skills and proficiency standards. At that conference an international convention on standards of training, certification, and watch keeping evolved and was aimed at standardizing levels of proficiency for the issuance of licenses to officers and crew by participating nations. Earlier conferences, such as ILO convention No. 109, dealt with wages, working conditions, and manning, while the IMCO Solas Convention of 1960 was responsible for setting standards of ship equipment for safe vessel operation. Although U.S. fleet operators are usually restricted to hiring U.S. citizen seafarers with skills certified by U.S. Coast Guard licenses and other certifications, ships of other nations are often manned by nationals of many nations with licenses or certifications that are sometimes difficult to evaluate.

5.3. Management of Liner Shipping

Liner shipping, as mentioned before, involves a large amount of selling of cargo space. Marketing, cargo booking, and other cargo-related activities are therefore major preoccupations requiring senior management involvement. A liner company usually has hundreds of staff in headquarters as well as in large representative offices at strategic ports. As most liner operators are members of liner conferences, their rates are generally fixed.[1] They must therefore attract added cargo by effective marketing, superior service, good customer relations, and astute tactical decisions. Their operating costs are largely fixed, independent of the amount of cargo carried; thus profitability largely depends on maximizing cargo revenues by attracting high value (freight rate) cargo and a larger-than-average conference share. Where conference shares are allocated to operators by tonnage or revenues, different tactics may be appropriate. Liner operations are also more constrained from both legal and regulatory points of view. Operators must thus maintain competent legal and government relations staffs as part of management. Operational management is usually divided by major services and often includes technical direction on a service basis. Superintendents are therefore assigned to particular groups of ships employed in a particular trade.

5.4. Management of Bulk Shipping[2]

In general, the organization of a corporate system for bulk cargo transport is carefully tailored to the needs of a particular company. The basic considerations in organizing bulk transportation services are shown in Table 5–2. The general, financial, and taxation questions outlined previously are also considered crucial to the optimal organization of bulk shipping enterprises.

Because many of the financial arrangements used in ship financing do not appear on the balance sheets of operating companies, firms having other profitable investment opportunities and/or limited amounts of capital generally do not own tonnage directly, but rather use charters and joint ventures to acquire shipping. Ownership,

---

[1] Although against most conference rules, discounting or rebating (sometimes deferred) is quite common.

[2] This section was contributed by Mr. John B. Cooper.

Table 5–2   Considerations in Organizing Bulk Shipping

Strength of demand for transportation
   Political and strategic conditions
   Season
   Demand by other commodities
   Demand by same commodity as used by firm
   Long-term changes in production, consumption, and method of distribution

Supply of vessels
   World order book: vessels on order, under construction, capacity and building
      times in shipyards
   Utilization of vessels
   Long-term changes in composition of world fleet

Market conditions
   Current spot and term prices (for subset of relevant vessel sizes and routes)
   Aggregate of past market behavior
   Volume of market activity
   Volume of scrapping, laid-up vessels

Expectations
   Forecasts of market level, operating costs, and shipbuilding prices
   Availability of backhaul arrangements

Nature of commodity using transportation
   Type, grade, quality
   Value per ton
   Seasonal or nonseasonal

Control over commodity source
   Degree of outright control
   Ability to schedule production and shipment

Control over commodity use
   Nature of use (continuous or intermittent)
   Ability to schedule use
   Volume of turnover
   Size of consignments acceptable

Availability of alternate modes of transport

Cost-Related Variables

Impact of transportation costs on firm's responsibility
   Percent transportation of total operating expenses
   Percent transportation in raw material costs

Expected costs of commodity shortage
   Costs of slowdown or shutdown
   Loss of sales, goodwill
   Probability of shortage under various arrangements

Costs of raw material shortage
   Cost of physical shortage
   Cost of capital in inventory
   Risk of spoilage

especially through an offshore subsidiary, is particularly favorable for integrated companies engaged in importing bulk commodities from outside the United States. In this case the shipping subsidiary provides a great deal of flexibility to the movement of funds within the corporate group. Before the repeal of the exemption of shipping income from subchapter "F" base income, the ability to move such funds was virtually unlimited. Thus the shipping subsidiary was a key in retaining earnings from overseas mines, processing plants, and so forth, and reinvesting them without paying a U.S. tax. This type of organization is shown in Figure 5–2. Figure 5–3 illustrates the general flow of funds in this organization structure. The trading company is used to funnel freight payment revenues from the domestic refining company to overseas venture companies dealing in other activities of the business. The shipping company itself plays little part in the net flow of funds, as its revenues generally are kept to a minimum required to service the debt resulting from the ship purchase. The vessels are generally time-chartered to a trading company owned by an overseas subsidiary. This company serves to channel the funds throughout the system. The whole structure is thus

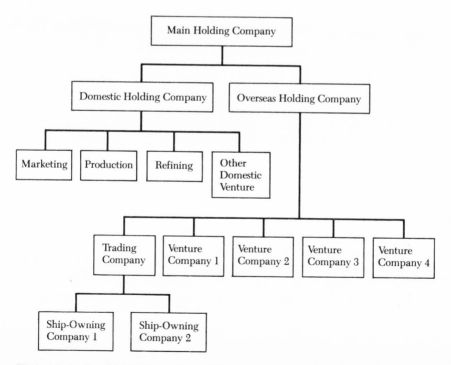

Figure 5-2 Possible Organization of Integrated Minerals Company Exploiting Advantages of Subchapter "F".

protected from the damage claims that could result from accidents involving the vessels or from other problems that might befall the operating company.

The repeal of the subchapter "F" exemption may bring changes in the optimal structure for holding ships. First, with the advantages of ownership through a separate holding company lost, many companies could revert to direct ownership by the parent company itself. This would bring organizational economies stemming from the elimination of offshore offices and reduction of bookkeeping required.

A second possible development from the current regulations will be the more extensive use of joint ventures. According to current regulations, income from a foreign corporation is subject to subchapter "F" when U.S. individuals holding more than 10 percent of the stock hold more than 50 percent of the voting power. The voting power is calculated by ignoring all American interests owning less than 10 percent of the stock. Thus, if five American companies own 80, 5, 5, 5, and 5 percent, respectively, the first company has 100 percent of the voting power. By establishing a joint venture on

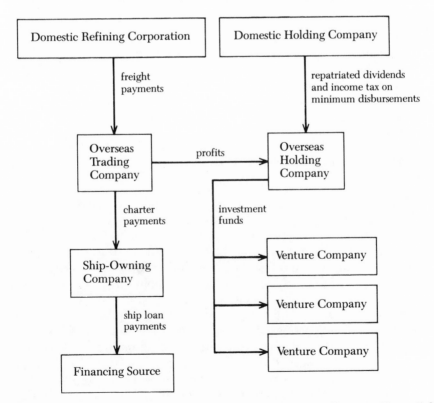

Figure 5-3 Flow of Funds in Import Corporation Structure Shown in Figure 5-2.

an equal basis, an American company can create a tax-sheltered situation at least as advantageous as the subchapter "F" exemption.

Typically, each partner will contribute 50 percent of the equity capital. The sponsoring partner then agrees to charter the vessel, which the joint venture is to operate for a long period. This charter is then used to obtain financing to construct the vessel. With this arrangement, each partner might contribute 5 percent of the vessel's cost, with the bank financing the remaining 90 percent. The profits of such an enterprise will not currently be taxed until returned to this country. If the same joint partner and bank are also used in the operation of other areas of the company's business, the arrangement will continue to provide the same ability to move funds between areas of the business on a pretax basis. In addition, it has the "advantage" of being nearly invisible on the sponsoring company's books, at the same time making 95 percent debt financing possible. This scheme is illustrated in Figure 5–4. The joint venture becomes the source of pretax profits that are transferred to the venture companies through corresponding joint-venture arrangements. Unquestionably, the joint venture will become increasingly popular, for it provides the following benefits:

- A means of satisfying all the concerns a country may have about utilizing vessels and equipment of its own nationality (such as 40–40–20 preference);
- A very large capacity for debt financing;
- Possible owner-management native to the business environment being served;
- Freedom from U.S. taxation;
- Understatement of company's bonds other than direct borrowing;
- Minimal effect of capital export restraints (when these are in force).

Most of the advantages stemming from joint ventures or (previously) from subchapter "F" corporations can only be fully utilized by an integrated company either serving foreign markets or importing foreign source commodities into the United States. If fully developed markets for the commodity and a well-developed price reporting system are available, obtaining as large benefits from these factors is impossible. Shipping ownership must be justified solely on a cost minimization basis. This makes ship ownership unattractive to American bulk exporting companies, and they usually do not own vessels. When they do have an interest in shipping, it is usually through investments in the stock of another company that is not a subsidiary. In this fashion a grain company owns a large interest in the overseas ship holding company of a major American corporation

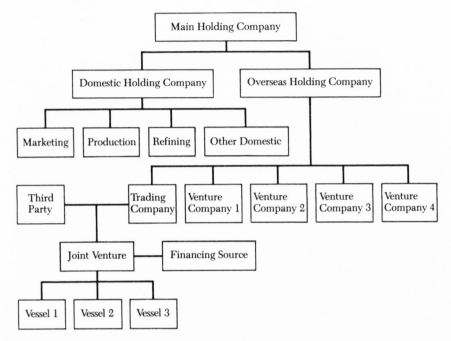

Figure 5–4 Possible Organization of Integrated Minerals Company Using Joint-Venture Partner.

operating bulk carriers and tankers under the American and other flags.

5.4.1. *Risks in Tramp or Bulk Shipping*

Shipping is a field where accurate assessment of risks and subsequent steps made to minimize exposure are very important to the profitability or even survival of ventures. Users and suppliers of shipping have somewhat different attitudes toward risk. Large, integrated firms using marine transportation tend to put a premium on risk reduction (at least in the transportation field) because of long lead times required to negotiate contracts the magnitude of those involved in shipping. In addition, ocean transportation is most frequently only a marginal contributor to the real revenue base of the company. Ocean shipping costs, however, often account for a large portion of the final cost of the commodities shipped and are considered as operational constraints by risk-averse firms.

Shipowners, on the other hand, tend to be much more risk prone. A study by the Institute for Shipping Research in Norway showed that "preference functions" could be derived for shipowners, many of whom are entrepreneurs. These studies indicate a marked preference for risk instead of risk aversion. Ship operators dealing with large companies can assume a role similar to that of an insurance company and agree to bear some of the long-term market risks in exchange for long-term charter payments in excess of the actual cost of delivering the shipping services.

A very complete study of the risk preference patterns of Scandinavian owners brings this point out very clearly.[1]

> *There is some positive relationship between the proportion of the fleet consisting of tankers and bulk carriers and the degree of risk preference of the owners.*
>
> *Measure of diversification and hedging is the proportion of fleet which is special purpose.*
>
> *Presumably, more risk prone owners would opt for short time charters, consecutive voyage agreements, and operations in the spot market while risk averse owners would tend to settle for longer term arrangements.*
>
> *As we have just seen, however, there is a negative relationship among Scandinavian ship owners between the degree of risk preference and the length of charter party they will accept. The least risk prone owners will find short term markets too risky and long term markets unprofitable. In the long run, therefore, they will be forced out of the pure tanker trades into trades where competition is less harsh and the risks smaller.*
>
> *Such alternatives do in fact exist. For these reasons we should accept the domination of Scandinavian shipping by the most risk prone firms.*
>
> *Regardless of the exact mechanism, therefore, we would expect the long-run industry structure to display a close relationship to the effective risk preference profile of the management.*

The risks that a shipowner assumes can be divided into business or market risks, operational or "catastrophe" risks, and foreign exchange risks. The foreign exchange risk, although large during the construction of a vessel, becomes small once the vessel is in operation and can be minimized by careful selection of the currency of payment. Those operational risks not covered by marine insurance or "general average"[2] can be kept to manageable proportions by ade-

---

[1] P. Lorange and V.D. Norman, "Risk Preference Patterns Among Scandinavian Tankership Owners," report by the Institute for Shipping Research, Bergen 1970. See also P. Lorange and V. D. Norman, "Risk Preference and Strategic Decision Making in Scandinavian Shipping Enterprises," Institute for Shipping Research, Bergen 1971.

[2] Under the "general average," certain expenditures to repair or salvage ships are for the account of both the ship and cargo. For example, should damage occur to a ship while it is loaded and the cargoes have to be discharged to repair the ship, the expenses from this operation would be divided between the owners of the cargo and the owners of the ship, according to their respective values.

quate working capital and the provision of sufficient "off hire" time to cover probable contingencies.

The business of market risk, however, is difficult to control using finance and insurance as tools. The market risk is, in fact, a two-pronged one. First, there is uncertainty regarding the accuracy of estimates of future bulk shipments. Second, there are uncertainties of the cost and availability of ocean transportation itself. The market risk is managed by the length of contractual commitments. In general, commodities with unstable volumes shipped or lack of regular patterns of destinations are not suitable for long-term contracts and are shipped in tonnage obtained on the spot market. Government financing or negotiation of sales also necessitates the use of shorter contracts, as the transportation arrangements are generally part of the negotiations.

The effect of uncertainty concerning cost and availability of shipping depends on current rate levels and expectations of the direction of future movements. For numerous reasons no formal options market has developed to institutionalize the risk of shipping rates. Although the charter market for shipping meets many of the criteria for a commodity suitable for options trading, the large value of individual transactions, coupled with the availability of working capital from other sources, rules out the development of an options market for tramp or bulk shipping. It is not, however, uncommon for a user of transportation to make long-term contracts of affreightment with concerns that do not own any vessels and who then fulfill the contracts with chartered tonnage (both spot and term charters). Nor is it uncommon for charters to be arranged with delivery of the vessel to occur up to eight months after agreement is reached. Informal arrangements of this nature are the principal means of handling market uncertainties.

To the extent that international marine transportation makes up a significant element of bulk cost, the options market for that cargo may serve to absorb transportation risks, as most bulk commodities are traded on various commodities exchanges.

5.4.2. *Cargo Sharing in Bulk Shipping*

Since the eighth session of the UNCTAD Committee of Shipping in 1977, in which general recommendations for cargo sharing in liner shipping were developed to lead eventually to a set of international regulations or an international convention, pressure to impose similar allocations on bulk shipping has been increasing. The experience with cargo sharing in liner shipping indicates that such regulation often results in noncompetitive freight rates independent of the supply/demand balance. In certain cases some degree of rationalization

could be achieved, although only where the regulation affected bilateral trade served by specialized bilateral shipping services. Bilateral liner cargo-sharing agreements, in which most participating operators served unregulated multiple markets or markets subject to
different and often contradictory cargo-sharing regulations, have
sometimes brought about inefficiencies, high costs, and subsequent
attempts at escape into protective regulation, including the rein-
troduction of conference-type arrangements. Another experience
with cargo sharing in liner trade, which is of increasing concern to
the bulk shipping industry, is the extent to which "holders" of cargo
shares have been able to license, subcontract, or charter tonnage
or space to carry their entitlement. The result has often been ineffective redistribution of cargo carried, as entitlements were simply
"sold" to the traditional carriers who now carried the cargo on behalf
of the holder of the cargo share. Presumably, similar developments
would encroach on any cargo-sharing regulation of bulk shipping.

Bulk shipping, more than any other component of international
shipping, and, in fact, most industries, depends on a free competitive
market governed by the demand for bulkable commodities in world
trade and the supply of shipping tonnage to carry these commodities
between the trading partners. Bulk shipping is diverse, and bulk
trades are subject to greater fluctuations in volume, trading routes,
and terms of trade. As a result, to be effectively served, bulk trade
requires the existence of highly flexible bulk shipping services capable of moving tonnage and services from one route to another.
This requirement includes the minimization of idle or ballast voyages,
which is essential to the maintenance of low bulk-shipping costs.
Cargo sharing requires the imposition of rights to cargo reservation
or sharing—in other words, regular employment of tonnage. Cargo
sharing, though, is not advisable, as bulk trades (and trading partners)
vary so much that any such regular tonnage allocation would result
in gross inefficiencies and high costs.

Another important consideration is the effect of such regulation
on the free competitive world bulk market. Although one may argue
that many commodities (such as petroleum) are already subject to
monopolistic market forces, recent developments have shown that
even such a highly cartelized market is subject to demand and supply
balances and cannot constrain free market forces solely by price
fixing. Production controls that are much harder to impose and which
by the nature of production usually lag behind such decisions are
an important ingredient. It may therefore be difficult to impose
cargo-sharing regulation even in monopolistic trades.

The cost of shipping is usually a significant part of the delivered
cost of the good, and many bulk commodities are traded at delivered
cost. As a result, it is not at all certain that inefficiencies or higher-

than-competitive costs of bulk shipping will not damage the exporter, which in many cases is a developing country highly dependent on bulk commodity exports for its foreign exchange income.

Bulk shipping serves bulk trade, and the two are highly inter-dependent, with bulk shipping moving to areas of high cargo demand. If bulk cargo-sharing regulation imposed tonnage assignments to specific (usually bilateral) trades, then we would essentially provide shipping capacity well above or below any bilateral trade in the commodity negotiated. The world bulk market, to maintain its capability, must assure exporter's and importer's choice of market and source of supply. The reasons for bulk trade among nations are affected by the demand and supply balance, and by various monetary, credit, political, quality, and other considerations, many of which are subject to change as a result of external and internal factors. Regulated bilateral bulk shipping would cause a dislocation of market forces and constrain trading partners, often against their will or best interest.

Interestingly, the OECD and socialist countries oppose bulk cargo sharing, while a predominant number of developing countries (with the exception of countries offering "open registry") voted for the imposition of such regulations. More than 50 percent of the world trade in dry bulk cargo is between developed countries, which furthermore own and control the vast majority of bulk shipping tonnage. Another consideration often overlooked by the proponents of dry bulk cargo sharing is the fact that developing countries do not have a monopoly in any one of the major bulk commodities in international trade. As a result, they are much more subject to market forces and affected by the cost of bulk shipping than are, for example, exporters of some important liquid bulk trades such as petroleum.

Major reasons for the preoccupation of developing countries with bulk cargo sharing can be summarized as follows:

- Earning of bulk shipping revenues;
- Control over bulk shipping and its terms, including terms of bulk trade;
- Foreign exchange earnings and balance of payment effects;
- Ownership of bulk shipping for prestige and equity buildup;
- Employment opportunities for nationals;
- Improving monopoly position where this is possible;
- Locking in of trading partner;
- Control over physical form of commodity in bulk trade.

The above criteria have different priorities and implications for different developing and, for that matter, developed countries. It is difficult to project the relative benefits and costs of each of the supposed rationales for bulk cargo sharing. The consensus, not only

among major bulk shipping operators and governments of major
maritime nations, but also among developed nonmaritime bulk trading countries, is that cargo-sharing regulation would invariably constrain the freedom of trade in world bulk markets and increase the
cost of shipping.

The counterargument is that both of these disadvantages would
be moot if bulk cargo prices were fixed on a worldwide basis and
if competition were taken out of the bulk market, presumably to
provide security and level of income for developing country (dry)
bulk exporters. Unfortunately dry bulk commodities are widely distributed, and many can be substituted. As a result, fixed bulk prices
and regulated bulk shipping may actually result in a complete relocation of the market and the elimination of some traditional suppliers, some of whom may be critically dependent on such export
revenues.

5.5. Shipping Management Information Systems (SMIS)

A management information system for a shipping company must be
designed to improve decision making by increasing shipping management's understanding of its environments in terms of costs, rates,
markets and related factors, and effective ways of dealing with resulting decision requirements. This applies to all levels of management, which for our purposes comprises every significant decisionmaker in the shipping company, both aboard ships and ashore in
the headquarters or outlying offices. As a result, we will not only
discuss the shipping management information systems (SMIS) requirements designed to keep shipping management informed, but
will also cover aspects of information transfer to and from decisionmakers at all levels aboard or ashore.

Decision making in shipping management requires an understanding of the problem that demands a decision and knowledge of available resources and constraints imposed by the environment, schedule
or service, budget or credit line, and other factors. It also requires
a knowledge of policy and criteria to be used. Without this knowledge, finding a proper approach to the solution of a problem in
terms of a decision is difficult. In other words, an effective shipping
information management system must really be designed to assure
more informed, effective, intelligent, and rational behavior over time
at *all* levels of decision making in a shipping company.

Management functions in a shipping company are comprised of
allocation of resources for the short-and long-term planning and control of the operations and other activities and thereby affect both

the near-term and future performance of the company. The following are among the activities usually comprised in a SMIS:

- Financial planning and decision making;
- Company or corporate planning for resource allocation (both short and long term);
- Company operations planning (long-term scheduling, routing, ship/fleet allocation);
- Shipping operations control (including ship scheduling, routing, cargo planning, conditions, maintenance, inventory and supply, finance, manning, and other).

Financial planning in shipping implies consideration of alternative courses of action in the expansion or contraction of resources to be acquired or sold, based on specifications or procedures consistent with the financial goals of the company. Planning includes selection of resources to be acquired and sources or resources to be used for such acquisitions, as well as allocations of available resources for the effective achievement of the financial objectives within any existing or imposed constraints.

Shipping operations planning is distinguished from overall shipping company and corporate planning. The shipping company is concerned with short-term operations planning; corporate planning places emphasis on the characteristic of longer-range requirements and the objectives of the shipping organization as a unit, comprising the shipping company and its owners, with proper consideration to requirements imposed by clubs, conferences, and governments. In shipping operations planning, on the other hand, the concern is with effective day-to-day operations of individual ships, fleets of ships and services, as well as terminal services.

Both company planning and operational planning are facilitated by the establishment of guidelines in terms of models. Such planning models can be explicit or implicit, normative or constitutional. The choice of the form and logic of the model depends largely on the planning horizon used. The objective of financial and operational control, as of any other control, is to obtain the desired behavior and result from the company or operation. Control can be pre-planned, imposed in real time, or introduced after the fact. The last really implies a feedback type of control, which assures learning from previous experience—an adaptive method of control. These various approaches can often be used as part of one SMIS, as the response times and capabilities of modern computers allow feedback control with practically real time response. Operational control requires the measurement of the status or performance of each resource of the company in terms of costs, revenues, conditions, service, and maintenance. This includes comparison with a standard of the operations under consideration, such as planned or budgeted costs, revenues, and other factors. Including detailed knowledge of the capability of direction of the activity, process, operation, or plan in the short term, under current operating conditions or within existing constraints, is also important.

Operational control requires classification or association of measurement of operational performance with required parameters. Similarly, to be able to pinpoint causes of deviation or potential change from the expected standard of performance, there must be a diagnostic capability. This requires a detailed understanding of the operations, the need and use of resources, and the short-term objectives to be applied.

We will next review the requirements for effective shipping management information systems, from the needs of management for planning and control of daily functions requiring decisions (owners/ operators) to approaches to long–term planning, control, and information handling. The purpose of a SMIS is to provide for the effective operation and performance of the enterprise. As noted in our discussion of shipping organization, the management structure of shipping companies can take many forms and can similarly be widely dispersed. The requirements for effective shipping management and control can be summarized as follows:

- Single line of command and direction and clear definition of authority in terms of responsibility and decision-making powers;
- Clear definition of decision requirements as well as structure of decision chains;
- Cooperation, functional integration, and operational separation of various decisionmakers and implementers—particularly important in a decentralized or matrix type of organization;
- Coordinated use of resources of the company (or ship) in accomplishing the goal and objective;
- Well-balanced resource assignment and utilization based on performance requirements measured against the goals and objectives of the company;
- Effective use of all resources.

Many planning and operational modeling methods can be used for effective planning and control. Not an integral part of a SMIS, they are often used to represent SMIS outputs or to evaluate the implications of certain decisions based on the SMIS. Among these are operations charts, operations flow charts, flow diagrams, procedure flow charts, sequence analysis, Gantt charts, schedule diagrams, multiple activity charts, balance charts, routing and network models, and scheduling charts and networks.

5.5.1. SMIS Requirements

Although simulation and other mathematical modeling techniques may be used as parts of a shipping management information system, the basic requirements are for data collection, assembly, aggregation, feedback, storage, transfer, and finally output in the desired or required format, which may vary with the purpose and the techniques used in a particular system. SMIS reporting structures and the definition of cost and profit or control and decision centers as part of an integrated shipping management control and planning organization are other main considerations that must be determined before an applicable information systems structure can be developed and the requirements of a SMIS established.

The effectiveness of computer aids to shipping managemment and control cannot be established by their contribution to various isolated phases of ship operations. Nor can their adoption be justified solely on the basis of resulting improvements in service, capacity, cost, or profit performance of individual ships or total resources of the company. The effectiveness of computer aids can similarly be evaluated only by considering shipping management planning and operational controls as an integral whole of the decision requirements to accomplish a given objective. The output of an SMIS usually consists of management reports in which progress is measured against plans and the best course of action to compensate for unexpected or unavoidable changes is determined. These reports may consist of resource assignment, schedule, utilization, revenue cost, cash flow, booking, ship orders in progress, inventory, and so on—data in a convenient summary form, issued on a weekly, monthly, quarterly, or annual basis, depending on the reporting level. In addition, the SMIS may issue schedule, route, or resource allocation orders that consist of plans for the performance of services, resource assignment to specific services or other requirements, and so forth. Such orders usually contain a feedback mechanism (to SMIS file) and feedforward (to affected decisionmakers), as well as links for information transfer relating to the performance of the various services or operations to other decisionmakers who may be affected. Ship, resource, and cargo status, puchasing, lead time, in-process inventory, equipment use, cargo handling, and other inventory control information forms are usually another set of outputs from the SMIS. Manpower allocation, manpower loading, manpower status, training, leave, vacation, payroll, hiring, lay-off, and other personnel information comprise the next type of output provided by the SMIS. Finally, there is usually concern with scheduled and unscheduled maintenance actions, casualty reporting, casualty action, services, and so on, both from the point of view of the implication on services as well as costs. All the above reports are not only concerned with status reporting but should also include forecasts of future needs, developments, and implications.

The purpose of installing a shipping management information system is, as mentioned, to improve shipping operations management and control. For effective ship management and operations control, careful study of the application of different numerical methods on a total systems basis is required. Although an integrated and well-designed shipping management and control system can introduce major improvements in cost, profit, capacity, and service performance, it may also substantially improve total resource utilization and improve user satisfaction, with a resulting increase in user goodwill and probably in user demand. These improvements, in turn, may increase net revenues or benefits. Such improvements are usually only derived if service planning forms an integral part of a well-coordinated total shipping management and control scheme. Indiscriminate application of computer aids may result in costly trimmings that provide only empty prestige without economic or quality of service benefits.

5.5.2.   SMIS Design

The design of a shipping management information system should commence with an analysis of the operations, organization, and controls. Where they exist, particular attention may be paid to management difficulties caused by lack of or late reception of the information required for timely decisions or administrative action. A review of the resulting problems, where practical and feasible, is usually instructive.

The design of the SMIS should proceed on several levels, starting with a review of documentation currently used in the shipping operations. Documents describing its formal organizational structure and objectives and its social, economic, and political context should be collected, reviewed, and analyzed to determine the requirements and constraints imposed by the organization and its environment. In the first instance, some preliminary problems may be uncovered, which can be identified with some aspects of the particular organization. Other factors inherent in the formal management organization and company structure and its relationship with surrounding institutions (for example, the nature of government regulation), registry, incorporation, and so forth may suggest lines of further investigation. The extent to which any or all of the shipping company's organizational characteristics can be changed should be assessed before attempting the design of the SMIS, which may include recommended or desired changes in decision sequences or power.

Analysis of existing documents will indicate the current percep-
tions of information requirements for each decision function, methods
of data collection or use of data banks, and format of data. Analysis
will show under whose supervision, in terms of position or administrative level, the collection and control of particular information
and its flow are located. Analysis will also indicate such things as
spheres of responsibility of decisionmakers at various levels. Knowledge of the nature and evolution of the current perception of the
information use and decision-making structure can help in developing
an updated description of the shipping company's managerial organization requirements for effective performance. The formal structure is also the starting point for the analysis of the informal decision-
making structure, which defines the real responsibilities. Informal
relationships and structures are developed constantly within a shipping organization as a result of real need or because of the large
dispersal of functions. Such an analysis provides valuable knowledge
of the perceived problems of the organizations and its operation,
particularly if these relate to information transmittal. The extent and
nature of the informal organization should be assessed, together with
its interaction with the formal structure and the other major sub-
systems of the shipping company. This includes evaluation of timeliness of decisions in such areas as implementation of technological
change. The extent to which the informal system can be shaped so
as to contribute to the management information systems should be
examined.

The social structure of employees and crews and the occupational
makeup of the labor force, particularly with regard to skill and level
of education, its organization, its unions and associations, its de-
mographic characteristics, and the rates of turnover and sickness/
accident, among others, must also be examined. The bearing of these
factors on the requirement for information, along with the problem
of correctly transmitting information, is obvious and is among the
most important inputs into driving the SMIS.

The technical system of the SMIS defines the levels at which the
information needs are identified and the point in the decision sequence structure at which the information is needed and generated.
Of importance is the sequence of information flow from the generator
of the information through the "processors" of the information to the
final "users" of the information. Functional problems and how they
relate to information flows are considerations that must be identified
to permit effective design of the SMIS. Also of importance is identifying operations that are candidates for automated or computerized
control procedures, both from a data as well as physical control point
of view. A typical example would be cargo planning.

A detailed specification of the information needed at each level, and, as a result, for each data bank, is required. The level of detail, periodicity, reliability, and other aspects of the input data varies from one functional specialization to another and must correspond to ideal requirements if the SMIS is to perform effectively. The organizational structure, objective, and environment of the shipping company will obviously affect the format of the information system design and the information delivery formats.

The success of the SMIS, however, will depend on its performance as an integrated "sociotechnical system"—not just as a system that replaces manual data collection, aggregation, and transfer. For this reason, alternative approaches for information handling must be evaluated to permit selection of an effective shipping management information system. Many different structures for MIS are available, and their choice and effectiveness in meeting the needs of a SMIS should be evaluated. An approach to the formulation of a SMIS design is shown in Figures 5–5 and 5–6.

Analysis of both the formal and informal structure of a shipping company should be performed, and consideration be given to social and technical requirements. Internal and external documents, statistical and financial reporting, and other requirements must be established. Similarly, data published by shipping and trade organi-

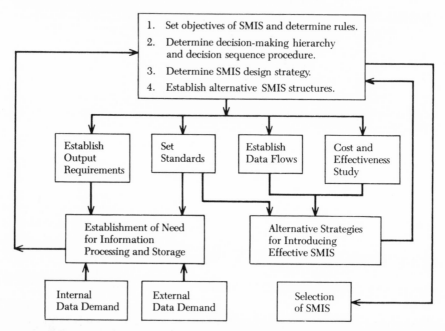

Figure 5-5　Organizational Information Handling: Design Strategies of Shipping Management Information Systems (SMIS).

zations and other types of published material should be evaluated for potential use in the SMIS. Interviews with shipping managers at various levels of the company, labor leaders, representatives of the shippers using the shipping service, suppliers of interfacing transport and other services, bankers, and others should be conducted to permit satisfaction of their needs.

Physical inventories and sketch maps/layouts can be made of the components of the technical system—ships, capital equipment, structures, and facilities. Work-study techniques may then be employed to determine how cargo coming into the system is handled and by whom; corresponding paper movements can be identified. The traffic-handling characteristics of the shipping services can be modeled and subjected to computerized analysis.

Designing an effective SMIS calls for clearly identifying and specifying data requirements by unit, input, output, and need, including estimates of the expected change in data requirements resulting from

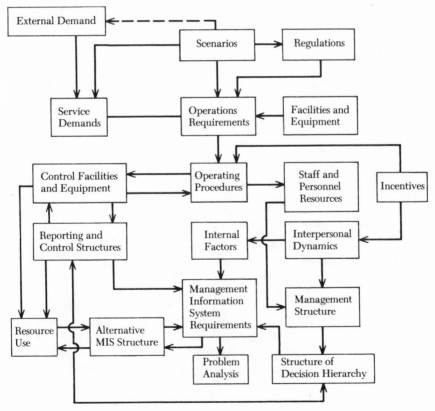

Figure 5–6 Structural Development of a Management Information System.

technological or operational changes. One important aspect is the establishment of the hierarchical relationship between information inputs and outputs (defining, locating, staffing, and specifying). That is, data should be collected by origin, data manipulation, data storage, software, output formats, and so forth to assure that the resulting SMIS truly meets the actual real-time and planning needs of the company.

The SMIS may be designed as an advisory system, whose main function is assisting the shipping managers at all levels of operations to view the implications of any decision. It may be designed as an operations control system, an operations planning system, or a combination of both these functions. If it is to serve as a control system, the data collected about real time status for use in control should be readily accessible for distribution. The SMIS does not make decisions as such, but should help in evaluating alternative strategies by the decisionmaker. Its output is an evaluation of the decision being studied, together with details of the labor, physical equipment, and procedures needed to implement the decision for operational functions. Usually an SMIS incorporates feedback which suggests improvements to the input/output decision, or in other words, the SMIS is used adaptively.

The need for an effective information system to assist in shipping management is largely imposed by the rapid expansion of shipping services and their increasing technical and operational complexity. Information requirements of each decision function, from long-term investment planning to the running of a ship or a crane by an operator, should be established and filled. Format, content, and intermittence of information transmittal should be established to assure that the management information system will provide all the information required (and no more), at a time and place useful to the decisionmaker and in a readily usable form.

The same applies to the development of information gathering systems. The central management information system program should be designed to manipulate, aggregate, store, retrieve, and transmit information required by the system. The program can be structured on a modular basis to permit rapid changes to the management information system in case operational, procedural, technological, or other changes in operations or management are desired. Modules are readily replaceable and changeable, and input/output formats can be designed for flexibility.

The most important aspect of any effort expended on an SMIS is the identification of existing and potential shipping problems and development of their resolution by direct actions in procedures, organizations, operating methods, etc., or by incorporating elements into the management information system that will diminish or eliminate the chances of recurrence or occurrence of these problems. A second important element of a management information system project is therefore the training of management and operating staff, not only in the applications and operations of the management information system but also in the effects the management information system has on their day-to-day functions, operations, and performance.

5.5.3. SMIS Functions

Shipping Management Information Systems deal with the planning and control of ships' functions and those at the ship/shore interface. Some of the major functions an SMIS can serve are listed below.

Financial Planning and Control
    Investment planning
    Vessel acquisition
    Financing analysis
    Accounts receivable
    Accounts payable
    Payroll accounts
    Insurance accounts
    Agents accounts

Cargo Booking and Planning
    Cargo booking
    Cargo assignment
    Cargo routing
    Cargo receipt and storage
    Cargo planning
    Cargo loading/unloading/sequencing
    Cargo inventory control
    Cargo gate control
    Damage identification and reporting

Operations Management
    Ship scheduling and routing
    Ship assignment and chartering

Ship Management
    General ship management
    Operations monitoring
    Survey records
    Maintenance planning
    Ship routing
    Damage reporting
    Ship manning
    Ship inventory
    Ship bunkers
    Ship condition management
    Cargo condition

Inventory Control
  Stores (consumables)
  Spare parts inventory control and ordering
  Bunker planning

Personnel Management
  Personnel planning
  Compensation studies
  Recruitment
  Leave and absence records
  Relief manning

The design of the SMIS will depend on company management requirements that affect its structure and scope, as discussed before, as well as methods and approaches used in communications, particularly between ship and shore. Ships communicate with other ships, with company offices, ship agents, and with various authorities. There are also intrashore and intershore office communications, which can be advisory, informative, controlling, or regulatory. Yet each transfers information, much of which is of potential use in the SMIS. Communication is by voice, visual, radio, satellite, computer, or other link.

Communications transfer information from input to output and may involve information modification or manipulation. Inputs and outputs can be continuous, intermittent, periodic, haphazard, fragmented, spontaneous, directive, or reactive. The purpose of communications is to allow decision making, action taking, record keeping, and so forth by managers onboard ship or ashore. The content and purpose of communications may be operational, legal, informational, recording, storage, retrieval, or data manipulation.

Distance, location, link availability, and accessibility will usually affect the choice of communication link and, as a result, the format of the information transferred. Therefore, integrating the design of the information and communication systems is important. In other words, in designing an SMIS, the function of the information system and role of communications system must be considered, and the format, origin, and flow of required information and generated information, including methods of information transfer, must be established.

5.6. Developments in Shipboard Computer Use

Great strides have been made recently in the adaption of computers to the performance of many ship and shipping management functions, as shown in Table 5–3. A large number of ship and shipping man-

Table 5–3 Computer Use on Shipboard

Operations Planning

Loading, cargo planning, stowage planning
Ship conditions planning, trim, stability, ballast planning
Inventory and supplies, including optimum bunker planning
Maintenance and repair planning, including repair scheduling
Routing: weather routing, commercial routing
Scheduling: ship and cargo scheduling
Allocations: fleet allocation, capacity allocation

Operations Control

Weather routing
Ship docking
Precise steering
Collision prevention
Ship motions control
Hull surveillance, machinery surveillance
Navigation control
Propulsion machinery control
Monitoring of ship (machinery conditions)
Cargo systems control (condition)
Cargo handling control
Communications: SMIS
Ship traffic control
Ship accounts, personnel, finance

agement operational planning and central functions now can be performed or assisted by the use of computers. Microcomputers are increasingly used to develop cargo stowage and ship ballasting plans ashore and on shipboard. Similarly, trim and stability calculations are now quite often performed using microcomputers or hand calculators. Weather routing can be performed using either shipboard or shore-based computers tied to the Marisat communication or similar satellite systems.

Computers are also now used in operations planning as well as operations control. They can be located both ashore and onboard ship. In many applications integrated compatible companywide computer systems are used. Together with the use of modern satellite communications systems, they allow near real-time integrated control of ship operations. This trend is expected to continue and will, in the future, include central control of most shipboard functions from engine settings to climate or cargo control and course setting. Similarly, monitoring, logging, analysis, and real-time transmittal of ship performance data are expected to provide future ship management with a new dimension of shipping management capability.

Appendix 5A

U.S. COMMODITY CODES

In 1969 the U.S. Department of Transportation carried out a study to develop the transoceanic (DOTTO) classification code to improve the compilation of trade data and prediction of U.S. commerce. The study also forecasted for 1970, 1975, and 1980 the shipping tonnages of the approximately two hundred commodities specified in the DOTTO code, as well as trade with the top-ranking U.S. trading partners, accounting for more than 95 percent of U.S. foreign trade. The shipping weights are also predicted for twenty-one broad groups of commodities having roughly similar transport characteristics.

5A.1. Data Base on Foreign Trade Statistics

Essentially two data sources can provide the foreign trade statistics on U.S. imports and exports on a detailed commodity basis. The first source is the U.S. Census Bureau, which compiles the U.S. trade data from reports furnished by the U.S. Customs Bureau. These statistics, designed to serve the needs of a wide range of users, include data presented in various arrangements and released in the form of reports, machine tabulations, and magnetic tapes. The second source is the International Trade Statistics Center of the Statistical Office of the United Nations. This office, on special order, supplies magnetic tapes that contain the trade flows starting with the year 1962 of most of the world's countries. The trade flows are given in the SITC code at the four-digit level in terms of value and quantity shipped. The basic United Nations sources for these data are the countries themselves. Thus, the U.S. trade flows are provided to the United Nations by the U.S. Census Bureau. The United Nations then converts these data into the SITC code. In the creation of the DOTTO code, Census Bureau data were selected as the basic data source, one reason being that, unlike the Census Bureau data, United Nations' magnetic tapes did not contain

135

shipping weight information for all commodities, but instead dealt in such units of quantity as barrels, yards, hogsheads, and so forth.

5A.2. Basic Commodity Codes

Basically, the DOTTO code is concerned with four commodity classification systems, from which several commodity codes are derived. The first system is the Tariff Schedules of the United States, Annotated (TSUSA), which is used to describe imports into the United States in reports to the Customs Bureau. The Customs Bureau transmits its data to the Census Bureau, which then processes and converts them to other codes. At present, and in recent years, the Census reports have used the Schedule A (Revised) code, which is an aggregation of the 10,000 TSUSA items into 2,200 items. Both codes use seven digits per item.

The second system, a seven-digit code, is that used in preparing Shipper's Export Declarations for submission to Customs; it is called Schedule B. These data are also transmitted to the Census Bureau, which reports them in the Schedule B code. The third system is the Standard International Trade Classification, Revised (SITC) code used by the United Nations to report international trade statistics. It is a five-digit code, based on the classification scheme of the Brussels Tariff Nomenclature (BTN). The fourth system of interest is the SIC industry code. Several commodity codes besides the eight-character product code are based on it. Some of them are described next.

Major revisions of Schedule A were published in 1964 and of Schedule B, in 1965. The object of the revisions was to create codes that, at least up to three digits, coincided with the SITC code, so that U.S. trade statistics could be compared readily with foreign statistics. A concomitant objective of the revision of Schedule B was to make it also compatible with the SIC-based (Standard Industrial Classification) product code used by the Census Bureau for presenting data on domestic output. The latter is not the same as the SIC industry code, which is a four-digit code used to classify industries and industrial establishments. The SIC-based product code is, as its designation implies, a code used to classify commodities derived from the SIC industry code. It is an eight-character code. The fifth and sixth characters may be alphabetic or numeric; the others are numeric.

Beginning in January 1978, export commodity information is collected in terms of the commodity classifications in the January 1978 edition of Schedule B, Statistical Classification of Domestic and Foreign Commodities Exported from the United States, which is based on the framework of the TSUSA classification system. The January 1978 edition of Schedule B, which superseded the 1971 edition, involved basic changes in the outline of the schedule as well as in the coverage and reporting numbers for individual classifications. Also effective January 1978, the Census Bureau reports the

Schedule B commodity data in terms of commodity groupings and major commodities in Schedule E, which is based upon the Standard International Trade Classification (SITC), Revision 2.

The Schedule A classification of import commodities, which continues to be based on data initially reported by importers in terms of TSUSA commodity classification, was also revised in January 1978 in order to accommodate SITC revisions which took effect at the same time.

5A.3. Correspondence Between Commodity Codes

It is not possible to develop an exact translation between any pair of the four systems. However, it has been necessary to publish tables of correspondences among all of them. In relating TSUSA classifications to SITC classifications, for example, the Census Bureau committee, which did the work, found that in many cases a group (of one or more items) in one code did not match exactly any group that it was possible to construct in the other code. Thus, many assignments had to be made on the basis of best judgment, usually taking into account what was the dominant commodity in overlapping groups. Any user of the tables of correspondence between TSUSA and SITC who must determine the exact details of a particular relationship may have to consult the U.S. Tariff Commission for an authoritative statement. Since the adjustments usually involve only the fourth and fifth digits of SITC and the fourth and higher-order digits of the TSUSA and SIC-product codes, and since the Census tape files used in connection with the DOTTO code aggregate to three- and four-digit derivative codes (S,T,W,A,B), most cases need not be concerned with the reconciliation of differences in the fine detail of the basic codes. However, it is necessary to reconcile precisely the sort of discrepancies just described in converting tonnage and value statistics from one of the derivative codes to another.

5A.4. Trends in the Use of Codes

As was noted, statistics disseminated by the Census Bureau are collected originally by the Customs Bureau, and commodities must be reported in codes, like TSUSA and Schedule B, that satisfy the tariff collection and export control functions of the U.S. government. At the same time, there is a firm wish to make U.S. statistics compatible with international statistics reported in the SITC code. Schedules A and B have been designed to satisfy these constraints, and there is a reasonable presumption that there will not be another major change in the commodity codes used by the Census Bureau for some years. Consequently, procedures have been worked out for converting from Schedules S, T, and W to A, B, and the DOTTO code that were mentioned previously. Subsequent minor changes can be made easily. It will also be possible to convert A and B to the SIC-based product code, which is something that DOT has expressed some interest in doing. It should be noted, however, that precisely the same problems were encountered in making a concordance between A (through TSUSA) and B to the SIC-based product code, as to the SITC code, and the same judgmental procedures were applied.

5A.5.　Other Commodity Codes

A number of different commodity codes are in use today. Each was developed for particular purposes. Attempts to unify these codes have failed so far, but continue.

- *Standard Transportation Commodity Code (STCC) Association of American Railroads, 1967.* This seven-digit code is based on the SIC industry code.
- *Commodity Classification for Transportation Statistics (CCTS).* This five-digit code was developed for the Census of Transportation. There is a concordance with the SIC industry code. The code is identical with the STCC up to its five-digit level.
- *Corps of Engineers (Department of the Army) Codes.* For some years prior to 1965 the Corps code, with some additions, used the Commodity Classification for Shipping Statistics (CCSS), which is a three-digit code based on the SIC classification. There is a concordance with the (old) 1958 five-digit B code and also with the S and T codes. Beginning with 1965, a new four-digit CCSS code, also based on the SIC, has been used. The old and new codes differ from each other and from the CCTS and the eight-digit, SIC-based product code.

5A.5.1.　*Formulation of the DOTTO Commodity Codes*

Histories of value and shipping weight of U.S. waterborne foreign trade shipments (imports and exports), both by commodity and by country, are readily available on magnetic tape. Compiled by the Census Bureau for annual U.S. waterborne imports and for annual U.S. waterborne exports, these tapes contain greater detail than necessary for obtaining overall values and shipping weights of shipments by country/commodity. To reduce the superfluous detail and the number of tape reels, the tapes must first be sorted and edited by country and by commodity, and then the value and shipping weight of tape records pertaining to each country/commodity pair for each year, for both imports and exports must be aggregated.

5A.5.2. *Transport Homogeneous Groups*

DOTTO commodity classifications were further aggregated into Transport Homogeneous Groups (THGs). THGs represent an attempt to bring together DOTTO commodities that have roughly similar transportation characteristics. From the viewpoint of transoceanic transportation planning and programming, this grouping should prove more useful than the underlying detail. The aggregation carries with it the additional benefit of increasing the probability of forecast accuracy through the operation of the "law of large numbers" or through adding offsetting errors.

Appendix 5B

STOWAGE FACTORS

The stowage factor is defined as the number of cubic feet that, according to experience, are taken up by one ton of a commodity packed in a specific way, once it is stowed on board a vessel. A stowage factor is needed to account for the variation in the relation between the weight and volume of the commodities carried. This variation affects the economic utilization of the capacity of vessels, considered in terms of both weight and measurement. Therefore, according to the nature of the commodity and the way it is packed for shipment, freight rates are fixed on the basis of weight or measurement, or shipping companies are left at liberty to choose between the two systems.

Stowage factors are required to convert freight rates to a common basis, expressed in terms of either weight or measurement. The stowage factor is established in approximate terms and may depend on the origin of the commodity, the type of packing used, and the grade of elaboration. For example, the degree of pressure to which a bale of cotton or wood pulp has been submitted may have a substantial influence on the stowage factor. Since it is a question of the number of cubic feet taken up by one ton of a commodity stowed onboard, the factor will also be influenced by the space usually lost, for instance, as a result of the shape of the barrels, bales, boxes, and so forth.

The greatest difficulty arises, however, in connection with commodities classified as of the same nature, but which in reality may differ widely (for example, spare parts for motor cars, certain types of machinery, etc.). The method adopted in such cases is to apply the stowage factor most nearly corresponding to the exact nature of the various commodities. For this reason the figures used on some routes may differ from those used on others. Hence, comparing the stowage tables given in various publications may prove a complex task since they often relate to commodities that are not exactly alike, or are basically concerned with conditions prevailing in specific trade flows.

A list of the stowage factors of commodities in South American trades is given in Table 5B–1. The source is shown in each case, and mention is made of the special problems encountered in some instances. Table 5B–2 presents stowage factors excerpted from Appendix C of the U.S. Federal Maritime Commission Report, "Puerto Rican–Virgin Islands Trade Study." Finally, Table 5B–3 presents specific gravities and densities of bulk commodities.

Table 5B–1   Stowage Factors of Commodities in South American Trades

Commodity	Cubic Feet per 1000 kg	See Source Notes:
Raw Materials		
1. Garlic, in crates or 12/28 kg boxes	75	1, 7
2. Raw cotton, in 180 kg bales	70	1a, 2, 3
3. Canary seed, in 60 kg bags	60	1, 3, 4
4. Crude asbestos, in 60 kg bags	60	2, 4
5. Paddy rice, in 60 kg bags	50	1, 2, 9
6. Sulphur in all forms		
in bags	37	4, 8, 10
in bulk	30	3, 4, 8
7. Barite (natural barium sulphate), in 220		
lb bags	15	7
8. Bauxite		
in bags	35	1, 4, 9
in bulk	30	1a, 4, 9
9. Kaolin		
in 50 kg bags	45	2, 4, 9
in bulk	40	4, 8
10. Forage barley		
in 50/60 kg bags	70	4, 5
in bulk	50	1, 2
11. Flax fiber, in 150 kg bales	120	1, 4
Jute fiber, in 180 kg bales	85	7, 8
12. Sisal fiber, in bales	100	5, 8, 11
Jute fiber, in 180 kg bales	60	2, 9
Fresh fruit:		
13. Pineapples, in 40 kg crates	125	2, 5, 12
14. Bananas, in stems or cartons	100	2, 5
15. Citrus fruit		
Lemons and grapefruit, in		
18/38 kg boxes	84	1, 8
Oranges, in 40 kg boxes	75	2, 7
in 60 kg boxes	90	1, 2
16. Apples, in 24 kg boxes	102	1, 4
17. Unworked granite	20	7, 8

Table 5B–1 (continued)

Commodity	Cubic Feet per 1000 kg	See Source Notes:
18. Greasy wool		
in 250 kg bales	80	2, 7
in 440/480 kg bales	100	1, 4, 8
19. Maize		
in 60 kg bags	55	1, 4, 9
in bulk	45	1, 4
20. Manganese ore, in bags or in bulk	20	1, 2, 9
21. Fish, chilled or frozen, in boxes	65	1, 6
22. Common salt		
in 30 kg bags	40	3, 4
in bulk	38	2, 9
23. Cotton seed in 35/50 kg bags	95	1a, 2
24. Soya seed		
in 60 kg bags	60	5, 7
in bulk	45	1, 9
25. Wheat		
in 60 kg bags	60	5, 7, 13, 18
in bulk	45	1, 4
Semi-Manufactures		
26. Fish oil, in 200 kg drums	90	1, 14
27. Asphalt/mineral tar pitch, in barrels or in bulk	50	8, 9
28. Husked rice	54	4, 9
29. Rolled oats, in 50 kg bags	70	1, 7
30. Semi-refined sugar, in 60 kg bags	45	2, 3, 4
31. Resin and resin acids	50	7, 8
32. Cocoa beans, in 60 kg bags	70	2, 3
33. Coffee beans, in 60 kg bags	65	2, 9
34. Beef, frozen	110	1, 2, 9
35. Malt barley, in bags	70	4, 6
36. Cork wood	220	4, 8, 9
37. Cattle hides, salted (18/24 kg each)	45	1, 2, 3
38. Railway sleepers, wooden	40	1, 7
39. Quebracho extract, in 50 kg bags	45	1, 2, 4
40. Ferro-manganese, ferro-chromium, ferro-nickel, ferro-silicon, and other ferro-alloys, in boxes or in bulk	20	7, 8
41. Dried fruit, in 11 kg cases or 27 kg cartons	55	1, 3
41a. Banana flour	70	5
42. Beef fat and tallow, in boxes or 200/220 kg drums	90	1, 7
43. Cereal (chiefly maize) flour, in 55/60 kg bags	70	1, 7

Table 5B–1 (continued)

Commodity	Cubic Feet per 1000 kg	See Source Notes:
44. Dried vegetables, in 60 kg bags	60	1, 2, 3
45. Sawn timber	90	2, 3
46. Logs, approximately 1000 kg each	40	2, 5
Balsa logs	320	3, 7, 15
47. Metal bars	10	1, 2, 9
48. Sodium nitrate, in bags	35	3, 9
49. Tea, in 35/45 kg cases or 27/33 kg bags	125	1, 7
50. Casings, salted		
in 180 kg bags	70	2, 4
in 260/330 kg casks	90	1, 7
51. Maté, canchada (not ground), in 60 kg		
bags or 28 kg cases	100	2, 16
52. Refined zinc	10	6, 8
Simple Manufactures		
53. Edible oils		
in casks or drums	75	1, 7
in bulk	39	1, 7
54. Lubricating oils and grease, in 200 kg		
barrels	60	8, 2, 9
55. Preserved olives, in 230/260 kg casks or		
barrels	70	1, 8
56. Stainless steel bars	15	7
57. Cellulose acetate, powdered or in grains	140	7
58. Sulphuric acid, in drums	40	7
59. Copper wire	35	7, 8
60. Iron or steel wire	50	4, 7
61. Alcoholic beverages (spirits), in cases	55	8
62. Industrial alcohol, in 200 kg drums	65	2, 7, 8
63. Cereal preparations	88	7
64. Refined sugar, in 60 kg bags	45	2, 4
65. Soluble coffee, in boxes	100	(estimation)
66. Casein, in 50/60 kg bags or 200 kg		
barrels	70	1, 4
67. Synthetic rubber, in bales, bags, or		
boxes	70	7, 8
68. Mechanical or chemical wood pulp, in		
bales	100	17, 18
69. Portland cement, in bags	40	7
70. Cigars, in boxes	140	4, 5
Cigarettes, in boxes	180	2
71. Nails and screws	40	7
72. Electrolytic copper, in 130 kg ingots	20	1, 7
73. Canned meat, in 30 kg cases		
(10/40 kg)	55	1, 2, 4

Table 5B–1   (continued)

Commodity	Cubic Feet per 1000 kg	See Source Notes:
74. Canned fruit, in cases	55	1, 3, 4
Canned vegetables (palmetto)	46	2, 5
75. Canned fish or shellfish, in cases or cartons	55	3, 6
76. Iron or steel sheets	15	7, 8
77. Hardboard	40	5
78. Beef extract and juices, in 60 kg cases	55	1, 4
79. Fertilizers/urea, in 60 kg bags	50	4, 7, 8
80. Meat meal, in 50 kg bags	60	1, 4
81. Fish meal, in 50 kg bags	55	1, 6
82. Cotton and flax yarn, in bales or cases	100	7
Woolen yarn, in cases	200	4, 7
83. Fruit juices, in casks or drums	70	1, 4
84. Refractory bricks	30	7, 8
85. Wool tops, in bales of approx. 310 kg	125	1, 4
86. Condensed milk, in 26 kg cases	45	2, 8
87. Powdered milk, in 31 kg bags or 18/20 kg cases	85	1, 18
88. Plywood	100	1a
Veneer, in bundles	70	4
89. Cocoa butter, in boxes or packages	55	4, 7
90. Margarine	55	4
91. Carbon black, in bags	110	7, 8
92. Newsprint, in 200 kg rolls	120	2, 4
93. Dried fish, in boxes	80	3, 4
94. Polyethylene, solid or liquid resins, in drums or bags	80	7
95. Cheese, in 48/68 kg cases	70	1, 4, 8
96. Rails	15	7
97. Jute, henequen, and other fiber bags for packing, in 250 kg bales	110	4, 5
98. Caustic soda (sodium hydroxide), in drums	30	7
99. Prepared soups or broths, in cases	55	7
100. Cotton textile goods, in boxes or bales	100 70	2, 4, 5, 7
Woolen textile goods, in boxes or bales	200	1, 4
Linen textile goods, in boxes	85	7
101. Copper tubes	70	7, 18
102. Iron or steel tubes	55	7, 18
103. Sheet glass, in boxes or crates	43	1, 18
104. Bottled wine, in 18 kg cases	70	1, 4

Highly Processed Manufactures

105. Carpets, in bales	200	4, 7, 8

Table 5B–1 (continued)

Commodity	Cubic Feet per 1000 kg	See Source Notes:
106. Electric bulbs (lamps)	200	7
107. Electric telephone and telegraph apparatus	140	18
108. Leather goods	105	5
	200	4
109. Ceramic sanitary ware	170	5
110. Motor cars	Various	
111. Motor car parts, spare parts and accessories	70	5
	140	18
112. Caffeine, in 50 kg boxes or 100 kg drums	110	5, 7
113. Leather footwear	120	4, 7
114. Processed rubber, mainly tires	150	2, 7
115. Clothing	120	7
116. Synthetic or artificial textile fibers	70	1a, 7
117. Books	70	7
Periodicals	60	4, 7
118. Agricultural machinery	70	18
119. Calculating, adding, and accounting machines	90	7, 18
120. Sewing machines	90	4, 7, 18
121. Washing machines, domestic	160	4, 18
Refrigerators, domestic	210	5, 18
122. Menthol (crystallized), in boxes	70	5, 7
123. Wooden furniture, in crates	175	7
Steel furniture	310	7
124. Dry cell batteries, in boxes	45	4, 7
125. Iron or steel containers for compressed or liquid gas	55	4, 7
126. Wheels for railways	50	8
127. Electric transformers	50	5, 7

SOURCES:
1. *The "MAR" Year Book*, Buenos Aires, 1966.
1a. *The "MAR" Year Book*, Buenos Aires, 1962–63.
2. "Notas sobre Estiva—Para uso dos Contra-Mestres de Terno," Sao Paulo, 1942.
3. *Puertos Chilenos*, Horacio Larrain Dooner, Santiago, 1966.
4. Data supplied by ELMA, Buenos Aires, 1967.
5. Data supplied by Lloyd Brasileiro, Rio de Janeiro, 1967.
6. Data supplied by Grace Lines, Valparaiso, 1967.
7. Joseph Leeming, *Modern Ship Stowage*, New York, 1963.
8. R. E. Thomas, *Stowage*, Glasgow, 1950.
9. *International Shipping and Shipbuilding Directory*, London, 1965.
10. Sulphur in bags. The stowage factor was calculated as 37, on the basis of data from ELMA corroborated by source 8, *Stowage*, where the figure given is 35/37 (in bags). However, source 3, *Puertos Chilenos*, and source 6, Grace Lines, mention 80 cubic feet per ton, presumably for sulphur in the natural state.
11. Sisal fiber, in bales. Stowage factor calculated as 100 cubic feet per ton, in line with sources 5 and 8. In sources 3 and 6, however, the figure given is 170 cubic feet.

Table 5B–1   (continued)

12. Pineapples, in crates. Stowage factor of 125 cubic feet applied, in conformity with the Brazilian source (2). ELMA, however, indicated 71 cubic feet per ton for pineapples in 45 kg boxes, and sources 7 and 8 gave 70/80 cubic feet.
13. For wheat in bags, sources 5 and 7 give 60 cubic feet, while the figure shown by sources 1, 4, and 9 is 50 cubic feet.
14. Fish oil in drums. The stowage factor applied was 90 cubic feet. According to source 1, it is 70/90 cubic feet for 200 kg casks or drums. In sources 7 and 8, however, it is given as 55/60 cubic feet.
15. Balsa wood. The stowage factor is 320 cubic feet per ton according to sources 3 and 7, and 185 cubic feet according to source 6.
16. Maté, in bags. The Brazilian source (2) shows 100 cubic feet, whereas source 7 gives a figure of 142 cubic feet per 1,016 kg, without taking into account the space lost in stowage on board.
17. Wood pulp, in bales. The factor applied was 100 cubic feet, according to experience in Brazil's, export trade, although other sources—7, 8, and 9—give lower figures, ranging from 52 to 75 cubic feet per ton.
18. Information received from Latin American shipping companies and other sources.

Table 5B–2   U.S. Federal Maritime Commission Stowage Factors

Commodity	*Average Stowage Factor*
Dry Containerized Commodities	
1. Fabricated textile products: dry goods (95%), nylon cloth, and flags	125
2. Canned fruits or vegetables: canned or bottled goods NOS (99%) and citrus pomace	50
3. Machinery or parts, NEC	90
4. Feed or feedstuffs: prepared foods for animals, fish or fowl (80%), animal food, livestock minerals, and urea animal feed supplement	65
5. Paperboard boxes or cartons	90
6. Household goods in packages, in shipper's containers, and loose in trailers	350
7. Household or office furniture, NEC: office furniture (13%), furniture NOS, and hammocks	300
8. Soap or detergent: cleansing, scouring, and washing compounds (50%); soap stock; laundry soap; and soap, NOS	90
9. Vitreous china plumbing fixtures	140
10. Leaf tobacco	110
11. Paints, varnishes, lacquers and enamels, including paint NOS (55%) and shellac varnish (10%)	60
12. Plastic materials, synthetic resins (85%), synthetic latex, expanded polystyrene, acetate powder, and air entraining solution	70
13. Footwear: shoes (90%) and boots	175
14. Mixed canned goods	75
15. Glass containers, caps, or covers: bottles or glass jars	110

Table 5B–2 (continued)

16. Refrigerators and parts	200
17. Fabricated plastic products: bags, cellophane, plastic products NOS (75%), cellophane products and articles, and plastic flower pots	200
18. Inner tubes, rubber	180
19. Confectionery or related products: cocoa (55%), cocoa butter, cocoa beans, and cough drops	75
20. Lubricating oil: form, lubricating (75%), machine NOS, and white	45
21. Steel pipe and fittings, iron and steel, not exceeding 8″ inside diameter	40
22. Small electric cooking appliances	250
23. Drinks, canned or bottled: malt (80%) and flavored	50
24. Tin mill products: tin or terne plate and tin	10
25. Toilet preparations	85
26. Meat or sausage, cooked, cured or dried, including smoked, preserved, and salted	50
27. Biscuits, crackers, pretzels, and snack items	200
28. Lubricants or similar compounds: Motor fuel antiknock compound (85%), hydraulic brake fluid, and hydraulic oil	75
29. Games or toys	180
30. Sanitary tissue or health products: tissue paper (25%), neck bands, toilet paper (28%), paper towels, and related articles (45%)	175
31. Beans, dry, ripe: in bags (95%) and NOS	45
32. Stationery: books (15%), tablet paper, and stationery and supplies (89%)	85
33. Yarn: synthetic (85%) and NOS	125
34. Paper products: boxboard (20%), cardboard (30%), corrugated paperboard (20%), pulpboard in rolls (20%), strawboard and chipboard	60
35. Wallboard	80
36. Paper cans, cups, or tubes	200
37. Table, kitchen, art, or novelty glassware	130
38. Structural metal products, iron and steel, tin cans	250
39. Cigarettes	110
40. Coarse paper or wrapping paper	80
41. Cooperage: empty wood barrels and empty wood tanks	600(SU)

Refrigerated Containerized Commodities

1. Fresh fruits or tree nuts NEC: fresh fruits and vegetables NOS	80
2. Meat, fresh and frozen	70
3. Poultry eggs: eggs in shell	200
4. Other dressed poultry, fresh, frozen: poultry NOS and frozen	90

Breakbulk Commodities

1. Passenger cars, assembled (vehicles, self-propelled): passenger cars NOS	280

Table 5B–2 (continued)

2. Trucks, tractors, or trucks assembled: trucks or commercial units NOS	300
3. Animals: calves NOS (75%), calves under one year NOS (15%), and cows and yearlings NOS	—
4. Animals: goats	—
5. Vehicles, self-propelled: buses	500

Breakbulk Dry Cargo Commodities

1. Lumber	55
2. Machinery	90
3. Iron and steel pipe or fittings, plain, galvanized, cast, or wrought	30
4. Cereals	120
5. Paper, wrapping, kraft, etc.	60
6. Cotton, in bales, not exceeding 100 cubic feet per 2,000 lbs.	100
7. Furniture	300
8. Lard	60
9. Electrical appliances, equipment, and materials, NOS	150
10. Cotton piece goods	100
11. Crepe	215
12. Beans, dried, in bags; garbanzos; peas, in bags; and lentils	45
13. Malt, in bags	80
14. Onions	60
15. Household goods, used in shippers' containers	300
16. Oils, other than lubricating	60
17. Canned or bottled goods	50
18. Feed and feedstuffs	65
19. Paper, tablet, writing, etc.	50
20. Flour	65
21. Clothing	200
22. Packing house products, NOS	80
23. Plastic products and materials	80
24. Iron and steel, structural	65
25. Paint, dry, liquid, or paste	60
26. Pigs feet, pickled, and pork in brine	80
27. Milk, condensed or evaporated	50
28. Machinery, air-conditioning or filtering	160
29. Paper boxes, cartons	120
30. Iron and steel sheets, other than in rolls or coils	20
31. Vehicles, self-propelled, commercial	225
32. Pulpboard, in boxes and in rolls	70
33. Stoves and ranges, other than electric	180
34. Hardware	110
35. Lavatories and plumbing material	150
36. Rubber and rubber goods	55
37. Paper bags	85
38. Paraffin, crude or refined	60
39. Insecticide	140
40. Dry goods	100

Table 5B–2 (continued)

41. Tires and tubes, rubber	225
42. Rice	60
43. Tractors, other than truck power units	115
44. Leather and leather goods	80
45. Bottles and jugs, vacuum	150
46. Oil, vegetable, hardened	60
Refrigerated Commodities	
1. Meats in barrels, boxes, cartons, or cans	70
2. Poultry, frozen	60
3. Refrigerated cargo	80
4. Eggs, frozen	60
5. Eggs, in shell	200
6. Cheese	42

SOURCES: Excerpted from Appendix C of the U.S. Federal Maritime Commission report "Puerto Rican–Virgin Islands Trade Study," April 1970. Operating data supplied by Sea-Land Service, Inc.; Seatrain Lines, Inc.; Motorships of Puerto Rico, Inc.; TMT Trailer Ferry, Inc.; South Atlantic and Caribbean Lines, Inc.; Lykes Bros. Steamship Company; Gulf Puerto Rico Lines, Inc. (FMC—Forms I–V).

Table 5B–3 Specific Gravities and Densities of Bulk Commodities

Item	Specific Gravity	Pounds/ Cubic Foot
Aluminum bronze	7.7	481
Anthracite (coal)	1.4–1.7	97
Asphalt	1.1–1.5	81
Bituminous (coal)	1.2–1.5	84
Brass (70% W, 30% Zn)	8.53	532
Brick (common)	1.8–2.0	120
Bronze (90% W, 10% Zn)	8.80	550
Cast iron	7.2	450
Cement, loose		90
Cement, set	2.7–3.2	183
Charcoal	0.4	25
Clay, dry	1.0	63
Clay, damp plastic	1.8	110
Coke	1.0–1.4	75
Concrete, plain	2.2	144
Concrete, reinforced	2.3	150
Cork	0.24	15
Corn, bulk	0.73	45
Cotton, flax, hemp	1.47–1.50	93
Earth, dry loose	1.2	76
Earth, dry packed	1.5	95
Earth, moist loose	1.3	78

Table 5B–3 (continued)

Item	Specific Gravity	Pounds/ Cubic Foot
Earth, moist packed	1.6	96
Flour, loose	0.4–0.5	28
Gasoline	0.75	468
Glass, common	2.4–2.8	162
Granite	2.6–2.7	165
Gravel, dry	1.6	100
Gravel, wet	1.8–2.0	120
Hay and straw, bales	0.32	20
Iron ore (hematite)	5.2	325
Leather	0.86–1.02	59
Lignite	1.1–1.4	78
Limestone	2.1–2.86	155
Limonite (iron ore)	3.6–4.0	237
Magnetite (iron ore)	4.9–5.2	315
Oats, bulk	0.51	32
Oil, vegetable	0.91–0.94	58
Oil, fuel	1.0	63
Oil, lubricant	0.9	56
Paper	0.70–1.15	58
Potatoes, piled	0.67	44
Rubber (goods)	1.0–2.0	93
Rubber (raw)	0.92–0.96	59
Salt	0.77	48
Sand, dry		100
Sand, wet		120
Sandstone	2.0–2.6	143
Slag	2.5–3.0	172
Steel	7.87	490
Sugar	1.61	100
Wheat, bulk	.77	48
Wood, seasoned	.35–.77	22–48

Chapter 6

COST ANALYSIS OF SHIPPING OPERATIONS

Previous chapters have reviewed the traditional functions of and recent developments in shipping and explored the structure, problems, and challenges of shipping management. Clearly, many forces affect the competitive situation of shipping; yet the failure or success of a shipping company ultimately rests on the actual allocation and operation of its ships. Even if the right ship has been selected, an economic trade route established, terminals provided, service sold, and everything possible done to generate the maximum income, the investment strategy used and operational phase of the cost structures remain decisive. Apart from directing the vessel movements, "operation" includes manning, loading, stowing, discharging, repair, maintenance, inspection, victualing, and a multitude of lesser activities. The operating department spends a major part of the company's revenue, but cost control is difficult. A company must await results of voyage accounts to determine the net profit. Chapter 6 discusses the financial and operating costs of ships.

6.1. Components of Shipping Operations

The components of shipping operations are (1) ship and crew, (2) terminal facilities, (3) supervision, and (4) administration. Of these components, the following cost items of an ordinary cargo ship must be controlled:

- Wages (straight time, overtime, and bonuses for deck, engine, steward's, and purser's departments)
- Subsistence and provisions
- Stores, supplies, and equipment in the deck department (consumable stores, rope, expendable equipment), the engine de-

153

partment (consumable stores, expendable equipment, and lubricants), and the steward's department (consumble stores, crockery, silverware, glassware, linen, etc.)

- Miscellaneous maintenance expenses not listed above, such as shoregang labor, loading stores, etc.
- Fuel
- Repairs (hull and deck department, steward's department, extraordinary drydock repairs, inspection and classification surveys)
- Insurance (marine, P&I, other)
- Charter hire (if applicable)
- Fresh water
- Launch hire and sundry vessel expenses
- Wharfage and dockage
- Pilotage, tug hire, towage
- Dues, quarantine, customs, and consular fees
- Stevedoring charges and expenses for rehandling of cargo
- Dunnage
- Hire of clerks
- Expense of cleaning holds and cargo tanks
- Lighterage
- Hire of guards and security
- Shore services (electricity, telephone, etc.)

The ship's ability to render effective service determines its value, which is determined by analysis and study of the following: efficiency, ease of maintenance, and reliability of loading and handling equipment; cargo ventilation and refrigeration equipment; capacity, condition, and arrangements of holds and tanks; ease of access; maintainability; and speed. These factors influence a potential customer and the shipper. Hull shape affects propulsion efficiency, hull construction cost, and maintenance. Terminal limitations on draft, length, or beam of ship (also imposed by locks and canals), governmental and international regulations and restrictions, and requirements of classification societies and underwriters all impose constraints that must be considered by the company or owner when choosing a particular vessel.

A ship operator must provide a place for the shipper to deliver cargo to be loaded on the ship and a place for a consignee to pick up cargo discharged from the ship—either the operator's own terminal or pier or a public or private facility. Selection of pier facilities is based on the adequacy of berthing space, size of wharf apron, transit shed, rail and motor access, channel width for barge loading, and supporting transportation and storage facilities.

The most important of the shoreside facilities is the stevedoring operation. Operators may employ their own stevedores, or work with a stevedoring company that maintains many of the special cargo-handling items. Longshoremen usually are hired as casual labor for a particular job. Gang size varies with port, cargo, and handling facilities. Maximum gang size is eighteen to twenty-five men. One gang working a hold consists of a boss, a hatchtender, a winch driver, six hold men, two dock men, and others as required for specific operations. Port and terminal management, charge estimates, supervision, and use of marine facilities are part of terminal operation. A detailed description of each of these aspects will be given later.

Decision making in the operation department of a cargo shipping company is largely decentralized. The organization of the department is as follows:

Dock and Wharf Division
Receiving cargo from shippers and agents
Loading or discharging vessel (may be contracted to a stevedoring company)
Delivering cargo to consignees
Acting as stevedores, etc. for other companies
Maintaining equipment

Marine Division
Safeguarding vessel's seaworthiness
Supervising repair work and annual drydocking
Providing for bunkering and stores
Preparing shipping articles and other papers
Supervising seagoing personnel
Supervising communications

Engineering Division
Supervising engine room maintenance and repairs
Supervising seagoing personnel

Steward's Division
Victualing the ship, providing supplies, etc.
Supervising seagoing personnel
Handling labor relations

The overriding factor and rallying point in operation is normally the schedule of the vessel. Operating efficiency depends on minimizing the number of days the ship is at sea and the turnaround time in port. Cargo booking and claims filing is often done by the traffic department, but all the paperwork connected with loading and discharging is handled by the operating staff. To obtain the advantages of bulk buying, larger companies concentrate all purchases in a combined purchasing division, which prevents overlapping procurement for different departments.

The major aspect of the ship's operation is manning. Duties and responsibilities onboard ships are well defined and concerned with efficient operation, maintenance, and safety of ship, crew, cargo, and passengers. To ensure vessel safety, the U.S. Coast Guard, for example, is required by law to fix minimum manning scales for all ships registered under the U.S. flag. Manning scales vary widely; usually high skill, high rates of pay, and small crews go together, as do low wages, lesser skill, and larger crews.

Generally, by international agreement, classification rules, and government regulation, a minimum complement consisting of licensed navigating officers, engineers, a radio operator, and ratings is required. The size depends on the type of ship, the type of engine and its output, and the service in which the vessel is employed.

6.2. Ship Operating Costs

Ship operating costs are usually divided into fixed and variable costs, with variable costs further divided into at-sea and in-port costs. Costs vary among countries, owners, and the service in which a particular ship is employed. The major cost categories are usually divided into:

Fixed Costs
1. Financing costs—Amortization, interest, etc.
2. Crew and manning costs
3. Insurance cost—Hull, P&I, etc.
4. Administration
5. Overhead

Variable Costs
In-Port
1. Fuel and lubricating oil
2. Maintenance and repair
3. Port dues
4. Supplies
5. Cargo handling costs
6. Brokerage
At-Sea
1. Fuel and lubricating oil
2. Maintenance and repair
3. Supplies

The above operating cost categories are discussed and analyzed in this chapter, and summarized for various major types of interest.

6.2.1. *Financial Costs*

Financial costs vary from owner to owner and depend on the terms of construction, mortgage, and other loans, as well as direct construction subsidies, shipyard prepayment discounts, owner- or government-supplied equipment, and more. As these terms vary widely, assume for our purposes that the financial costs to the owner equal linear repayment of total capital costs over a twenty-year period plus average (midlife) interest costs, with no credit for scrap or residual value after twenty years. From this, the annual and daily financial costs for various ship types are derived and presented in Table 6–1. Financial costs of secondhand tonnage are difficult to determine because expected useful life and the acquisition terms of such tonnage vary widely.

No separate financial costs for U.S.-built tonnage are indicated because cost parity equates these to foreign costs for vessels used in the foreign trade of the United States, which qualify for cost-parity construction differential subsidy. As a result, financial costs of U.S.-built tonnage should roughly equal that of foreign-built tonnage. Although U.S.-built ships generally qualify for government-guaranteed mortgage loans and therefore lower cost (8.75 percent in 1978) financing, a 10 percent interest rate assumed for world shipbuilding is applied to U.S.-built vessels as well. The reason is that certain other requirements, such as a three-quarter point loan insurance charge payable to the government, make the effective rate of interest paid by a U.S. owner larger than the quoted rate of the government-guaranteed mortgage bonds, and close to the 10 percent in recent years. In fact, U.S. rates have in recent years risen to well above the two-digit level (12 to 15 percent) as a result of the sharp increase in the U.S. prime lending rate during 1980–1981. Foreign shipbuilding loan rates, on the other hand, have in some cases been maintained well below 10 percent as a result of government aid or loan interest subsidy to ailing shipbuilding industries. Unit prices of newbuildings for recent years are shown in Table 6–2.

6.2.2. Crew and Salary Costs

Crew and salary costs are only weakly dependent on ship size and type. In recent years, crews on most U.S. vessels averaged thirty-two men, with an increasing number of vessels operating with significantly lower manning. The average burdened cost of a crew member on a U.S. vessel (including wages, medical insurance, social insurance, overtime, uniform allowance, family benefits, extras, vacation, repatriation, and so forth) was $51,020 per year in 1980. Comparative foreign vessel crew costs averaged $29,800 per year. Typical U.S. and foreign crew salary costs are summarized in Table 6–3, which includes a multiplier effect accounting for the number of men per slot (relief crew) in a manning scale. Foreign crew costs are an average of OECD manning costs using about 50 percent of low-cost crew at the lower ranks.

Table 6-1 Vessel Financial Costs (in 1980 prices, U.S. dollars)

Vessel	Size (DWT)	Annual Cost ($ million)			Daily Finance Cost ($)		
		Depreciation	Interest	Total	Depreciation	Interest	Total
Bulk carrier (nonself-unloading)	20,000	0.66	0.66	1.32	1,799	1,799	3,598
	30,000	0.92	0.92	1.84	2,520	2,520	5,040
	50,000	1.34	1.34	2.68	3,679	3,679	7,358
	100,000	2.29	2.29	4.58	6,279	6,279	12,558
	150,000	3.28	3.28	6.56	8,999	8,999	17,998
	200,000	4.19	4.19	8.38	11,494	11,494	22,988
	250,000	4.89	4.89	9.78	13,400	13,400	26,800
Bulk carrier (self-unloading)	20,000	0.85	0.85	1.76	2,432	2,432	4,864
	30,000	1.20	1.20	2.40	3,266	3,266	6,532
	50,000	1.76	1.76	3.52	4,822	4,822	9,644
	100,000	2.83	2.83	5.66	7,758	7,758	15,516
	150,000	3.95	3.95	7.90	10,850	10,850	21,700
	200,000	5.01	5.01	10.02	13,720	13,720	27,440
	250,000	5.86	5.86	11.71	16,066	16,066	32,132
General cargo	10,000	0.44	0.44	0.88	1,199	1,199	2,398
	20,000	0.77	0.77	1.54	2,120	2,120	4,240
	30,000	1.07	1.07	2.14	2,920	2,920	5,840

Containership (excluding container inventory)	10,000	0.79	0.79	1.58	2,169	2,169	4,338
	20,000	1.42	1.42	2.84	3,895	3,895	7,790
	30,000	2.00	2.00	4.00	5,474	5,474	10,948
	40,000	2.50	2.50	5.00	6,854	6,854	13,709
	50,000	2.97	2.97	5.94	8,136	8,136	16,272
RoRo vessel (excluding trailer inventory)	5,000	0.43	0.43	0.86	1,183	1,183	2,365
	10,000	0.83	0.83	1.66	2,268	2,268	4,536
	20,000	1.42	1.42	2.84	3,895	3,895	7,790
	30,000	1.98	1.98	3.96	5,425	5,425	10,850
Tankers	20,000	0.55	0.55	1.10	1,505	1,505	3,010
	50,000	1.12	1.12	2.24	3,083	3,083	6,167
	100,000	1.90	1.30	3.80	5,213	5,213	10,426
	150,000	2.75	2.75	5.50	7,525	7,525	15,050
	200,000	3.50	3.50	7.00	9,581	9,581	19,162
	250,000	4.07	4.07	8.14	11,149	11,149	22,298

Note: interest 10 percent; depreciation twenty-year; no scrap credit.

Table 6–2   Recent Average World Shipbuilding Prices (in dollars per DWT)

Ship Type	DWT	1977	1978	1979	1980
General cargo	10,000	602	694	782	876
	20,000	541	621	694	773
Dry bulk carrier	20,000	460	532	601	707
	50,000	392	443	498	537
	100,000	367	400	422	458
Containership	10,000	1,101	1,278	1,441	1,584
	20,000	995	1,142	1,307	1,422
	40,000	875	1,014	1,147	1,251
Tanker	20,000	385	447	508	550
	50,000	310	358	406	448
	100,000	266	309	347	380

SOURCES: *Fairplay* (various issues); *Motorship*, Annual Review of Shipbuilding, 1981.

Crew costs vary widely. In a recent United Nations Study[1] it was found that 1975 payroll costs for a typical thirty-two-man tanker crew varied from an average of $328,000 per year for a developing country crew to $482,000 per year for a British crew, $380,000 per year for a Greek crew, $850,000 per year for a Norwegian crew, and $1,750,000 per year for a U.S. crew.

There have been many discussions on the methods of computing crew costs. Crew costs were traditionally computed to include wages, pension, vacation pay, health insurance, sick leave pay, food, travel costs to join vessels or return home on leave, and various miscellaneous costs such as supplies and insurance. However, other costs— such as capital and maintenance costs of crew accommodations, crew administration, crew replacement, medical expenses not covered by health insurance, agents fees for crew arrangement or commissions for providing crews and similar expenses—are usually not included in computing manning costs. Another cost that is increasingly relevant is the cost of providing advances and pay in various foreign currencies. Interest and exchange costs for these expenditures have become significant as a result of high interest rates and rapidly fluctuating exchange rates. It can be shown that these "hidden" costs can add as much as 30 to 80 percent to crew costs. While information on pay scales is usually available, other crew or manning costs are much harder to determine. These vary not only among nations and owners but also according to the type of officer or rating, his union

---

[1] Comparative labor costs, UNCTAD V, Item 14(b), Supporting Paper TD/222/ Supp. 4, Manila 1979.

Table 6-3 Crew and Salary Costs (1980 dollars, including all benefits)

Vessel	DWT Size	Manning Scale	Annual Cost ($ million)		Daily Cost ($)	
			U.S.	Foreign	U.S.	Foreign
Containership	50,000	31	2.53	1.29	6,941	3,538
General cargo	30,000	30	2.45	1.25	6,717	3,427
Bulker-tanker	20,000	29	2.37	1.21	6,493	3,315
	100,000	32	2.61	1.33	7,153	3,647
	150,000	33	2.69	1.37	7,374	3,757
	200,000	34	2.77	1.41	7,591	3,866
	250,000	34	2.77	1.41	7,591	3,866
Tug/barge	20,000	12	1.13	0.64	3,108	1,753
	50,000	13	1.22	0.69	3,353	1,894
	80,000	13	1.22	0.69	3,353	1,894

SOURCE: Interviews with U.S.- and foreign-flag operators.

Note: U.S. crew costs, full costs assuming no operating differential subsidy, including all relief crew costs, vacations, benefits, etc. Foreign-flag typical OECD vessel.

Table 6–4 Typical Insurance Costs (1980 dollars)

DWT	Bulker Annual ($ thousands)	Daily ($)	Self-unloader Annual ($ thousands)	Daily ($)	Tanker Annual ($ thousands)	Daily ($)	Tug/Barge Annual ($ thousands)	Daily ($)
20,000	195	534	219	599	188	515	151	414
50,000	364	997	405	1,109	352	964	252	690
100,000	572	1,567	628	1,720	522	1,430		
200,000	1,040	2,349	1,134	3,107	902	2,465		

SOURCE: Interview with operators.
Note: Average age, 5 years.

Table 6–5 Average Maintenance and Repair Costs (1980 dollars)

Vessel DWT	Bulker Annual ($ thousands)	Daily ($)	General Cargo Container Annual ($ thousands)	Daily ($)	Tanker Annual ($ thousands)	Daily ($)	Tug/Barge Annual ($ thousands)	Daily ($)
10,000			390	1,067				
20,000	364	997	468	1,277	390	1,067	286	783
50,000	455	1,247	650	1,778	481	1,317	364	997
80,000	520	1,425			552	1,513	429	1,175
100,000	546	1,495			572	1,566	468	1,282

SOURCE: Interviews with owners and operators.

affiliation, if any, and the route or service of the ship on which he signs. While it is comparatively simple to determine manning cost for scheduled liners, computing manning costs for a tramp ship, for example, may be very hard.

6.2.3. *Insurance Costs*

Insurance costs depend on many factors such as where and by whom insured, degree, if any, of self-insurance, perils insured against, value of cargo and ship, performance record of operator/owner, quality of licenses of officers, and others. As a result, only general rates of hull and machinery insurance can be quoted. The average annual and daily cost of such insurance is shown in Table 6–4. In addition there is cargo protection and indemnity (P&I) insurance. Cargo insurance may or may not be carried by the operator, and P&I coverage is usually provided by "P&I clubs." These clubs were established as the result of the increased hazards and consequent exposure of owners/operators resulting from increased ship size, increased ship speed, and new laws enforcing environmental and social responsibility. Although originally established on the basis of mutuality or straight sharing of claims, P&I has developed into a method for effective assessment of contribution by each participating shipowner to the losses of the club. Clubs usually pool their exposure and use reinsurance extensively.

Personal and indemnity insurance coverage usually includes the following claims:

- Personal claims, such as death, injury, illness medical expenses, noncovered repatriation, loss of personal effects, damage to personal property, unpaid wages, and more.
- Property claims (collision damage to other ships; damage to ships without collision, such as explosion, fire, or wash; damage to port installations; contractual liability to equipment; pollution-caused damage, including secondary pollution as well as cleanup and other environmental costs).
- Cargo claims, loss or damage by the shipowners' fault, including inability to recover cargo's share of general average.
- Miscellaneous claims, such as fines against the ship, and various other claims covered under an "omnibus" clause.

The subject of marine insurance is complex; yet the cost of marine insurance has become a major element in ship operating costs and must therefore be considered in the financial and economic evaluation of ship performance.

6.2.4. *Administrative and Overhead Costs*

Administrative and overhead costs vary by type of operation, service, nationality of operator, and location. Administrative costs, including agent's fees and other expenditures related to liner vessel or fleet administration, are generally 22 to 35 percent of operating costs. In tanker, bulk carrier, and tramp type vessel operations, administrative costs, including overhead, cargo and ship broker fees, and other expenditures related to vessel administration, are generally 8 percent of total vessel operating costs.

6.2.5. *Port Costs and Dues*

Port costs and dues depend on the route of a vessel, as port and canal tariffs differ widely. These costs usually constitute 2 to 8 percent of the operating cost of a dry or liquid bulk carrier (average 5 percent), assuming cargo loading and unloading charges are not assumed by the vessel and all cargo is delivered free on board (FOB) and discharged at the cost of the consignee. Port costs and dues for general cargo ships, container, and RoRo ships can be significantly higher, depending on ship size and route served.

6.2.6. *Maintenance and Repair Costs (M&R)*

M&R costs vary with the route served by a vessel and fluctuate widely from year to year. The average expenditures for M&R costs are shown in Table 6–5 (page 162).

6.2.7. *Supply and Miscellaneous*

Supply and miscellaneous costs average 3.8 percent of total operating costs of vessels. These costs are fairly independent of the route served or vessel type or size.

6.2.8. *Fuel and Lubricating Oil Costs*

The major difference in the operating cost between U.S.- and foreign-built vessels today is in fuel cost. Most U.S.-built vessels are propelled by steam turbine plants, while over 85 percent of all foreign-built carriers (owned and built) are propelled by diesel engines. The daily fuel consumptions are presented in Figure 6–1. Daily fuel cost may be calculated using Figure 6–1 and the following average 1981 fuel costs: bunker C, $185 per ton (1980 cost = $160 per ton); diesel oil, $280 per ton (1980 cost = $240 per ton). Also assume that diesel-

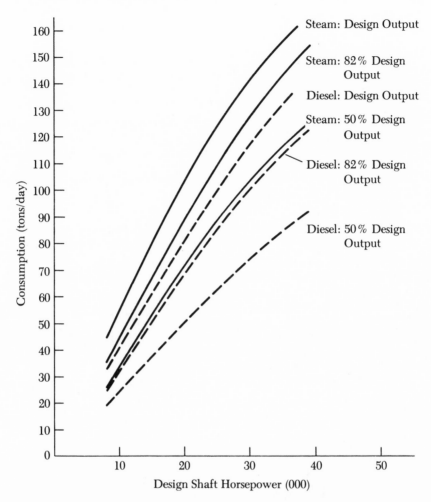

Figure 6–1 Fuel Consumption for Steam and Diesel Propulsion.

propelled vessels use a blended heavy residual oil either part time during maneuvering because they are driven by heavy fuel-burning, direct drive diesels, or full time when equipped with engines designed for mixed fuels. The cost of fuel used by diesel-propelled vessels is therefore assumed to average $199 per ton. Small RoRo and similar vessels, universally equipped with medium- to high-speed diesels, can be assumed to burn diesel oil exclusively at a cost of $280 to $320 per ton. Typical daily fuel and lube oil costs are given in Table 6–6.

Table 6–6 Daily Fuel and Lubricating Oil Costs at Design Output (1980 dollars)

Engine Type	Design SHP	Daily Fuel Consumption (Tons)	Daily Fuel Cost ($160/ton)		Lub. Oil Cost	Total	
			Bunker* ($180/ton)	Diesel ($240/ton)		Bunker ($180/ton)	Diesel ($240/ton)
Steam	10,000	55	8,800		360	9,160	
	20,000	102	16,320		520	16,840	
	30,000	142	22,720		640	23,360	
	40,000	179	28,640		800	29,440	
Diesel	10,000	40	7,200	9,600	900	8,100	10,500
	20,000	79	14,220	18,960	1,400	15,620	20,360
	30,000	117	21,060	28,080	1,800	22,860	29,880
	40,000	147	26,460	35,280	2,100	27,560	37,380

SOURCE: Based on engine manufacturers data.

* Blended heavy fuel.

For chartered bulk vessels, costs per ton can be calculated, based on reported voyage charter and short-term time charter rates using the following formula:

$$\text{cost per ton} = \frac{\left(\dfrac{L}{v} + t_o\right)\left(\dfrac{w \cdot c_s}{30} + r_d c_d\right) + \dfrac{L}{v} r_b c_b}{\left(w - r_v \dfrac{L}{v} - w_o - t_o r_d\right)}.$$

L = round-trip travel distance (miles);
v = average distance covered per day at sea;
t_o = time in port in days;
w = ship's deadweight;
w_o = allowance for water and stores;
c_s = average charter rate per DWT per month;
c_b = bunker fuel price;
c_d = diesel fuel price;
r_b = bunker fuel consumption tons per day;
r_d = average of diesel fuel consumption, tons per day at sea and in port.
r_v = 1/1 $(r_b + r_d)$

6.3. Characteristics and Dimensions of Shipping Operations

Ship dimensions and designs have undergone major changes in recent years. The primary reason for this departure has been the overriding importance of fuel costs in shipping operations. The trend since 1974 is toward slower, shorter, and more full-bodied vessels, which have lower wetted surface areas and resistance at lower speed. Fuel savings of 20 to 40 percent per ton mile of transport are achieved with speed reductions of 15 to 20 percent. The average design speed of new general cargo ships is now 17.2 knots, while new mainline containerships generally have design speeds of 19.3 knots. Also, tanker and dry bulk carrier speeds have come down to below 15 knots. In addition to fuel savings, significant reductions in ship light weight, particularly in the weight of the hull and main propulsion machinery, are also achieved.

To the operator, the ship characteristic of most concern is the cargo capacity in terms of deadweight or volume in tons. A cubic measure such as the number of containers that can be loaded may also be used. A reduction in fuel consumption per mile obviously permits a higher proportion of a ship's total deadweight or volume to be used for the carriage of payload cargo. When new vessels are compared to vessels of equal displacement and endurance built seven or more years ago, increases in payload deadweight per unit of ship displacement are on the order of 3 to 8 percent. This trend is expected to continue and to foster new developments in ship propulsion, cargo transfer, ship steering, and seakeeping technology.

Ship dimensions are usually defined by length, beam, depth, draft, and hull form. Hull forms can be expressed by a variety of form factors such as the block coefficient, which is the ratio of the actual submerged volume of the ship divided by the volume of a rectangular box with the same length, beam (width), and draft. The block coefficient is therefore a measure of fullness of a ship's hull. In ship design it is convenient to express ship characteristics in terms of non-dimensional ratios such as the block coefficient. This permits more effective comparison of designs and establishment of operating characteristics for a vessel. The most important non-dimensional ratios are:

$$\text{Length/beam ratio} \quad = L/B$$
$$\text{Beam/draft ratio} \quad = B/T$$
$$\text{Block Coefficient} \quad = \frac{\text{Submerged Volume}}{L \times B \times T} = C_B$$

where

$$\text{Length, in meters} = L$$
$$\text{Beam, in meters} \quad = B$$
$$\text{Draft, in meters} \quad = T$$
$$\text{Block coefficient} \quad = C_B$$

While the length/beam ratio has generally been reduced by 4 to 12 percent for most ship types and sizes built in recent years, both the beam/draft ratio and the block coefficient have been increased by about the same percentage. The length/beam ratio and block coefficient mostly affect resistance and are therefore largely dependent on the desired speed of a ship. The choice of beam/draft ratio on the other hand, affects stability and is itself influenced by the requirements imposed by limiting water depth.

A typical formula used to determine a vessel's displacement in terms of the various dimensions discussed is as follows:

$$\text{Displacement} = \frac{L \times B \times T \times C_B \times 1.025}{OH}$$

where the coefficient 1.025 is the saltwater correction and *OH* is the 'overhang ratio,' with

$$\text{Overhang ratio} = \text{Length overall/length between perpendiculars}$$
$$\text{or } OH = LOA/LBP$$

6.3.1. *Containerships*

Considering the different major ship types next, we start with the characteristics and dimensions of containerships. Since their introduction in the early 1960s, containerships have grown from ships with a carrrying capacity of 280 to 520 twenty-foot equivalent (TEU) containers and speeds of 12 knots to ships with capacities of 2000 to 3000 TEU and speeds in excess of 26 knots by 1974. Subsequent design speeds of new containerships have dropped to under 20 knots, with a consequent change in ship form. The block coefficient of fast containerships built in the early 1970s varied from 0.53 to 0.58 with the deadweight coefficient varying from 0.57 to 0.70. Mainline containerships built now usually have block coefficients of 0.57 to 0.66, with deadweight coefficient as high as 0.76. The length /beam, beam/ draft, and length/depth ratios vary slightly with length, as larger ships need proportionately less beam for stability. Draft was not a major consideration in the past because containerships were volume limited. Newer containerships with containers stacked 4 or 5 high on deck require use of much of their ballasting capacity for the maintenance of effective stability. As a result many of the newer containerships are designed for larger effective or operating drafts than earlier designs. Characteristic dimensions of containerships are presented in Figure 6–2. Containerships in most trades are volume and not weight limited. As a result, relationships between TEU capacity and deadweight or displacement are usually not useful. Container cargo may have weights of 2 tons per TEU for empty containers and up to 17 tons per TEU for very dense container cargo. Many ships would become weight limited if the average cargo weight per TEU were 17 tons. In general, containerships carry cargo with an average density of 10 tons per TEU. For this average density an approximate relationship for the computation of ship carrying capacity is:

$$\text{Number of TEU} = 0.0134 \times L \times B \times D,$$

where D = depth of hull, in meters.

Interest has developed recently in various hybrid types of vessels for the carriage of containers, such as dry bulk carriers with deck-loaded containers, RoRo-containerships, and barge carriers serving as potential containerships. The main purpose is usually to achieve better and more balanced capacity utilization on the different legs of a voyage. As a result there are now numerous types of ships in container shipping designed for efficient operations on particular routes. The greatest change, however, has occurred in the development and use of container feeder vessels. Capital intensity of

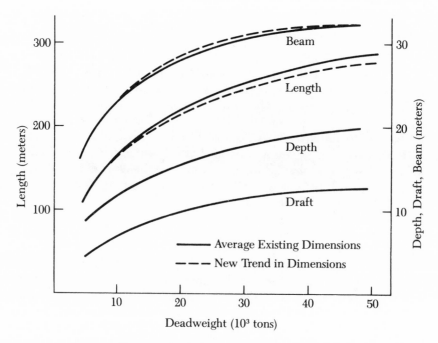

Figure 6-2   Containership Dimensions.

containership operations has forced most mainline operators to curtail the number of mainline vessel port calls. This has caused a tremendous demand for container feeder services, many of which have grown into feeder and regional container collection and distribution systems. Many new concepts of self-sustaining or self-loading/unloading as well as non-self-sustaining container feeder vessels have been developed and introduced. While the majority of these vessels use traditional lift-on/lift-off and cellular on-board stowage methods, others use shelf-type stowage served by vertical and horizontal conveyor methods.

6.3.2. *Trailerships and RoRo Vessels*

Trailerships or Roll-on/Roll-off (RoRo) vessels, also operate at a much lower speed today than ships of this type built before 1974. Roll-on/Roll-off vessels are volume intensive and as a result require a large depth. Their length/depth ratio is as a result lower than that of any other type of ship, including passenger vessels. RoRo vessels usually have low stability because of the low density of their cargo. As a result many RoRo vessels are now built as combined container-trailer or dry cargo-trailer vessels. Typical characteristics and dimensional ratios for RoRo vessels are shown in Figure 6–3.

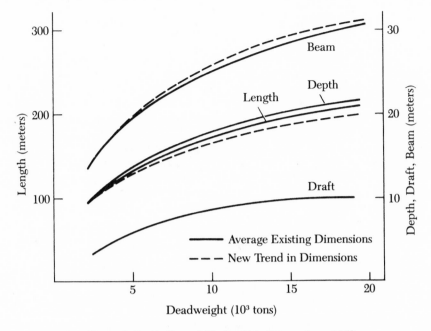

Figure 6-3 RoRo and Trailer Ship Dimensions, 1978.

RoRo vessels have suffered major losses in recent years. Many of these vessels lost their stability under damage conditions, when complete cargo compartments were flooded, causing the ships to capsize. The lack of sufficient transverse subdivision of this type of ship has come under increasing attack. Major changes in RoRo vessel design and arrangement should therefore be expected. RoRo vessels are increasingly used for medium- to long-distance routes and often carry significant numbers of containers stacked on their vehicle decks. Developments such as the LUFF container-frame system permit prestacked containers to be rolled on or off the trailership deck. These and other developments have increased the cargo volume utilization of such ships and allow them to compete with cellular containerships on longer routes. The average design speed of new RoRo vessels is now 19.1 knots. Most existing RoRo vessels currently serve on short or feeder routes.

6.3.3. *General Cargo Ships*

General cargo ships are now designed for speeds averaging 16.0 knots, and many, particularly those serving in irregular or tramp service, actually operate at speeds in the 14 to 15 knot range. The

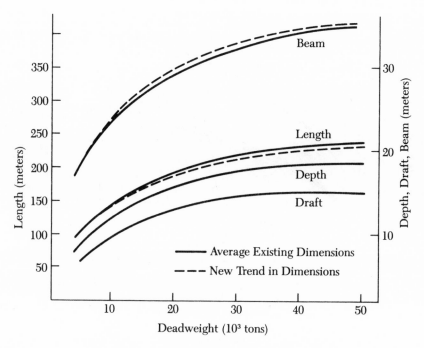

Figure 6-4 Breakbulk Ship Dimensions, 1978.

dimensions of typical general cargo or breakbulk vessels are shown in Figure 6–4.

There is a renewed interest now in pallet carrier types of general cargo ships and "standard" general cargo ships that can be converted to small bulk carriers, RoRo, partial containerships, or combined carriers. The flexibility provided by such ships is of interest for service on the minor trade routes, where insufficient volumes of cargo of particular physical forms prevents effective and frequent service by specialized carriers such as containerships, RoRo vessels, or bulk carriers.

6.3.4. *Dry Bulk Carriers*

Dry bulk carriers must be divided into subcategories such as carriers for dry bulk ore, coal, or grain. Ore, mineral, and coal carriers usually carry the densest of dry bulk cargoes, while grain carriers hold the least dense. In between are cement, fertilizer, phosphate rock, and other specialized dry bulk carriers. Dry bulk ships are more and more frequently designed for a specific trade and commodity, particularly if they are to be used in proprietary service. As a result, there are numerous types of dry bulk carriers, too many

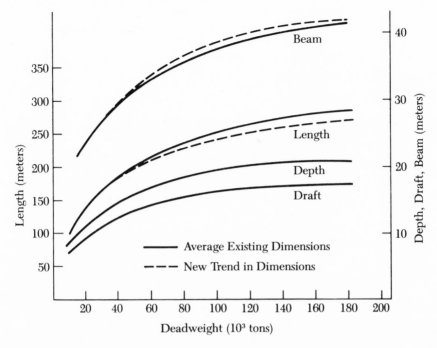

Figure 6-5   Mineral Bulk and Ore Carrier Dimensions, 1978.

to describe here. In fact, many dry bulk carriers are designed for more than one specialized service—for example, oil and ore carriers (OBO). Here we will discuss only mineral ore, coal, and grain carriers. Dry bulk ships designed today are very full-bodied, slow vessels with design speeds of 13 to 15 knots, with most operating at speeds of less than 14 knots. The usual problem for dry bulk carriers, as for tankers, is the lack of return cargo, a fact that imposes a requirement for large amounts of segregated ballast capacity. While this is not difficult to arrange on carriers of high-density cargo such as ore, it does pose some problem in the design and operation of grain carriers. Most dry bulk carriers are non-self-unloading. In fact, with the exception of Great Lakes ore ships and some other usually short-distance carriers, the vast majority of dry bulk carriers is non-self-sustaining. Typical dimensions of mineral bulk and ore carriers are shown in Figure 6–5, while those for typical grain carriers are shown in Figure 6–6.

6.3.5.   Tankers

Finally, considering tankers, we again find an increasing trend toward fuller, slower vessels, particularly among long-distance crude

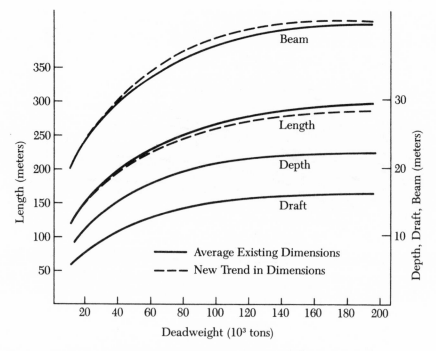

Figure 6-6   Grain Carrier Dimensions.

tankers. Segregated ballast and maximum tank size requirements are also affecting ship dimensions and configurations, and in particular deadweight capacity to displacement ratios. Should double bottoms become a requirement as well, dimensions of tankers would change even more radically. The dimensions of typical crude oil tankers are shown in Figure 6–7. Because of the value of their cargo and the shorter route distance of these trades, product and chemical tankers usually have somewhat finer lines and operate at higher than the 13.8 knot speed of large crude tankers today.

6.4.   Shipping Investment Costs

Shipping is a highly capital-intensive, complex business operated in the world of international finance. The replacement cost of the world's shipping fleet is estimated to be well in excess of $280 billion in 1980 terms. With a decreasing economic life of ships (large tankers are often scrapped after 8 to 10 years), increasingly complex technology, and escalating shipbuilding costs, total annual investment in newbuildings is expected to be well over $17 billion per year by 1985 and to grow to $25 billion per year by 1990. Similarly, as noted

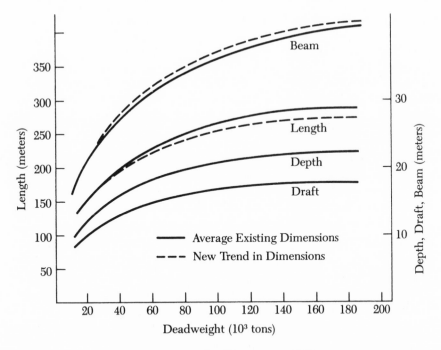

Figure 6–7 Tanker Dimensions, 1978.

before, financial costs are assuming an ever greater importance in ship operating cost, and together with fuel expenditures usually comprise 60 percent of total costs. Ship management is thus forced to be particularly alert to opportunities for reducing ship financing costs.

6.4.1. *Shipping Investment Financing*

The numerous ways to finance ship acquisition and effective design of an investment financing strategy are as important as the proper selection of a ship design and the timing of its acquisition. Ship financing offers many more opportunities than financing of practically any other asset. Ship financing involves choice of flag, domicile of ownership, and country of ownership. These may affect eligibility for subsidy, special credit terms, tax benefits, and more. Many countries and, in particular, major shipbuilding countries, offer concessionary financing terms to domestic and foreign buyers of ships produced in their country or equipped with engines or other major components manufactured there. Similarly, many countries offer special financing and/or tax concessions to owners of vessels registered under their flag. An effectively designed financing strategy may save as much as 40 percent of the total financial cost of vessel acquisition over the life of the ship. Such strategy is therefore a dominant factor in the profitability of a shipping venture. As an example, consider alternative financing terms offered shipowners in recent years:

- *OECD Standard Conditions:* 70 percent of price over seven years at 8 percent; 30 percent deposit (not financed). (Many owners, particularly those capable of chartering a new vessel before delivery, are also able to finance much, if not all, of the 30 percent deposit. Such financing is usually at prevailing prime rates unless covered by government guarantees such as the U.S. government's construction loan guarantee.)
- 70 percent of price over eight years at 8 percent; 20 percent of price over five years at 12 percent; 10 percent deposit (not financed).
- 30 percent of price as outright grant or subsidy, with remaining 70 percent at 9¾ percent over a fifteen-year period.
- 85 percent of price at 9¼ percent, payable over twelve years; 15 percent deposit (not financed).

These financing terms may in many cases be as important, if not more, than price and delivery schedule. In recent years, for example, some shipbuilding countries such as Korea have consistently underbid Japanese shipbuilders; yet the latter were able to maintain their market share, largely as a result of favorable financing terms offered with the help of the Japanese government. Obviously, any analysis of ship financing alternatives must include cash flow, tax, risk, and other exposures. Other factors influencing financing decisions are the (1) extent of the grace period, (2) time the first installment is due, (3) currency in which loan and interest are payable, their stability and expected change with respect to currency of principal revenues, and (4) the frequency of repayment and interest payments (annual, quarterly, etc., also beginning or end of period). All the above factors have a major influence on the cost of financing. It is interesting, though, that many shipowners make but superficial evaluations of the impact of financing alternatives available or offered to them, at a time when increasing competition by state-owned companies and greater involvement of government in shipping regulation and capacity allocation make operating costs an increasingly important factor. With more cargo and/or revenue sharing, effective cost control will become the primary determinant of shipping profitability.

6.4.2. *Financial Incentives to Shipping*

To counter competitive and other aspects influencing utilization of shipbuilding capacity and the maintenance or growth of national shipping, innumerable incentives have been devised and are offered by various nations. They consist of fiscal and nonfiscal incentives and include such varied approaches as revenue guarantees, cargo protection, subsidies, easy credit, investment grants, differential bunker costs, government-paid insurance, and more. Let us consider some of the more recently offered fiscal incentives first.

Credit Terms. In addition to the standard OECD terms for ship export (70 percent of price at 8 percent for eight years), there are numerous deviations from this standard, even by OECD countries. Some countries provide longer-term credits or, by combining credits for the ship with credits for major ship components such as machinery, are able to extend shipbuilding loans up to 90 percent or more of the ship's price. Furthermore, special credit conditions are usually associated with loans for newbuildings for domestic use. In the United States, construction loan mortgages guaranteed by the government cover as much as 87.5 percent of the nonsubsidized price of a newbuilding.

Domestic ship credit schemes in Belgium permit the government to provide loans of up to 80 percent of ship price for fifteen years at 3 to 5 percent interest. Danish owners, for example, ordering vessels from a Danish or EEC yard qualify for loans of 80 percent of price at 8 percent interest over ten years. Sweden, on the other hand, extends loans of 70 percent of price over twelve years at 8 percent. Some countries, such as Norway and Sweden, offer special credit terms to owners in developing countries, often at zero interest over twenty-year periods.

Investment Grants. Another financial incentive to shipping that is often used is investment grants. These are usually given only to owners residing in the shipbuilding country. England, for example, provided 20 percent investment grants for ships ordered for British registry during the period 1966–1970. Germany, on the other hand, continues to offer 17.5 percent investment grants. Some owners have misused investment grants by setting up shop in a particular country solely for the purpose of qualifying for the offered investment grant.

Subsidies. Direct shipbuilding subsidies are used by many countries. The United States was probably the first country formally to offer a "cost parity" subsidy for newbuildings ordered by U.S.-flag operators (only liners until 1970) for use in the U.S. foreign trade. Other shipbuilding countries offer similar construction subsidies, usually based on real or imagined differences in cost or other competitive factors. Numerous operating cost subsidies are also offered by various governments varying from U.S.-style operating (cost) differential subsidies to government provision of marine insurance, or the subsidization of ship bunker prices.

Depreciation Allowances. Although most countries permit accelerated depreciation, some countries, such as England, allow depreciation at will for shipowners, whereby the asset can be written off 100 percent during a year if desired. Norway allows the addition of a 25 percent allowance to be added to the price of the ship in calculating accelerated depreciation. The effective use of flexible and generous depreciation rules often permits an astute shipowner to save significantly in taxes, particularly if depreciation can be used to offset large trading profits in a particular year.

Taxation. In addition to the exemption from tax and/or duty on ship bunkers and supplies, many countries make major concessions in taxing shipowners. In Germany, for example, profits from foreign shipping operations of a German-domiciled company are calculated separately, and only 80 percent of these profits are taxed at 50 percent of the tax rate applicable to the full amount of profits. There is also relief from capital gains tax in the United States, England, and other countries that permit the rollover of capital gains without tax against use of the funds for the purchase of replacement tonnage.

Sale and Leaseback. This incentive scheme has many variations. Governments will either buy a newbuilding for their own account and lease it to an operator or buy a vessel from an owner for leaseback to the owner, using cheap funds raised by the government at its much lower and often tax-free interest rate. Governments may also use funds raised by international borrowing or from large development institutions such as the World Bank or its regional affiliates.

Government Ownership or Ownership Participation. This incentive is similar to sale and leaseback, where financing is provided by the government.

6.4.3. *Nonfiscal Incentives*

Among nonfiscal incentives, revenue guarantees and cargo protection or preference are probably those most commonly used. These incentives are usually considered discriminatory, and governments are thus cautious in their use. The practice is usually restricted to domestic shipping, the shipping of clearly defined government cargo, or cargo subject to a bilateral sharing agreement. Exchange regulations and currency values may provide both fiscal and nonfiscal incentives or disincentives and must be seriously studied in any effective design of shipping financing. Another incentive is to make available special rates of taxation and other conditions to crews.

6.4.4. *Fiscal Disincentives*

Some countries impose a tax on nonresident shipping, which often leads to double taxation of such companies. Such action is usually designed to favor national shipping. Some countries, including the United States, reciprocate by taxing profits of foreign owners whose government taxes U.S. operators. Singapore goes one step further by actually taxing freight receipts of such owners. Few countries, however, have at this time developed effective countermeasures.

In summary, planning of shipping requires analysis of the large number of incentives and disincentives offered in order to decide on a financing strategy that provides a combination of low financing costs and taxation and ultimately leads to maximization of net profits.

6.5. Ship Cost Formulation

The price of ships has traditionally borne some relation to the cost of ship construction. As a result, basic ship dimensional, operational, and other parameters could be used to estimate the cost and therefore price of any type of ship.[1] Ship cost estimates in turn could readily be obtained by determining first the weights of major subgroups such as hull, main propulsion machinery, accommodation, and so forth. Next, by using relative productivity in terms of manhours per unit of installed or erected weight, unit labor, and unit material or equipment costs, the building costs of various types and sizes of vessels in different countries could readily be estimated.

The glut of world shipbuilding capacity and the increasing use of direct and indirect aids to shipbuilding in many countries of the world have resulted in large distortions in the offered or delivered prices of ships. In many cases it even affects the cost of the ships to the builder because the costs of engines, steel, labor, and other inputs to the builder may similarly be distorted by the various subsidies and aids. The price of ships is today affected by:

1. *Direct Government Subsidies or Aids to the Builder*
   - Cost parity subsidies
   - Labor incentive pay

---

[1] See *Ocean Transportation* by E. G. Frankel and H. Marcus, MIT Press, 1972, Part 4, "Study of Shipbuilding Costs," by E. G. Frankel.

- Sales or export subsidies
- Loss reimbursement subsidies
- Capital investment loans or subsidies
- Other

2. *Indirect Government Aids to the Builder*
   - Tax incentives—investment tax credits
   - Export tax credits—tax deferral, etc.
   - Loan interest subsidies or low-cost government loans
   - Supply credits or supply of government-owned materials at non-market costs
   - Labor cost and employment incentives (partial payment of labor cost by direct worker compensation)
   - Subsidies to suppliers of materials and equipment
   - Exemption from duty on imported materials and equipment
   - Special government guaranteed foreign exchange rate
   - Low-cost or subsidized use of facilities or equipment
   - Other

3. *Direct and Indirect Aids to the Buyer or Owner*
   - Construction and investment cost loan subsidies or low-cost subsidized mortgage (also government mortgage loan guarantees like U.S. Title XI)
   - Export credits or negative sales tax
   - Foreign exchange conversion subsidies
   - Direct mortagage loan at below-market costs
   - Supplier credits
   - Other

As a result of the above direct and indirect aids to the builder and/or buyer available in many shipbuilding countries, purchasing and building decisions are increasingly affected by financing and other available aids. Competition among shipyards in different countries is frequently a factor of the aid packages those countries are able to offer and obtain.

Under these circumstances, it is extremely difficult to determine "real" ship costs and prices. Recently, for example, an owner bought identical ships from two yards in two different countries for prices that differed by over 9.2 percent. The reason was simply that the higher priced vessels were covered by a financing and aid package which readily made up for the difference in the "purchase price" of the vessels. As a result, we will not discuss ship costs or prices as a function of ship parameters here but simply review ship costs to the owner or purchaser in market terms. It will be noted that ship costs vary widely. In general it can be assumed that higher priced vessels will be covered by incentive packages that will retain their competitiveness in the international marketplace. Costs in this discussion refer to costs to the buyer and may include some incentives which differentiate these costs from the seller's price.

6.5.1. General Cargo Ship Costs

The costs of general cargo ships of a certain size, speed, and deadweight capacity vary widely because of differences in the following:

- Cost and size of the accommodations
- Capability and extent of cargo handling equipment installed
- Degree and level of sophistication of automation, communication, and navigation equipment installed
- Degree of customization or standardization of vessel
- Length of production run for vessel

Crew sizes on general cargo ships vary from 21 to 57 depending on age, design, nationality, route, and control of the vessel. Older ships serving developing countries usually have much larger crews than newer ships serving the industrialized nations' ports. The same large variations in crew size are not experienced with containerships or bulk carriers. The average 1980 cost of a single-screw general cargo ship can be expressed as:

$$C(GC) = 1382 \; WS + 980,000 \left(\frac{SHP}{1000}\right)^{b} + 420,000 \left(\frac{DISP}{1000}\right)^{0.86},$$

as derived by a multivariable regression from sample data, where

$$WS = \text{Hull weight}$$
$$SHP = \text{Installed shaft horsepower}$$
$$DISP = \text{Displacement of Ship in tons}$$
$$b = \text{Coefficient dependent on type of propulsion plant,}$$
$$\text{with } b = 0.60 \text{ for direct drive diesel and } b =$$
$$0.56 \text{ for medium speed diesel.}$$

The above formula applies to vessels built in series of three. If ships are built in longer runs, then ship costs will usually benefit by a cumulative learning curve such as that shown in Figure 6–8 with a 93.5 percent slope. This shows that the average cost of a ship in series of three is equal to 90 percent of the first ship cost. When built in series of 10 ships, the average ship cost declines to 80 percent of first ship cost. These ship and learning costs are based on published data in various international magazines and journals, as well as interviews with different owners and shipyards. The costs are the actual investment or capital costs to the buyer after direct subsidies to the builder or buyer but do not include financing costs (including incentives) and other indirect aids to the builder or buyer. General

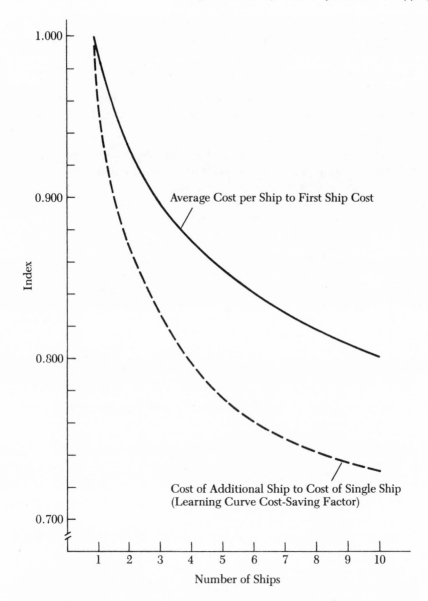

Figure 6–8   Learning Curve Cost-Saving Factors. (Cumulative average learning curve slope = 93.5%.)

Table 6–7   Typical General Cargo Ship Costs (1980 delivery, millions of dollars)

DWT	Foreign			U.S. (Before Subsidy)*		
	Low	Average	High	Low	Average	High
5,000	4.61	5.12	5.73	9.72	10.85	12.82
10,000	7.98	8.82	10.14	16.30	18.12	20.84
15,000	11.12	12.33	13.81	21.38	24.30	27.45
20,000	14.13	15.60	17.90	27.68	31.00	35.08
25,000	17.09	18.86	21.69	32.52	37.80	43.81

SOURCE: Regression of data published in various journals such as *Fairplay, Motorship*, etc.

* Estimates, as no general cargo were built in 1980. Low, average, and high refer to level of manning, automation, cargo equipment, and propulsion system.

cargo ship costs are summarized in Table 6–7. The escalation of these costs between 1980 and 1981 averaged 18.2 percent.

6.5.2.   Containership Costs

Containership costs are also highly variable, and costs for a ship of a given DWT capacity are not necessarily indicative of cost in terms of TEU capacity. Ships with the same DWT capacity may differ by as much as 20 percent in their effective capacity in terms of TEUs or container carriage capability. The average 1980 cost of a single-screw cellular containership can be expressed as follows:

$$C(CS) = 1790\,WS + 1,180,000 \left(\frac{SHP}{1000}\right)^b + 62,000 \left(\frac{DISP}{1000}\right)^{0.76},$$

as derived by multivariable regression from sample data. The value of the coefficient b is the same as in the general cargo ship formula. Similarly, learning curve benefits are the same as in the general cargo ship example, although fewer containerships are built in long series than general cargo vessels. The escalation of these costs between 1980 and 1981 averaged about 20 percent. The design speed of containerships delivered in 1980 averaged 19.72 knots. Typical (1980) containership costs are summarized in Table 6–8.

6.5.3.   Tanker Ship Costs

The cost of tankers has been depressed by the lack of orders, particularly for large crude tankers. As a result, the cost of such vessels is appreciably lower per ton of erected steel or outfit than other types of ships. This trend is expected to continue at least until 1987, when sufficient ships in this overtonnaged sector of the shipping market have been retired.

Table 6–8   Typical Containership Costs (1980 delivery; single-screw, diesel propelled, millions of dollars)

DWT	Foreign	U.S. (Before Subsidy)*
5,000	8.30	16.92
10,000	15.90	32.59
20,000	28.40	56.82
30,000	41.00	82.92
50,000	59.62	116.26

SOURCE: Regression of data published in various journals such as *Fairplay* and *Motorship*, or obtained from owners.

* Estimates, no containerships built in U.S. in 1980. Containerships (30,300 DWT) listed in Table 6C-1, ordered in 1981, delivery expected 1983.

Table 6–9   Typical Tanker Costs (1980 delivery; single-screw diesel, millions of dollars)

	Foreign		U.S. (Before Subsidy)*	
DWT	Crude	Product	Crude	Product
20,000	—	15.96	—	33.09
50,000	22.40	27.98	45.92	57.63
100,000	38.00	—	77.91	—
150,000	55.00	—	109.82	—
200,000	70.00	—	136.00	—

SOURCE: Regression of data published in various journals such as *Fairplay* and *Motorship*, or obtained from owners.

* Estimates or extrapolation of published data.

Table 6–10   Typical Dry Bulk Carrier Costs (1980 delivery, millions of dollars)

DWT	Foreign	U.S. (Before Subsidy)*
20,000	14.20	28.40
30,000	18.86	38.39
50,000	26.88	53.76
100,000	45.80	90.68

SOURCE: Regression of data published in various journals such as *Fairplay* and *Motorship*, or obtained from owners.

* Estimates or extrapolation of published data.

Tanker costs vary widely among product and crude oil tankers, and specialized chemical, LNG-LPG, wine, milk, and other tankers. The range of tankers is too broad to be covered here. Furthermore, many of the LNG, LPG, chemical, and specialized tankers are custom-designed and incorporate features particular to their route and service.

Considering crude and product tankers, multiple regression of recent (1980) non-U.S. cost data gives the following results:

Crude Tankers

$$C(CT) = 1180 \ WS + 940{,}000 \left(\frac{SHP}{1000}\right)^b + 286{,}000 \left(\frac{DISP}{1000}\right)^{0.81}$$

Product Tankers

$$C(PT) = 1298 \ WS + 980{,}000 \left(\frac{SHP}{1000}\right)^b + 305{,}000 \left(\frac{DISP}{1000}\right)^{0.86}$$

The average design speed of these crude tankers (50,000–200,000 DWT) was 15.0 knots, while the average design speed for product tankers (20,000–50,000 DWT) was 16.1 knots. Typical 1980 tanker costs are summarized in Table 6–9.

6.5.4. *Dry Bulk Carrier Costs*

Dry bulk carrier costs, as mentioned before, also vary widely with service, route, method of cargo handling, and more. Dense cargo bulk carriers such as ore carriers or coal carriers provide less cargo volume and therefore require less hull steel than equal DWT capacity grain carriers for example. For our purposes only a general indication of the average costs of dry bulk carriers can be presented. The average non-U.S. 1980 cost of a dry bulk carrier can be expressed as

$$C(BC) = 1260 \ WS + 1{,}020{,}000 \left(\frac{SHP}{1000}\right)^b + 315{,}000 \left(\frac{DISP}{1000}\right)^{0.85}$$

The average design speed of a dry bulk carrier delivered in 1980 was 15.2 knots. Typical 1980 dry bulk carrier costs are summarized in Table 6–10.

Appendix 6A

ITEMS OF VESSEL COST ANALYSIS

Vessel Data

Vessel data include purchase price, additions, present value, total investment, special survey due date, fuel consumption, speed/power/displacement, age and remaining life.

A. Crew Cost
   Number of crew
   Wages
   Crew travel
   Crew provisions
   Crew supplies
   Crew per diem (waiting or travel)
      Total crew costs

B. Stores
   Deck
   Engine
   Lubricating oil
      Total stores costs

C. Repairs
   Deck: Voyage
         Survey
         Casualty (noninsured)
   Engine: Voyage
           Survey
           Casualty (noninsured)
      Total repairs

D. Insurance
   Hull value × average premium
   P&I
      Total insurance

E. Other Costs
   Wireless fees and costs
   Entertainment: Port
                  On board
   Classification and fees
   Other miscellaneous costs
      Total other costs

F. Administrative Costs
   Management fees
      Fixed
      Commission
   Chartering commissions
   Brokerage commissions
   Administrative expenses
      Office and agents expenses
      Certified public accountants
      Legal fees
      Membership
         Total administrative costs

G. Taxes

Total fixed operating costs = A + B + C + D + E + F + G.

Variable Vessel Operating Costs

a. Fuel costs
b. Port dues and tonnage charges
c. Canal dues
d. Pilotage
e. Special services
f. Cargo-handling costs

Total variable operating costs = a + b + c + d + e + f.

Appendix 6B

VOYAGE PROFITS COMPUTATIONS

$$\text{Revenues} = R = \left[\sum_i \sum_{jk} W_{ijk} \times r_{ijk} \times E_j - B_{ijk} + DM_j \right]$$

where W_{ijk} = cargo type i loaded at port j for port k

$\quad r_{ijk}$ = freight rate for cargo-type i loaded at port j for port k

$\quad E_j$ = exchange rate at port j

$\quad B_{ijk}$ = brokerage commission at port j for cargo-type i carried to port k

$\quad DM_j$ = demurrage received in port j

$$\text{Expenses} = C = \sum_i \sum_{jk} (P_j + L_{ij} + DIS_k$$
$$+ D_{ik} + CV_{jk} + CPT_j + DB_{jk})A$$

where P_j = port costs (dues, etc) in port $j = 1 \ldots m$

$\quad L_{ij}$ = loading costs of cargo-type i in port j

$\quad D_{ik}$ = discharge cost of cargo-type i in port k

$\quad DIS_k$ = dispatch cost at port k

$\quad CV_{jk}$ = voyage costs from port j to k at given speed v_{ij} and with cargo load CL_{jk}, resulting in displacement DPL_{jk}

$\quad CPT_j$ = port time costs in port $j = 1 \ldots m$

$\qquad = PT_j \times SCP$ = time in port $j \times$ ship cost per unit of port time

$\quad DB_{jk}$ = other disbursements on voyage jk including ports j and k

$\quad A$ = administrative costs as a percentage of operating costs

Voyage profits $= [R - C]$

Annual profit $= N (R - C)$

where N = number of trips per year

$$N = \frac{365}{VT}$$

$\overline{VT}$ = average total voyage time

$$= \sum_n \sum_{jk} \left(D_{jk}/v_{jk}^n + PT_j^n \right)$$

where D_{jk} = distance between ports j and k

v_{jk}^n = voyage speed between ports j and k on voyage number n

PT_j^n = port time in port j on voyage number n

$$\text{Annual voyage costs} = \sum_n CV^n = \sum_n \sum_{jk} CV_{jk}^n = \sum_n \sum_{jk} [VT_{jk}^n] FC$$
$$+ [VT_{jk}^n \times BC_{jk}^n \times FF]$$

where CV_{jk}^n = cost of nth voyage during year

FC = fixed cost of ship per unit time

BC_{jk}^n = bunker consumption per unit time on voyage n
between ports j and k

FF = fuel cost per unit of fuel used

$BC_{jk} = Me^{S_{jk}}$

VT_{jk} = voyage time on voyage number $n = D_{jk}/v_{jk}^n$

where M and S are constants, depending on vessel type, speed, and displacement, and S_{jk} on the route characteristics between ports j and k while $e = 2.718$.

$$\text{Annual port time costs} = \sum_n \sum_j PT_j^n \times SCP$$

where

PT_j^n = port time in port j on voyage n

$SCP = (FC + BCP \times FF)$
= ship cost per unit of port time

where FC = fixed cost of ship per unit time

BCP = bunker consumption per unit time in port

FF = fuel cost per unit of fuel used

The above are gross profit and loss voyage computations. To compute the net operating income, a depreciation, or depletion, allowance and interest costs must be included. Then taxable income can be computed. These prices vary from $2325 per DWT to $1161 per DWT for handy-sized products tankers. Although there are usually variations of 20 to 30 percent in ratio prices, which account for differences in powering, engine type, ship arrangement, and so on, the price differences are now larger than historically experienced.

Appendix 6C

U.S. SHIPBUILDING PRICES

U.S. shipbuilding prices are subject to larger fluctuations than those in other shipbuilding countries because of the limitation of the U.S. market, the variations in government-sponsored, or naval, shipbuilding, and changes in the availability of government aids. During 1981, U.S. shipbuilding prices rose by an average of 16.8 percent over 1980 prices. Typical prices for ships under construction or on order in U.S. yards in August 1981 are shown (MarAd records) in Table 6C–1.

Table 6C–1 Prices for Ships under Construction in U.S. Yards, 1981

Ship Type	DWT	Engine*	SHP	Each of	Estimated Price ($ million)
Containership	30,300	(D)	43,200	3	110.0
Tanker	33,900	(D)	14,720	2	71.0
Tanker (products)	43,000	(D)	17,000	1	100.0
	37,500	(T)	11,300	2	50.0
	37,500	(D)	11,400	2	51.0
	44,000	(D)	11,400	3	51.0
	31,000	(D)	14,200	1	36.0
RoRo/container	23,500	(T)	32,000	1	61.0
	23,500	(T)	32,000	2	68.7

SOURCE: U.S. Maritime Administration, Department of Commerce, Monthly Report, Dec. 1981.

* D = Diesel, T = Turbine.

Appendix 6D

EFFECT OF THE ECONOMIC RECOVERY TAX ACT OF 1981 ON SHIP LEASING

Leasing has become a major factor in shipping. It involves the leasing of ships, containers, terminal equipment, and other equity or operating assets and offers opportunities to expand or build a shipping operation. On August 4, 1981, Congress passed the Economic Recovery Tax Act of 1981, which introduced major changes in fundamental federal taxing principles and thereby in U.S. fiscal policy. It reduces the role of social objectives, including that of income redistribution in tax policy, and attempts to introduce incentives for greater savings, investments, and productivity.

Some of the highlights of the Act affecting ship leasing are that companies are now allowed to buy and sell tax credits and deductions through "safe harbor leasing," which assumes that sellers of tax benefits are usually to receive only a fraction of their value. The reason behind this change in tax policy is that, in the past, companies with insufficient taxable income could not benefit from investment tax credit (ITC) and similar programs, through an offset of their credits and deductions. The Safe Harbor clause of the new law is part of the Accelerated Cost Recovery System (ACRS) as proposed. Under this clause, reductions in taxes that the buyer of credits has purchased do not show up until future years because only the ITC can be claimed immediately. Under the new rules, buyers of credits are also allowed to escape being hit with a big tax liability in the event the seller was liquidated in bankruptcy.

Under this new legislation, both U.S.- and foreign-built ships which are registered in the United States and are "owned" by a U.S. taxpayer can be leased under leveraged leases for terms matching available foreign shipyard financing and containing nominal purchase options at the conclusion of the lease term.

In the past, unlike U.S.-flag ships, very few foreign-built ships were leased because long-term (20 to 25 year) debt was not readily available and because foreign shipyard debt generally did not exceed eight years and did not match equity investment requirements for a leveraged lease. Foreign-flag ships or ships owned by a foreign corporation that is not a U.S. taxpayer do not qualify to take advantage of this new legislation.

6D.1.   Safe Harbor Clause Guidelines

1. The lessor's minimum investment should be not less than 10 percent of the adjusted basis of the property.
2. The term of the lease cannot exceed the greater of 90 percent of the useful life of the ship or 150 percent of the class life of such ship.
3. At the end of the lease, the lessee may have a purchase option at a fixed price and the lessor may have a payment to the lessee at a fixed price, and such purchase option or payment may be at more or less than the fair market value.
4. No recapture of ITC and tax depreciation in the event of bankruptcy and disposition of the ship is allowed.
5. Rents or lease payments may be offset against leveraged debt.
6. Both the lessor and lessee must affirmatively elect to treat the lessor as owner of the ship.

6D.2.   Reaction of the Leasing Companies

Leasing companies, including those operating at least in part as general partners to limited partnerships of private investors, have in the past been very much in favor of capital investment incentives such as those in the 1981 tax law. However, the new provision which allows corporations to sell their tax credits on newly purchased equipment has the potential for cutting deeply into lessors' businesses.

Companies without profits or with surplus credits from the past can now sell investment tax credits and depreciation allowances for cash, which effectively reduces their cost of purchase of equipment or ships. The purpose of the provision is to encourage capital spending by corporations, including those without profitable operations. It is also designed to improve the quality of productive capital assets of corporations. There are some who argue that this capitalization of unprofitable companies results in inefficient resource allocation, particularly as it also results in a tax reduction for profitable companies who are not really a beneficiary or user of the capital asset involved.

6D.3. Examples

Assume company A buys a ship for $20,000,000 with a useful life of more than ten years, yet does not have enough profits to offset against ITC and other tax benefits immediately. A may therefore sell the ITC and depreciation rights to company B. A now received both a cash payment and a note from B for the balance, making B the lessor of the ship. The maximum payment B can make to A is $4.776 million. B would also give A a note with an interest rate of, say, 12 percent for the balance of $15.224 million, calling for 10 annual payments of $2.694 million to cover annual interest and capital payments. A then leases the ship back from B for an annual rental of $2.694 million. At the end of ten years, A terminates the contract by buying the ship back for $1. Company B therefore receives ITC and the tax benefits accruing from the depreciation of the vessel, while company A receives a cash payment of 23.88 percent of the investment cost, which reduces its capital cost for the ship while maintaining full rights to the exclusive use, if not ownership, of the ship for the ten-year period of the lease, whereafter the ship's ownership reverts to company A for the "token" payment of $1.

The above example assumes that company B makes the maximum possible payment allowed under the law to company A. This may not be attractive enough to company B. As noted in the examples below, the benefit to B depends on the applicable interest and discount rates, as well as the corporate tax rate of B and the duration of the lease.

Considering the issue in more detail, we present in Table 6D–1 an example where only 10 percent of an investment, say $1,000 out of an investment cost of $10,000, is paid by the lessor B to company A. B pays the remainder of $9,000 in ten installments of capital and interest against a note given to A. A pays B lease or rental of $1,593 per year which is equal to the annual capital payment installment and interest payable by B to A. Assuming an interest rate of 12 percent, the total and net present value of revenues, ITC, tax savings due to depreciation and tax due to profit are presented and the net present value (NPV) of the total savings for B are computed for a discount rate of 10 percent and 15 percent, when the NPV of total savings are $789 and $719, respectively.

In Table 6D–2 we present the cash flow of an example where B puts up 20% of the investment, or $2,000, for a $10,000 investment. With a 12 percent interest rate, the NPV of the total savings for B would be $287 with a discount rate of 10 percent and $145 with a discount rate of 15 percent.

Table 6D–1   Cash Flow Analysis for Initial Investment of $1,000 (10% of $10,000 required)

Company B

Year	1 Revenue	2 Depreciation	3 Interest	4 ITC	5 Tax Savings Due to Depreciation	6 Rev. − Int. (Repayment Part)	7 Tax On 6	8 Total Savings 4 + 5 − 7
1	—	1,000	—	1,000	460	—	—	1,460
2	1,593	1,000	1,080	—	460	513	236	224
3	1,593	1,000	1,020	—	460	573	264	196
4	1,593	1,000	900	—	460	693	318	142
5	1,593	1,000	780	—	460	813	374	86
6	1,593	1,000	660	—	460	933	429	31
7	1,593	1,000	540	—	460	1,053	484	(24)
8	1,593	1,000	420	—	460	1,173	540	(80)
9	1,593	1,000	300	—	460	1,293	595	(135)
10	1,593	1,000	180	—	460	1,413	650	(190)
	1,593	—	60	—	—	1,533	705	(705)
NPV (D.R. = 10%)	$9,789			$1,000	$3,358		$2,569	$1,789
NPV (D.R. = 15%)				$1,000	$2,861		$2,142	$1,719

Total Benefit to B in Present Value Terms = $1,789 − $1,000 (initial payment from B) + $2,569 (Maximum Tax Deduction). Company A − Total Benefit = $1,000 (initial investment) = $789 (D.R. = 10%). (This occurs because of the difference between the rental it pays and the interest it receives. The actual value would depend on when company A starts to make profits.) Total Benefit to B in Present Value Terms = $1,719 − $1,000 = $719 (D.R. = 15%).

Table 6D-2 Cash Flow Analysis for Initial Investment of $2,000
Interest Rate = 12%. Discount Rate = 10%. Repayment Period = 10 Years. Tax Rate = 46%.

Company B	1	2	3	4	5	6	7	8
Year	Revenue	Depreciation	Interest	ITC	Tax Savings On 2	Rev. − Int. (Repayment Part)	Tax On 6	Total Savings 4 + 5 − 7
—	—	2,000	—	1,000	920	—	—	1,920
1	1,416	889	960	—	409	456	210	199
2	1,416	889	906	—	409	510	234	175
3	1,416	889	800	—	409	616	283	126
4	1,416	889	693	—	409	723	332	77
5	1,416	889	587	—	409	829	381	28
6	1,416	889	480	—	409	936	430	(21)
7	1,416	889	373	—	409	1,043	480	(71)
8	1,416	889	267	—	409	1,149	529	(120)
9	1,416	888	160	—	409	1,256	578	(169)
10	1,416	—	53	—	—	1,363	627	(127)
NPV (D.R. = 10%)				$1,000	$3,421		$2,134	$2,287
NPV (D.R. = 15%)				$1,000	$2,924		$1,779	$2,145

Total Benefit to B in Present Value Terms = $2,287 − $2,000 = $287 (D.R. = 10%). Total Benefit to B in Present Value Terms = $2,145 − $2,000 = $145 (D.R. = 15%).

Chapter 7

SHIPPING FINANCE

While liner shipping operations generally require a large amount of specialized knowledge, bulk or tramp shipping operations are much simpler and need only have a basic organization. Operation of the very largest, most modern vessel requires a crew of only thirty to thirty-five, while support/service personnel and office staff may number as many as twenty. Thus, to any large-scale user of marine transportation, the establishment of a ship-operating subsidiary is nearly always a viable approach to its shipping problems. This applies particularly to bulk transportation users that are generally large-scale users, such as oil, steel, chemical, and grain companies. The bulk shipping industry structure is largely shaped by the needs of this type of concern. Decisions as to who owns shipping or what types of contracts are drawn all stem from basic corporate policy, which, in turn, is shaped by tax laws, the types of financing available, the financial structure of the company, and the rules governing that financial strategy.

7.1. Financial Arrangements and Flow of Funds

Three characteristics of marine transportation provide flexibility in how it fits into the organizational structure of user companies. first, once employment of a vessel is secure, the operation is largely self-financing, with very little requirement for equity capital. Second, ships receive favored financial and tax treatment in most countries of the world. Third, because of the nature of maritime law involving insurance claims and the difficulty in firmly setting a fair transfer price for shipping, a shipping company or subsidiary is often offered opportunities to move within a corporate family funds that would not otherwise be available.

The general goals of a large corporation when determining policies for organizing marine transportation are as follows:

- To obtain the transportation required at a predictable price, which is not far in excess of marginal cost;
- To organize and finance the operation with a minimum commitment of the user's financial resources;
- To minimize the overall taxes paid by the whole operation;
- To retain at least sufficient control to allow overall coordination of the operation;
- To minimize risks, including foreign exchange, business, political, and casualty losses.

Figure 7–1 shows the options of a multinational operation to raise funds to finance its operation. Equity financing, while tending to minimize financial risks, is the most expensive method of raising funds. As such, most operations borrow heavily to finance liquid assets or use contracts with the parent firm to allow others to borrow money to finance the asset.

Ships are one of the most liquid forms of real property, and, as pointed out before, 80 to 100 percent of a vessel's cost is often debt financed. This is not the case with many other types of equipment associated with production manufacturing or service industries. The

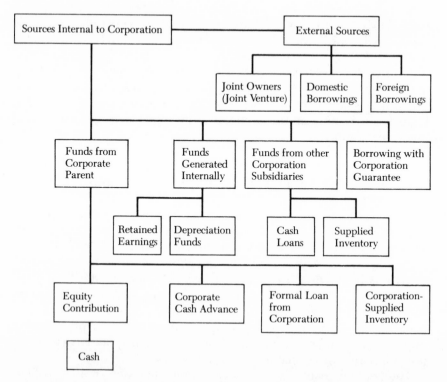

Figure 7-1   Sources of Funds to Finance Multinational Corporation.

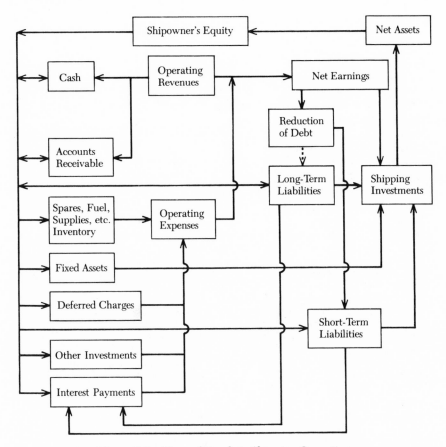

Figure 7-2 Flow of Funds in Shipping Operations.

capital costs associated with most industrial investments are usually sunk and represent poor collateral for loans unless backed by a financially strong company. Usually the shipping portion of the operations does not require a strong equity position from a parent company. Thus the scarce equity resources are free to finance less liquid and potentially more profitable areas of the business.

The flow of funds and common transactions in shipping operations can be summarized as shown in Figure 7–2. Flow of funds are used to determine changes in the balance sheet of a shipping company by summing the sources and use of funds as in Table 7–1. Balance sheet information for a shipping company is usually derived from the financial performance data of individual vessels (Table 7–2).

Funds flow analysis begins with accounting statements, which usually contain a variety of accounting and other adjustments in conformity with practice, policy, or requirements. Table 7–3 is a

Table 7–1   Sources and Uses of Shipping Company Funds

Sources of Funds	Uses of Funds
Decrease in cash	Increase in short-term investment
Decrease in inventories	Increase in assets
Decrease in assets	Increase in accounts receivable
Decrease in investments	Increase in prepaid expenses
Decrease in receivables	Increase in net properties or fixed assets
Increase in long-term debt	Increase in deferred charges
Increase in deferred income tax	Decrease in equity
Increase in minority interest	Decrease in accounts payable
Increase in common stock	Decrease in dividends payable
Increase in equity	Decrease in notes payable
Increase in other capital assets	Decrease in long-term debt due in one year
Profit from operations*	Decrease in accrued taxes
Increase in retained income	Decrease in insurance reserve
	Loss from operations*

* Before accounting writeoff.

Table 7–2   Factors in Vessel Financial Performance Analysis

Fixed assets	*Capital accounts*
Book value of vessel	Share capital (if ship incorporated
	as separate corporate entity)
Current assets	Profit and loss account
Accounts receivable	
Voyage suspension account	*Profit on vessel's trading, including:*
Balance at bank	Depreciation
	Legal fees
Total assets	Mortgage interest
	Tonnage tax
Less current liabilities	Audit and bookkeeping
Amount due to associate companies	General agents' fees
Amount due to general agents	Conference membership fees
	Deposit interest received
Accounts payable	Net profit/deficit for the year
Less secured bank loan	Balance brought forward
Less principal	Profit/deficit carried forward
Less accrued interest	

typical consolidated balance sheet for a shipping company that shows changes in each of the accounts shown from the preceding two years. These changes are used to determine the consolidated flow of funds from which we derive the change in financial position statement (Table 7–4).

The key sources in this statement are an increase in long-term debt from $7,266,500 to $26,484,000, and an increase in working capital. Balance sheet changes, however, do not usually provide a complete view of changes in funds flows, and some items may have to be reduced in detail to provide the information necessary for planning and decision making. The important function of funds flow analysis is to identify significant elements in the performance of the shipping company that reflect management decisions on investment, operations, charters, and ship or capacity commitment, and financing.

7.1.1. *Financial Performance Evaluation*

The effectiveness of business results is usually measured by comparing the following financial ratios:

- Current assets/current liabilities
- Cash and marketable securities plus receivables/current liabilities
- Inventory turnover
- Total debt/total assets
- Long-term debt/capitalization
- Net sales/total assets
- Net profits/total assets
- Net profits/total net worth
- Net profits/net sales

Usually ratios are divided into those used in cost and operational expense analysis, profit analysis, and contribution analysis. In the first category, a shipping company would evaluate

$$\text{cost of service ratio} = \frac{\text{net revenue} - \text{cost of service}}{\text{net revenues from shipping service}}$$

or

$$\text{gross margin ratio} = \frac{\text{net revenue} - \text{cost of service}}{\text{net revenue}}.$$

Profit analysis is usually concerned with the profit margin = net profit/net revenue. Net profit can be computed before or after interest and taxes, depending on the prevailing conditions.

Expense analysis is usually concerned with the ratios of expenses to net revenues. Finally, contribution analysis deals with the effect particular costs such as fixed costs have on profit. In addition, there is often a need to evaluate the effectiveness of management of capital, or assets. For this purpose the turnover ratio = net revenue/gross assets or profit ratio = net profit/net assets may be useful measures. In addition, it is usually beneficial to draw up statements of operations and retained earnings and a financial summary, such as those shown in Tables 7–5 and 7–6, respectively.

Owners and lenders may require measures that relate net profit to net worth or common equity or earnings per share of publicly

Table 7-3 Consolidated Balance Sheet—Good Shipping Company

	Year Ended Dec. 31, 19——	Year Ended Dec. 31, 19——
ASSETS		
Current Assets:		
Cash	$ 5,794,000	$ 3,840,500
Marketable securities, at cost which approximates market	—	4,992,000
Accounts receivable, less reserve of $5,897,000 in 1974 and $3,960,000 in 1973	21,892,000	23,034,500
Due from U.S. government for vessels under construction	3,678,500	4,883,000
Shipbuilding contract in progress, less billings of $114,937,000	37,035,000	—
Construction and escrow funds	3,016,000	—
Prepaid expenses and other assets	3,655,500	2,789,000
Total current assets	75,071,000	39,538,000
Vessels, property and equipment, at cost less accumulated depreciation of $79,509,000 in 1974 and $75,235,000 in 1973	97,115,000	148,143,000
Construction, escrow and other funds	12,638,000	12,803,000
Prepaid charter hire	24,839,000	25,705,000
Deferred preoperating expenses	4,875,000	6,990,000
Other assets	6,432,000	5,190,000
	$220,970,000	$238,370,000

LIABILITIES

Current Liabilities:

Notes payable-banks	$ 22,166,000
Accounts payable and accrued liabilities	35,390,000
Current portion of long-term debt	27,196,000
Estimated loss on uncompleted shipbuilding contract	—
Total current liabilities	84,752,000
	3,075,500
Unterminated voyage revenues less expenses	120,268,500
Long-term debt	1,953,000
Other liabilities	8,594,500
Deferred charter income	1,023,000
Deferred federal income tax	

Stockholders' equity:

Capital stock-$1 par value; authorized 30,000,000 shares, 13,706,764	
outstanding after deducting 3,900 shares in treasury	6,353,500
Paid in capital	1,759,000
Retained earnings	10,091,000
	18,703,500
	$238,370,000

	$ 12,214,500
	31,606,500
	53,180,000
	6,584,500
	104,085,500
	4,245,500
	93,126,500
	4,354,000
	5,619,000
	522,500
	6,353,500
	1,698,000
	465,500
	9,017,000
	$220,970,000

Table 7-4 Consolidated Statement of Changes in Financial Position—Good Shipping Company

	Year Ended Dec. 31, 19___	Year Ended Dec. 31, 19___
Sources of Working Capital		
Loss before extraordinary items	$ (9,625,500)	$(11,172,000)
Charges (credits) not affecting working capital:		
Depreciation	7,918,500	9,368,500
Deferred federal income tax	(500,500)	(650,000)
Amortization of prepaid charter hire, deferred charter income, and deferred preoperating expenses	1,319,000	2,694,500
Prepaid and deferred and other charges and credits included in loss on disposal of vessels, equipment, and other assets	644,500	
Increase (decrease) in unterminated voyage revenues less expenses	1,170,000	(97,500)
Total from operations	926,000	143,500
Proceeds from sale of vessels, equipment, and other assets	10,267,500	8,040,000
Construction differential subsidy for vessels under construction	7,137,500	11,732,500
Decrease in construction, escrow, and other funds	165,000	1,364,000
Proceeds from borrowings	19,155,000	20,922,000
Transfer of vessels under construction to shipbuilding contract in progress	46,337,000	
Other	1,020,500	1,743,500
	85,058,500	43,945,500

Application of Working Capital

Additions to vessels, property, and equipment	18,814,500	40,059,000
Addition to prepaid charter hire	3,748,500	9,004,000
Reduction in long-term debt	46,297,000	21,521,500
	68,860,000	70,584,000
Increase (decrease) in working capital	$ 16,198,500	$ (26,638,000)

Changes in Working Capital

Cash	$ 1,953,500	$ (3,195,500)
Cash in restricted accounts	(4,992,000)	(2,455,500)
Marketable securities	(1,142,500)	4,992,000
Accounts receivable	(1,204,500)	5,060,000
Due from U.S. government for vessels under construction	37,035,000	(3,000,000)
Shipbuilding contract in progress	3,018,000	
Construction and escrow funds	866,500	(1,254,500)
Prepaid expenses and other assets	9,951,500	(11,164,000)
Notes payable-banks	3,783,500	(8,455,000)
Accounts payable and accrued liabilities	(26,484,000)	(7,266,500)
Current portion of long-term debt	(6,584,500)	
Estimated loss on uncompleted shipbuilding contract		
Increase (decrease) in working capital	$ 16,198,500	$ (26,639,000)

**Table 7–5   Consolidated Statement of Operations and Retained Earnings—
Good Shipping Company**

	Year Ended (Date of end of acct.-year)	
Freight and charter revenues	$172,711,000	$149,146,500
Operating expenses	121,205,000	114,861,000
Marketing, general and administrative expenses	24,110,000	23,374,000
Interest expense	110,653,000	8,365,000
Depreciation	7,918,500	9,368,500
Loss on uncompleted shipbuilding contract	6,584,500	—
Loss on disposal of vessels, equipment and other assets	2,346,000	—
Deferred federal income tax (credit)	(500,500)	(650,000)
	182,336,500	160,318,500
Loss before extraordinary items	(9,625,500)	(11,172,000)
Extraordinary items	—	(376,000)
Net loss	(9,625,500)	(11,543,000)
Retained earnings at July 1	10,091,000	22,639,000
Retained earnings at June 30	465,500	10,091,000
Loss per share (based on average number of shares outstanding:		
Before extraordinary items	$ (.70)	$ (.81)
Extraordinary items	—	(.03)
Net loss	$ (.70)	$ (.84)

owned stock. Similarly, cash flow per share often represents important additional information. Lenders will be primarily concerned with various debt ratios, such as current assets to current liabilities, total debt to total assets, long-term debt to net assets, total debt to net worth, or equity and net profit to interest payable. These ratios are all related, as noted before, and should really be considered as part of a performance evaluation system, in which performance data are folded sequentially into the ratios. The ratios together provide an indication of a shipping company's operational, management, and financial performance.

7.1.2.   Tax Considerations in the Selection of Registry

Since a vessel is considered a portion of the country of its flag of registry, a preferred procedure under existing U.S. law for organizing a subsidiary shipping company is to register the vessel with a flag-of-convenience country. The ship is owned by a corporation domi-

Table 7-6 Five-Year Financial Summary—Good Shipping Company

	1979	1978	1977	1976	1975
Results for the year					
Revenues	$172,711	$149,146	$105,151	$ 80,699	$ 49,910
Operating expenses	131,205	119,861	76,685	56,799	27,537
Marketing, general, and administrative expenses	24,110	23,374	15,792	9,087	3,292
Interest expense	10,653	8,365	7,541	7,410	3,722
Depreciation	7,918	9,368	11,032	9,523	6,088
Loss on uncompleted shipbuilding contract	6,584	—	—	—	—
Loss on disposal of vessels, equipment, and other assets	2,366				
Federal income tax (credit)	(500)	(650)	(2,250)	(2,050)	(1,645)
Total expenses	282,336	160,318	158,802	80,770	42,284
Income (loss) before extraordinary items	(9,625)	(11,172)	(3,150)	(71)	(7,625)
Extraordinary items	—	(376)	(2,079)	(188)	(1,094)
Net Income (loss)	(9,625)	(11,548)	(5,229)	(259)	(8,719)
Expenditures for vessels, property, and equipment	18,814	40,059	35,968	31,559	50,962
Year-end position					
Current assets	$ 75,071	$ 39,039	$ 41,493	$ 26,956	$ 22,398
Current liabilities	104,085	84,752	57,966	53,206	40,048
Vessels, property, and equipment—net	97,115	148,143	137,601	138,125	122,578
Total assets	220,970	238,370	226,027	194,311	166,338
Long-term debt	93,126	120,268	120,868	97,592	83,988
Stockholders' equity	9,017	18,703	30,239	35,354	34,968
Shares of common stock outstanding	6,853	6,853	6,344	6,842	6,340
Per share data					
Income (loss) before extraordinary items	$(.70)	$(.81)	$(.23)	$(.005)	$(.56)
Net income (loss)	(.70)	(.84)	(.38)	$(.02)	$(.64)
Stockholders' equity	.66	(1.36)	(2.21)	$(2.58)	$(2.55)

ciled either in that country or in a tax shelter country. A country that offers a flag of convenience may not necessarily provide a satisfactory tax shelter as the country must also have a stable, easily converted currency and a well-developed banking system. If 10 percent or more of the subsidiary in the tax shelter (usually Bermuda, Bahamas, etc.) is owned by a U.S. company, the income from the operation is classed as subchapter "F" income. Prior to 1962 no income tax was payable on such income until it was returned to the United States as profits or until the company was liquidated, in which case it was treated as capital gains. After 1962 the rules were changed so that tax was payable as income was earned. However, specifically excluded from the "base" income were proceeds from "use, lease, or servicing" of ships or aircraft in foreign commerce.

These changes provided real tax savings to companies operating steamships as part of an integrated business because the profits from ship operations could be used to finance other areas of activity, such as mine development or oil drilling. Recently, the exemptions of profits from steamship operations from holding company base income have been removed. However, for local expansion, under present rules, a foreign-operating company can generally use funds without paying the U.S. tax. This change in tax laws will bring a gradual change in the method of organization because it eliminates nearly all advantages of an offshore holding company as a vehicle to own ships.

A second aspect of U.S. tax law, recently revoked, which had a large effect on organization and ownership patterns, was the reduced taxation of dividends received from "Less Developed Country Corporations." One of the goals of U.S. tax policy is to stimulate investment in developing countries. As a vehicle to implement this policy, the Less Developed Country Corporation was created in the U.S. tax code. A Less Developed Country Corporation meets the following criteria:

- It is a foreign corporation.
- It is engaged in active conduct of trade or business.
- At least 80 percent of its income is from sources within underdeveloped countries.
- At least 80 percent of its assets consist of (1) business property located in less developed countries, (2) cash or bank deposits located in less developed countries, (3) stock or obligations of another LDCC or of a less developed country, (4) assets equivalent to an insurance company's unearned premiums and ordinary and necessary reserves, and (5) obligations of the United States and certain other U.S. property.

The following were general advantages of a Less Developed Country Corporation:

- Dividends, interest, etc. are not included in subchapter "F" income to the extent they are invested in less developed countries.
- If the company is liquidated, the proceeds are treated as dividends. However, if the company has been owned by share owners for ten continuous years, the proceeds from liquidation are taxed as capital gains.
- In computing minimum dividend distributions of the parent company holding the LDCC, the income of the LDCC is excluded.
- The interest-equalization tax does not apply.

The Less Developed Country Corporation (LDCC) allowed businesses to set up much the same structure as before, with a parent holding company in a less developed country holding interests in mining, transportation, and so on, all incorporated in less developed countries. This structure allowed the profits of one area of the company to be invested in other areas without paying U.S. taxes. This portion of U.S. regulation had one addendum: as vessels registered in countries belonging to the English Commonwealth can fly the English flag, they do not represent, for this purpose, assets invested in less developed countries. Thus the flags of registration of vessels that are owned in this fashion are limited to Panama, Honduras, and Liberia—the conventional flag-of-convenience countries. Any non-Commonwealth country, such as Indonesia, Thailand, or Peru, can legally be used, but these countries generally place restrictions on ownership, crew nationality, or other factors that make them relatively unattractive for ship operation. The LDCC provision of the tax code was revoked in 1976.

Another point concerning the mechanics of organizing a ship holding company is that unless a ruling is obtained in advance that the organization of such a subsidiary is not part of a plan to avoid U.S. taxes, an excise tax of 27.5 percent is levied against any stock or securities transferred. This is avoided if the vessel itself, rather than the funds to buy it, are transferred. Thus, it is commonplace for one company to own a vessel during its construction and to transfer it to a second operating company on its completion.

7.1.3. *Controls of Investment in Shipping*

A tool occasionally used to help control cash flows affecting the U.S. balance of payments is controls on direct foreign investment. These controls can exert a large influence on patterns of ownership because of the large sums required to finance the operation of modern tonnage.

In 1968 a program of voluntary controls on direct investment was converted to a mandatory program. Its purpose was to restrict direct investments by U.S. investors in foreign ventures. Essentially, a direct investor is one who possesses as much as a 10 percent interest in a foreign venture. Net investment is the sum of (1) net capital transfers to and from foreign business ventures and (2) the direct investor's share of any reinvested earnings or losses in the foreign venture. For purposes of this program, the nations were divided into three classes. Schedule A countries are generally the less developed or emerging nations. Schedule B countries are such countries as Great Britain, Australia, New Zealand, and the Middle East oil-exporting countries. Schedule C countries are those countries not highly dependent on U.S. capital, such as Western Europe, the Sino-Soviet block, and South and Southwest Africa. The limits on net investment set in 1971 were as follows:

- Schedule A countries—110 percent of 1965–1966 net investment.
- Schedule B countries—65 percent of 1965–1966 net investment.
- Schedule C countries—35 percent of 1965–1966 net investment.

Long-term foreign borrowing and funds generated from depreciation were excluded from net investment calculations. In general, allowed investment could not be shifted between regions—that is, between A, B, or C. These regulations are still in force but with vastly relaxed limits. In particular, the largest investment allowed without becoming subject to the regulations at all has been raised from $100,000 to $1,000,000.

Because of the extremely high debt-equity ratios possible in ship financing, this kind of regulation can have a very strong effect on the kinds of organizations that are most economical for integrated ship operations. Furthermore, because charter payments are not counted as direct investment for the purpose of enforcing those regulations, ship operations can easily be used to circumvent investment controls entirely. A ship can be purchased using money borrowed outside of the United States, using charter payments from the U.S. company planning to use the ship as collateral. As long-term charter payments frequently are sufficient to amortize a vessel's cost in five years (sometimes even two years), they have the effect of transferring large amounts of money essentially for investment purposes without subjecting the "investor" to direct investment controls.

7.2. Financing of Shipping

A thorough study of financial strategies available to a shipping company requires the modeling of the capital flows through the shipping
company, including the environment with which the company in-
teracts. Figure 7–3 shows the major flows of capital in a shipping
company. It shows the flow of capital through the shipping company,
both input and output of capital, and the flow of the operational
investment and financial decisions. These decisions are dependent
on and heavily influenced by the flow of capital through the company's activities. The financial decisions deal with sources and purpose of available capital and include an evaluation of the port's capacity to undertake various forms of new financing, based on
expected or projected net revenues. Note that even in the aggregate,
capital or cash flows are fairly complex. Capital or cash inflows and
outflows often participate in internal feedback loops designed to
assure both control and internal distribution. The method and type
of financing used by a shipping company will determine the scope
of its operations and the size and type of debt load the company can
carry. As a result, financial planning is the most important factor
influencing a company's investment decisions. Consequently, it also
affects financial strategies, the expected returns from capital investments, its growth rate, and other factors that in turn determine the
availability of future financing.

The approach to and method of financing is among the most important decisions for shipping management. Terms, as well as provisions of financing, must be considered, as they affect the degree
of control of company management over operations. Sources of financing may insist on prior claims to the income of assets. The
resultant cost of capital and degree of control surrendered to obtain
financing will influence the investment decision.

Any shipping company, to ensure its continued viability, must
constantly examine and undertake new investments designed to
maintain required capacity and productivity. One of the most important tasks of shipping management, it is as essential as control
of daily operations of the company. New investment projects must
be located, identified, and adequately described. Next, an estimate
of initial cost and potential earnings must be made. This should be
tied to an estimate of the uncertainty and risk involved in both these
earning estimates and future cost estimates. The financial decision
process considers the amount of available capital, the cost of capital,
and the tax considerations involved in the various projects. The top
management must also determine the desired rate of return on proj-

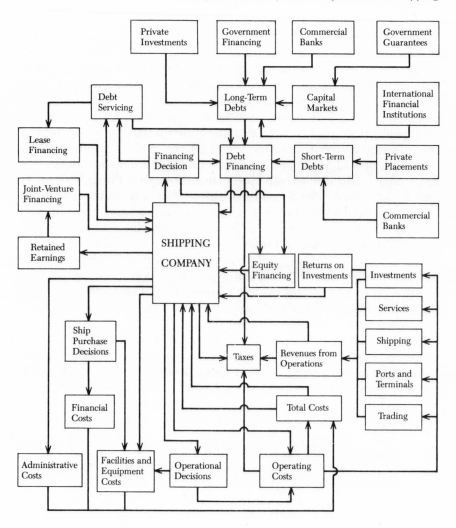

Figure 7–3 Shipping Company Capital Flows.

ects to be undertaken by the firm. These factors, combined with the expected returns from the project, will indicate a new present worth or return on investment of each project considered. This information, along with other noneconomic measures, such as the company's identification with the project and public relations, will determine which projects are to be undertaken. In turn, it will feed back into the financing decision process to complete the feedback loop.

7.2.1. *Capital Budgeting of Shipping Developments*

Shipping investments are capital assets and are used by the company to produce services. Such development investments or allocations of capital are usually carefully planned. A plan for expenditure of capital assets is a capital budget. The process of determining how much and when to spend capital assets and which assets to acquire is capital budgeting.

Capital budgeting can be short run or long term. Short-run capital budgeting usually involves the current and forthcoming (two to five year) periods. Long-term capital budgeting for shipping developments generally extends over a period of twenty to twenty-five years and often involves consideration of the appreciable uncertainties involved. Capital budgeting considers both the cost and benefit of each development and consequent investment opportunity.

Different or alternative shipping investment projects should generally be evaluated on the basis of the cash flow resulting from each project. The project should only be undertaken (or selected from among the alternatives) if its cash flow meets certain criteria. Cash flow for any period—that is, the costs and benefits associated with the project—can be computed as follows: Net cash flow from project = (cash inflows − cost outflows) = (project revenues − operating expenses, excluding depreciation, − capital expenditures − taxes). (Taxes are usually assessed on revenues minus expenses, including depreciation.)

Future cash flows from a project are usually uncertain. Expected or estimated costs and revenues must be used in the determination of expected or estimated net cash flow. If data are available, statistical theory permits statistical measures to estimate the degree of uncertainty of different potential levels of cash flow. Today, investment costs and benefits (revenues) involve indirect and often unquantifiable factors, such as environmental costs or social benefits.

After the cash flow has been estimated or determined for an investment, an evaluation must be made of the merit of this investment relative to alternative investments. If the investment is unique and not essential, a decision must be made whether the investment should be undertaken at all.

7.2.2. *Financial Performance Computations*

To compute expected or real financial performance of a ship, fleet of ships, or other assets, a cash flow analysis should be undertaken. Revenues are first determined by computing the inflows of funds from nondebt sources.

Gross revenues, period $t = R_t = \sum_{ij} P_{tij} \times M_{tij} + RO_t$

where

P_{tij} = amount of cargo of type i carried on route j during period t;

M_{tij} = applicable freight rate for cargo type i on route j during period t;

RO_t = other revenues during period t.

Operating costs, period $t = C_t = (OS_t + OP_t) + OC_t$

where

OS_t = at-sea operating cost, period t;

OP_t = in-port operating cost, period t;

$(OS_t + OP_t)/N_t$ = average voyage cost, period t;

and

N_t = number of voyages, period t;

OC_t = other costs, period t.

Net operating revenues = $I_t = R_t - C_t - \sum_k D_{tk}$

where

R_t = gross revenue, period t;

D_{tk} = depreciation, year t, type k.

Taxable income, period $t = TI_t = TI_t = (I_t - D_t)$,

where

D_t = depletion allowance.

Investment tax credit = $ITC_t = \overline{ITC}_{t-1} + \sum fZ_{t1} ITC^1$,

where

$\overline{ITC}_{t-1}$ = unused ITC from previous year;

f = fraction of investment Z_{t1} qualifying for investment tax credit (including energy investment tax credit);

Z_{t1} = investment-type 1 in period t;

ITC^1 = rate of investment tax credit.

Deferred income tax is the next item to be computed, based on available shelters. From this, potential tax can be computed, based on alternative deferral strategies. Alternative taxation approaches should be considered to determine net revenues after tax and to use investment tax, deferred tax, and similar clauses of the tax law to affect tax rate, after tax income for period t, and ultimately the overall financial performance of the investment.

7.2.3. *Financial Evaluation*

Several financial criteria for investment evaluation are in use. Table 7–7 presents each method, its symbol, and its formula. The most important criteria are listed as follows:

- Internal Rate of Return (IRR)
- Net Present Value Method (NPV)
- Payback Period Method (PP)
- Accounting Rate of Return Method (ARR)
- Capital Recovery Factor Method (CRF)
- Minimum Average Annual Cost Method (AAC)
- Present Worth Method (PW)
- Equated Interest Rate of Return Method (EIRR)

These various financial methods for investment evaluation are discussed in Appendix 7A. Financial evaluation is only one part in the evaluation of shipping investments.

7.2.4. *Choosing Among Alternative Financial Criteria*

Suitably general economic criteria, such as net present value (NPV) and equated interest rate of return (EIRR), can be used to optimize the development or performance of a shipping investment project with respect to its technological and competitive environment. Different economic criteria may be used as objective functions in the choice among alternative ship operating and procurement projects, decisions, strategies, or plans. Choosing which criterion to use to make decisions about an investment or operational plan is dependent on managerial and other objectives. The choice represents a method of quantifying those objectives. Each of the criteria has certain characteristics of potential value in particular situations. For example, while the EIRR does not reflect the effects of reinvesting profits, the use of NPV does. Both NPV and EIRR are calculated using assumptions about future revenues. EIRR, however, is less sensitive to an error in prediction than is NPV.

NPV can be used to formulate explicit guidelines for managerial action regarding vague issues. An example is the determination of conditions under which depositing profits into a tax-exempt reserve fund would be advantageous.

Table 7–7   Basic Financial Criteria for Shipping Development Projects

Criteria	Symbol	Formula
Maximum annual profit	AP	$F_m = [R_m - E_m]$
Minimum cost/ton-mile	CTM	$CTM = \dfrac{1}{n} \sum\limits_{m=1}^{n} (E_m/TM_m)$
Maximum profit/unit investment	PUI	$PUI = \dfrac{1}{P}\left[\sum\limits_{m=1}^{n} (R_m - E_m) \right]$
Maximum annual profit/unit investment	APUI	$APUI = \dfrac{1}{nP}\left[\sum\limits_{m=1}^{n} (R_m - E_m) \right]$
Maximum profit/average investment	PAI	$PAI = \dfrac{2}{nP}\left[\sum\limits_{m=1}^{n} (R_m - E_m) \right]$
Capital recovery factor	CRF	$CRF = \dfrac{B}{P} = \dfrac{r(1 + r)^n}{(1 + r)^n - 1}$
Minimum average annual cost	AAC	$AAC = E + CRF \cdot P$
Net present value	NPV	$NPV = \sum\limits_{m=1}^{n} \dfrac{CF_m}{(1 + r)^m} - P$
Present worth	PW	$PW = \sum\limits_{m=0}^{n} (E_m/(1 + r)^m)$ $= P + \dfrac{E}{CRF} = \dfrac{AAC}{CRF}$
Equated interest rate of return	EIRR	$0 = \sum\limits_{m=0}^{n} (CF_m/(1 + p)^m)$
Internal rate of return	IRR	$P = \sum\limits_{m=1}^{n} \dfrac{CF_m}{(1 + r)^m}$
Payback period	PB	$P = \sum\limits_{m=1}^{Y} \dfrac{CF_m}{(1 + r)^m}$
Accounting rate of return	ARR	$\text{Max. } ARR = \dfrac{\text{average annual benefit}}{\text{investment}}$

Symbols
  B = Annual payback amount
  F_m = Annual profit in year m
  R_m = Revenues in year m
  E_m = Expenses in year m
  TM = Ton-mile transport effort
TM_m = Ton-mile transport effort in year m
  P = Principal or initial investment
  Y = Number of years required for payback
  n = Planning horizon in years
  p = Discount rate
  r = Rate of interest or internal rate of return
CF_m = Cash flow in year m

7.2.5. *Example of Financial Evaluation of Shipping Projects*

Taking as an example alternatives for a container feeder vessel shipping investment, assume that we have a choice between a vessel costing $3.0 million, with a net annual cash flow over a five-year period of $0.9 million, and another costing $2.0 million, with an annual net cash flow of $0.610 million. Using the four different evaluation methods, we obtain the following results (given that we assume a technological change will make either system obsolete within five years after installation). (Take cost of capital as 10 percent.)

It is seen in Table 7–8 that although the NPV of Vessel A is 25 percent higher than that of Vessel B, the IRR of the latter is higher— 16.2 percent instead of 15.2 percent. Also, payback period and ARR are shown to be highly insensitive and indicate here invariance between the two alternative systems, notwithstanding the great superiority of Vessel A in terms of NPV. These results would be even more pronounced if the period were extended to ten years.

7.3. Financing Alternatives

A major difference exists in the financing of ships acquired by U.S. owners for U.S. registration as compared with the methods used by owners (including U.S. owners) who purchase ships abroad. U.S. ship financing is largely affected by the traditional U.S. government approach to the provision of government aids to national ship operators and builders, as well as by other clauses of the maritime laws. Many of the following methods of ship financing are increasingly being used and may have attractions to U.S. owners in the future. Some may require changes in U.S. law.

- *Joint-Venture Financing:* International joint ventures that pool their financial resources and markets and share their risks are becoming increasingly popular.
- *International Financing:* Lower-cost foreign financing, mortgaging, or other involvement of foreign financial institutions are being used.
- *Venture Capital Financing:* Numerous venture capital sources may consider ship financing, particularly with high leverage.
- *Lease Purchase Financing:* As with containers and similar equipment, present tax laws make use of lease purchase, leverage leasing, or other approaches more attractive.
- *Private Placement Financing and Leaseback:* General and limited partners are financing new or existing tonnage and leaseback.

Table 7–8   Financial Comparison of Alternative Investments

System	Vessel A	Vessel B
Investment	$3,000,000	$2,000,000
Net cash flow (annual) for next five years	$ 900,000	$ 610,000
NPV	$(900 × 3.791 − 3000) × 1000 = $412,000	$(610 × 3.791 − 2000) × 1000 = $313,000
IRR	15.2%	16.0%
Payback period	3.33 years	3.28 years
ARR	0.300	0.305

- *Ordinary Sale and Leaseback:* Tax writeoff, depreciation, and other rights to "new" owners are being transferred.
- *Space Leasing:* Similar to space chartering, space leasing is for a longer period or on a permanent basis.
- *Government financing under some bilateral or unilateral financing terms* is being offered by numerous industrial countries to owners in LDC countries, owners registering ships in LDC countries, or simply to owners ordering or purchasing ships from domestic sources.
- *Vendor Financing:* Shipyards, equipment manufacturers, and charterers are now offering financing.

These alternatives and many more are now available to owners. Tax laws, aid, or subsidy terms, loan repayment, and grace terms vary throughout the world. Owners will continue to have many opportunities to design attractive financing schemes which, though unconventional, may offer great advantages over the traditional approaches used in U.S. shipping.

The increasing importance of intermodal transport introduces both new opportunities and challenges. In financing intermodal ocean transportation, the ship investment is often no longer the principal investment. In container, integrated trailer, barge carrier, and other modern intermodal shipping systems, the investment in containers, trailers, barges, and related terminal equipment often greatly exceeds the investment in ships. Also, the economic and/or operational life of such equipment is usually much less than that of the ship or ships. Therefore, equipment must be replaced one or more times over the life of the ship. The resulting proportion of present value investment in intermodal equipment is therefore even higher than the actual investment, in proportion to the investment in ships. This problem has resulted in the development and use of many novel and imaginative equipment-financing approaches, some of which, as discussed before, may also offer new and lucrative alternatives to conventional ship financing.

Appendix 7A

CRITERIA FOR FINANCIAL EVALUATION

7A.1. Internal Rate-of-Return (IRR) Method

The project's value is assumed to be its rate of return, commonly referred to as its "internal rate of return" (r). If the net cash flow estimated to be generated by the project in period m is CF_m, then the internal rate of return r on the initial investment P is the average percentage of P that would give us the same average net cash results in each period m over the economic life n of the project. In other words, it gives us the percentage of earnings on the initial investment. To determine the internal rate of return, we write

$$NPV = \sum_{m=1}^{n} \frac{CF_m}{(1 + r)^m} = 0.$$

Note that r is the interest that makes the present value of the investment P over its economic life n equal to zero. In this method, a project's returns are assumed to be measured by how much its IRR exceeds the cost of capital.

7A.2. Net Present Value (NPV) Method

The net present value of an investment is determined by adding the present values of all profits, losses, and investments over the investment's life. The profits and losses are discounted at an adjusted cost of capital r. This criterion tells us whether it was worth borrowing the money at that rate. If the NPV is positive, the investment is worthwhile, relative to its cost

221

of capital. (Any residual or salvage value of the capital assets should be included in the last period cash flow as a receipt.)

$$\text{net present value of project} = \sum_{m=1}^{n} \frac{CF_m}{(1 + r)^m} - P,$$

where r is the assumed cost of capital. In this method, the NPV of a project is a direct measure of the relative profitability of the project. If the cost of capital is not constant over the period n of the project, then

$$\text{NPV} = \sum_{K=1}^{n} \frac{CF_K}{\prod\limits_{j=1}^{K} (1 + r_j)} - P$$

where r_j is now the interest rate in the jth year

$$j = 1, ..., K.$$

The NPV method is usually considered to be a more rational basis for project financial evaluation. A project with a high internal rate of return, for example, does not necessarily have a high net present value. Therefore, choosing the project with the maximum internal rate of return from among the alternatives is not always a good basis for selection. Similarly, the internal rate of return of a project is not necessarily unique. One exception is where alternative, mutually exclusive investments each require the same initial outlay and earn that investment's internal rate of return until some predetermined future date. Here, the initial investment and the reinvestment period are assumed identical for all alternative projects, and the resulting IRR is an effective measure of the relative merit of the alternative investments.

The analytical value of the NPV method is dependent on how well the net cash flow CF_K can be determined and what interest rate is used to discount the profits. Once the CF_K's and r are determined, the NPV gives the most reliable representation of the investment's performance, as it involves no simplifying assumptions. The NPV, however, is subject to the underlying discount rate, which is usually taken to be constant over the economic life of the project. The underlying discount rate, though, varies usually over time. This makes the approach less reliable.

7A.3. Capital Recovery Factor (CRF) Method

The capital recovery factor takes explicit account of the time value of money. It is employed by dividing the initial investment by the yearly profit and then solving for p, the annual rate of return, analytically, or, more often using interest tables. (Strictly speaking, this criterion holds only for constant yearly profit. In practice, an average figure can be used without much loss of accuracy, as long as yearly profit does not vary too much.) The CRF is, in fact, the annual rate of return corrected for a finite investment life. Furthermore, if we divide the numerator and denominator of the right-hand side of the formula by $(1 + r)^n$ and let n go to infinity, the result will yield

$$CRF = r.$$

Those investments, where profitability p is greater than cost of capital r, are favorable; investments with the highest CRF are presumably most favorable if the duration of the investment is not an important item.

Another way of thinking about CRF is as one form of average annual proceeds per dollar of outlay, with yearly proceeds assumed to be fairly constant. If this constraint is imposed, there is no problem about ordering the receipts since they are equal from year to year.

The CRF shown in Figure 7A–1 appears to be only marginally useful. Where high, long-term performance of an investment is desired, other criteria, such as net present value, give more complete information. If, on the other hand, the investor desires a high immediate rate of return but is not concerned about the long run, the profitability p is more useful.

7A.4. Minimum Average Annual Cost (AAC) Method

The minimum average annual cost converts the cost of investment and operation into a yearly figure by using the CRF to convert P to an equivalent annual expenditure. This criterion has very limited applicability in choosing among investments, as it does not account for any revenues. It can be useful if alternatives have equal (but unknown) incomes, equal lives, and if revenues and expenses are constant from year to year. Such a case might arise in the instance of a captive demand and capacity. That situation does not occur frequently.

The meaning of CRF here is vague. Previously, we said that the interest rate to be used in (or found by) the CRF is the internal profitability of the investment. Hence, since profits are unknown, there is no definable profitability. An adequate substitute is the desired profitability of the system as a whole if the investment being considered is a subsystem of the overall operation. If the investment is intended to be a business unto itself, one could raise the cost of capital r after properly correcting for risk. This is allowable because r is, in effect, the lower limit of the acceptable range of p.

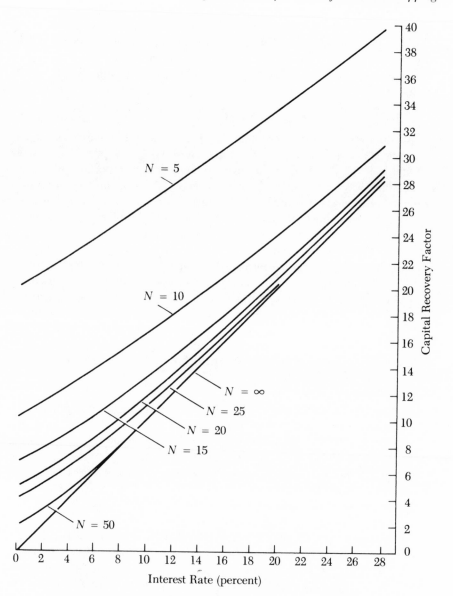

Figure 7A–1 Capital Recovery Factor Versus Interest Rate.

7A.5. Present Worth (PW) Method

This criterion is related to net present value, with the difference that it includes only expenditures. It is useful in the case of a captive fleet, as is true with some of the previous criteria discussed. If the annual expenditure is constant over the life of the investment, then

$$PW = P + \frac{1}{CRF} E,$$

which, when combined with the definition of average annual cost, gives

$$PW = \frac{AAC}{CRF}.$$

7A.6. Payback Period (PP) Method

The criteria is the length of time it takes to recover the initial investment of the project. The project whose initial investment is recouped in the shortest period is assumed to be superior to all alternative projects.

To compute the packback period, we can use either real or present value net cash flows (based on the cost of capital)

$$P = \sum_{j=l}^{Y} \frac{CF_j}{(1 + r)^j},$$

where r = cost of capital and Y = payback period. In most calculations of payback period, r is assumed to be zero. This method ignores past payback period returns and the patterns of returns during the payback period, as well as the effects of reinvestment or cost of capital factors.

7A.7. Accounting Rate of Return (ARR) Method

In this method the average annual after tax accounting benefit (net revenue or profit) obtained from the selection of a particular project is divided by the capital cost of the project, or:

$$ARR = \frac{\text{average annual benefit from investment}}{\text{investment}}.$$

7A.8.   Equated Interest Rate of Return (EIRR) Method

The formula for EIRR is

$$0 = \sum_{m=0}^{n} \frac{CF_m}{(1 + p)^m}$$

where p is solved for implicitly.

The rate of interest p, which sets the net present value (NPV) equal to zero is the equated interest rate of return. This is the cost of capital that would make the investment a breakeven proposition. If p is greater than the actual cost of capital r, the investment is profitable.

The NPV and EIRR criteria contain basically the same elements. Some writers have praised the EIRR method at the expense of NPV because it computes an explicit interest rate while the NPV uses an assumed rate. This is only partially true, as the profitability p is meaningless by itself. It must be compared with an appropriately chosen cost of capital. If the investment under consideration has more than one period of net loss, several values of p may satisfy the polynomial that defines the EIRR. In that case, the pairs of adjacent p's define limits between which the cost of capital must fall to make the venture profitable.

7A.9.   Minimum Required Freight Rate (MRF)

Another approach is to compute the minimum required freight rate as a measure of profitability of the shipping project or investment.

Let L = loan to be repaid over n_1 years;

I = total investment;

C_o = operating expenses/day (all fixed and variable expenses except for financial costs);

r = expected average percentage increase/year in operating expenses;

i_1 = interest payable on loan;

P = percentage loan capital of total investment;

i_2 = required interest on owner's equity (opportunity cost of equity).

Cash flow requirements in year t (assuming linear repayment over n_1 years):

$$CF_t = L\left[\frac{n_1\text{-}t}{n_1}\right] i_1 + \frac{L}{n_1} + PI\left[i_2 + \frac{1}{n_2}\right] + C_o \cdot 365 \cdot r$$

for $t \leq n_1$ or n_2.

MRF_t = minimum required freight rate/day during year $t = CF_t/365$

The above does not consider the scrap value of the ship, assumed zero at n_2, where n_2 is assumed to be the economic life of the ship, with $n_2 \geq n_1$.

Appendix 7B

ELIGIBILITY OF FOREIGN CITIZENS FOR PARTICIPATION IN U.S.-FLAG SHIPPING

Eligibility for participation in U.S. government aid programs to U.S. flag shipping is restricted to U.S. citizens as defined in Section 905(c) of the Merchant Marine Act of 1936, under which a corporation, partnership, or association may be considered a citizen of the United States only if it is a citizen within the meaning of Section 2 of the Shipping Act of 1916.[1] Section 2 defines citizenship for corporations, partnerships, and associations with respect to a "controlling interest." For coastwise (Jones Act) operation, 75 percent of the stock or ownership rights must be owned and controlled by citizens of the United States, while for government aid programs affecting U.S.-flag shipping in the U.S. foreign trade, a majority of the stock or ownership rights must be owned and controlled by citizens of the United States. Furthermore, according to the Shipping Act of 1916, the "President or other Chief Executive Officer and Chairman of the Board of Directors," as well as a majority of the number of directors necessary to constitute a quorum, must be United States citizens.

Therefore noncitizens can participate in the benefits of U.S. coastwise shipping and government aids to U.S. foreign shipping through a minority interest in a company in foreign trade and an interest of up to 25 percent in a company in the domestic trade.

Direct foreign participation can be in the terms of a joint venture, partnership, or stock ownership, while indirect participation may involve time charter of a ship owned by a U.S. citizen, space charter on such a ship, or similar arrangements.

---

[1] Abstracted from H. Clayton Cook, Jr., "Ship Finance," Seatrade Academy, Conference on American Shipping, December 1981, New York.

Chapter 8

ECONOMIC ISSUES AND OPPORTUNITIES FOR AMERICAN SHIPPING

American domestic and foreign trade provides the major demand for American shipping. Although cross-trading is important for some foreign-going U.S.-flag operators and for many U.S.-owned foreign-flag vessels, U.S. trade still provides most of the revenues for American shipping. The volume of trade and therefore the derived demand for shipping depends to some extent on the cost of shipping. Some trades have a higher elasticity of demand with respect to shipping or transport cost than others, depending on the degree of essentiality of the commodity involved and the uniqueness of the origin and destination in that trade. Therefore, trade in essential commodities that are available only from one source in the quantities and/or qualities required will be inelastic with respect to shipping costs. Shipping costs as a percentage of the landed costs of goods are nearly always lower for higher–value commodities.

The increased dependence of the U.S. on lower value, raw, and semifinished material imports and the lack of U.S. bulk shipping capacity have the potential for greater American vulnerability to higher bulk shipping costs, particularly if cargo sharing or similar restrictive practices are introduced into bulk-shipping trades.

U.S. bulk trades are expected to continue to expand, particularly in trades with the LDCs, although some U.S. bulk trades, such as coal, phosphate, and so forth, with OECD countries will grow substantially as well. The largest rates of growth in the 1980s should be in trades with the developing countries in the Far East, South East Asia, and the Middle East. South American and African trades will probably grow at a lesser rate. By 1985, Pacific liner trades are expected to comprise over 50 percent of all U.S. liner trade.

A major issue facing the U.S. is the government's role in international trade. While many of the world's governments have specified trade policies and in fact often participate in or assist the foreign trade of their nation, the United States has traditionally advocated free trade. This is increasingly difficult to achieve now with growing intervention or control by foreign governments in international trade. Governments of most centrally planned economies essentially control all their foreign trade, while others such as many LDCs resort to significant direct or indirect involvement by government in their foreign trade. Among OECD nations we similarly find governments that directly or indirectly influence their country's foreign trade through encouragement of trading combines or groupings that operate with the support and consent of their government. Many of these developments contradict the central U.S. policy objective for improvements toward free trade through the reduction in government-imposed barriers to trade, flow of funds, or free choice of means of transportation. At this time over half of the world trade by value is controlled by governments or trading companies. An increasing amount of Japanese trade (70 percent in 1980) is controlled by trading companies, and more governments are assuming control of the major trades of their nations.

Government and trading-company or similar control of trade obviously affects the terms and choice of shipping. It may also influence the mode and route choice. Issues of increasing concern to U.S. shipping are:

1. Demands for exclusion of government-owned or traded cargoes from cargo sharing under the UNCTAD Code.
2. Diversion of U.S. cargo to Canadian and Mexican ports, and resulting diversion to non-U.S. shipping.
3. Increased involvement of foreign governments in shipping.
4. Expanded definition of "national shipping" by many governments to comprise all shipping capacity under their control. This includes tonnage owned by nationals, by other flags of registry, space-chartered tonnage, and more.
5. Increased involvement of foreign governments in the control and ownership of shipping.

Other issues include the potential establishment of shippers' councils in the United States. These groups would be able to exert great pressures on shipping and particularly on liner conferences.

A major opportunity exists in the rationalization of shipping. Many plans and proposals have been developed, aimed at achieving a more rational use of shipping capacity in U.S. trade, and thereby lowering the cost of transportation of U.S. trade. The existing structure of shipping does not encourage such an approach. With increasing intervention in the free trade approach to shipping, rationalization may be required to offset the effects of new constraints, which generally reduce capacity utilization and increase costs of shipping.

8.1. Management of Technology and U.S. Shipping

U.S. technology has been instrumental in introducing some of the major changes in the types of ships used in world trade and the methods of shipping developed in the last few decades. Container ships, barge carriers, container feeder ships, oceangoing barges, slurry carriers, and others all originated in the United States. Yet while these technologies were developed in the United States, many of our foreign competitors have enthusiastically advanced them well beyond United States' use. Therefore, leadership in many of these and other technologies has passed to foreign interests better able to integrate their use or marshal the increasing private and public capital resources needed for the continued development of these technologies. While this is largely due to the lack of U.S. commercial shipbuilding capacity and use, it is equally affected by the inability of U.S. shipping to take a leading role in technology development and by the traditional reliance of U.S. shipping management on government participation in or the financing of technological developments.

It is interesting to note, though, that the majority of technological breakthroughs achieved in shipping in the United States were developed through private and not public initiative, notwithstanding the comparatively small private exposure to and involvement in shipping research and development. This seems to indicate that imagination and initiative are still very much alive in the United States, but that the industry lacks the close support by government which is essential to allow technological development to be fully exploited and technological advantages to be maintained.

This approach is quite different from the role taken by other major maritime countries, particularly Japan, where government works closely with industry in the development, application, and extension of new technology. Another factor is the lack of technological coordination between the suppliers and users of shipping. Again, U.S. owners/operators are handicapped by their inability to closely work with shippers in developing and adapting shipping technology to both operator and user needs, a requirement for effective introduction and effective use of new technology. In many other countries, and again Japan is an outstanding example, owners/operators and users collaborate closely. This is obviously much easier in Japan where nearly 70 percent of the foreign trade is controlled by the major trading companies, many of which have their own shipping companies.

The U.S. Maritime Administration has repeatedly attempted to obtain industry "inputs" into their research programs, yet considering the range of federally supported maritime research, few projects ever find an application or are of potential practical use. In the past, an inordinately large percentage of federal maritime research funds went to "Nuclear Ship" and similar programs. Now a significant portion is spent on maintaining major goverment research facilities such as CAORF (ship simulator), projects of the National Maritime Research Center, and various programs such as the NDF Communications program.

While relevant research and technology development is performed at these facilities, there appears to be a large gap in the U.S. between research and application. The percentage of U.S. research projects that never lead to applications is larger than in many other major maritime nations, such as Japan and England, where maritime research is controlled, funded, and often performed at least partly by independent maritime research organizations jointly established, supervised, and funded by government and industry. It appears that this type of approach fosters closer supervised and more coordinated research with a greater chance of direct application.

Obviously many other factors, such as the total size of the U.S. maritime industry and the size of individual maritime companies, are important as well. A major issue, though, appears to be that many U.S. shipping and shipbuilding companies do not really recognize the value of research and development either in the short or long term. Research and development expenditures are particularly attractive under today's tax incentives, yet few in the industry have ever studied the benefit/cost effectiveness of maritime research. Competition is a reason often advanced for the lack of effective industry-wide cooperation in maritime research. This is curious considering that U.S. shipping is probably operating in a less competitive internal environment than shipping in most other countries.

Considering the fact that we probably have the oldest fleet among all major industrial nations, and may not be able to count on continued direct support by the federal government, some major decisions on composition and technology of fleet replacement are obviously required. While some U.S. operators and naval architects have been tremendously innovative and have introduced significant advances, the further developments of these same technologies has often been assumed by interests abroad.

A large storehouse of technology and knowledge is available in the United States which—though often developed for other purposes—

offers some unique opportunities for U.S. shipping. It appears that new approaches must be found to organize the transfer of technology and develop effective applications.

8.1.1. *Technological Developments*

Container shipping has for over twenty years now been the primary technological development in general cargo shipping. In recent years, the main concern has been the integration of intermodal container transport. While some large (3000 TEU plus) container vessels have been built, there is a trend toward systems and not ship economies of scale. Fewer port calls, larger port consignments, and more effective intermodal point-to-point transport are today's major considerations. Greater use is made of feeder vessels (or barges) for coastal or short ocean route distribution and gathering of containers. Efficient container shipping is today rationalized as a system. Slower steaming, fewer port calls, larger port consignments, greater use of feeder vessels, unit trains, and integrated track or barge services are all part of this rationalization or system approach. It also includes such operational considerations as pooling, space sharing, space chartering, and others which permit greater utilization of capacity. This trend is exemplified by the new Mexican and other land bridges, as well as numerous ocean or coastal container feedership or barge services throughout the world.

The average containership ordered during the next five to ten years will probably be a slow or medium-diesel driven, full-bodied, 18 to 20 knot vessel with a 1500 to 2000 TEU capacity. Containerships will change to permit the handling of various sizes of high-volume containers of up to 50 feet in length and 10 feet in height. Similarly, there is increasing interest in RoRo vessels for both RoRo and batched containers as well as outsized cargo and wheeled cargo handling. Future RoRo containerships (1986 and later) may include block container handling capability with double-width cells above and possibly below deck, which would permit use and handling of blocked containers, two containers wide.

A parallel development in portable container lifts and vertical conveyors is an attachment to a ship's side that can lift containers two or four high from alongside a vessel to a transfer rail on the ship's deck for sliding into the particular deck slot. This type of equipment is of particular use for dry bulk carriers (coal, grain, etc.) designed to carry on-deck containers that are too high or wide to be served by ordinary shoreside gantry cranes.

A major issue in the more extensive use of RoRo trailer and containerships is the transverse watertight subdivision of such ships. The many recent ship casualties indicate a need for a drastic departure from the traditional design and arrangement of such vessels. There are numerous technological solutions varying from trunked ramp arrangements and scissor lifts to hybrid longitudinal and transverse stepped subdivision.

Bulk carriers offer many opportunities for technological developments, particularly in coal carriers. The primary concern is usually effective unloading with shoreside or shipboard equipment. New scrapers and belt and buckle chain methods that offer higher discharge rates are available or being perfected. Another future approach might be to unload via bottom dumper gates onto enclosed conveyors sealed against the bottom of the hull of a discharge ship. Similar advances are being offered in the area of slurry handling, dewatering, mixing, and discharging of pulverized dry bulk cargo.

Increasing use will also be made of integrated tug-barge systems for dry bulk transport, particularly for applications where major terminal delays can be expected and drop and swap type of operations provide significant potential savings.

Tanker developments will be increasingly affected by double hull/bottom and ballast segregation and subdivisioning requirements, with primary developments in short- to medium-distance crude carriers and a multitude of diverse product carriers to meet increasing requirements for product segregation. *LNG/LPG* and other types of gas carriers will probably be based on new concepts of containment and barrier design currently being investigated.

Marine propulsion plant research in the U.S. has been in steam and gas turbine propulsion and in propeller or thruster investigations. Comparatively little research has been devoted to marine diesel or other reciprocating internal combustion engine developments. Here it would be wise to learn from Japanese, Korean, Taiwanese, and similar experiences that are based on the development of improved technology founded on some of the most advanced existing internal combustion engine technology. In particular, the integrated use of microprocessors to control fuel injection, pressure, temperature, and other settings, many of which are currently controlled by mechanical or electronic sensors through direct feedback, may provide significant advances which could allow U.S. marine power plant development to catch up with or overtake developments abroad.

Cargo handling and stowage or control systems are probably the most important technology affecting shipping costs and therefore competitiveness. Many of the developments in the U.S. space, air/transport, and chemical industries could be readily adapted to marine use, but again, we find a void in U.S. technology application.

8.1.2. *Opportunities for U.S. Technological Developments*

Although, as mentioned before, much of advanced maritime technology has originated in the United States, its further development, refinement, and innovative application has more often advanced abroad than domestically. Examples are computer applications for shipping management information systems, cargo planning, ship weather routing, container terminal control, and other systems. Although shipboard use of microprocessors for ship management, or satellite communication-based ship weather routing systems were first introduced in this country, many more, and often more advanced, applications of these technologies are now found abroad.

It is now necessary for U.S. shipping to leapfrog many of these developments to attain a measure of our traditional competitiveness. To achieve this we require greater coordination and collaboration in maritime technology research and development. While it is important for us to continue basic long-range research, it is equally important to effectively fill the gap of short-term technological developments. To allow this we need a much greater involvement of the U.S. shipping industry in maritime research and technological development. The U.S. maritime industry is near the bottom of all U.S. industries in its commitment and contribution to technological research and development. Even among transportation modes, proportionately less is spent by the U.S. shipping industry than by the road, rail, or air transport industry. If we are to turn our industry around, we will require a greater commitment and contribution by the industry, particularly now when the federal government increasingly transfers the responsibility of development to the private sector.

8.2. Issues in Government Policy and Regulation Affecting U.S. Shipping

U.S. policies and regulations affecting American shipping have been described in a companion volume.[1] U.S. shipping policies are prescribed by the various Shipping and Merchant Marine Acts which introduced various direct maritime aid programs such as the Construction Differential Subsidy (CDS), Operating Differential Subsidy (ODS), Capital Construction Fund (CCF), and Title XI Ship Mortgage Loan guarantees.

There are similarly many indirect aid programs, as well as legislation under which certain trades are reserved for U.S. shipping,

---

[1] E. G. Frankel, *Regulation and Policies of American Shipping,* Boston, Mass.: Auburn House Publishing, 1982.

or which provides for preferential treatment of U.S. shipping. During recent months potential changes in U.S. maritime policy have been considered, and there are indications that some of the subsidy programs may be modified or revived. The reasons are that notwithstanding the existence of these programs the U.S. Merchant Marine has been subjected to a continuous decline since 1945. At the same time, U.S.-owned shipping under foreign registry now comprises over four times the active U.S.-flag tonnage. Furthermore the U.S. finds itself increasingly isolated in its encouragement of free trade, open conferences, reduced trade barriers, and free competition in international shipping. Compared to their foreign competitors, U.S.-flag shipping companies generally operate with disadvantages such as the following:

- Higher ship investment costs;
- Larger ship operating, and particularly fuel, costs;
- Greater degree of government control and restriction affecting shipping management;
- Stricter ship design and operating rules;
- More stringent limitations on sources and methods of ship finance;
- Stricter limitations on the selection and size of crew or manning.

While the various government policies have the objective of furthering the development and vitality of the U.S. Merchant Marine, many of the programs and regulations have been counterproductive. Restrictions imposed by them have affected U.S. shipping management initiatives and often reduced or even eliminated incentives for efficient operations.

While U.S. shipping companies participating in U.S. Maritime Subsidy Programs are restricted from ownership of foreign-flag vessels, foreign citizens, including foreign shipowners, can acquire a minority interest in a U.S.-flag coastwise or foreign-going company.

Many issues in government policy and regulation affect U.S. shipping. Current U.S. maritime policy has evolved from shipping and maritime acts legislated long ago, at a time when the U.S. was supreme in world trade, its economy was far ahead of that of any other nation, and its industry was by and large without competition. Times have changed, and the economic and political conditions under which U.S. foreign trade and shipping operate are distinctly different now. Cost parity as an aid program for U.S. shipping has become a self-defeating concept at a time when basic labor costs are nearly identical in advanced industrial nations. Even more important is the fact that the world's nations depend less and less on U.S. trade, particularly for U.S. industrial exports. Finally, the decline of U.S. political and economic influence has resulted in virtual isolation of this country in many approaches affecting international trade and shipping.

Many of our closest allies and trading partners give lip service to the free trade principles we advocate while simultaneously entering into all kinds of restrictive agreements or imposing trade restrictions themselves. Some are indirect restrictions affecting entry of U.S. goods or participat on of U.S. shipping, but many new and imaginative methods of reserving cargo, combining shipping capacity, cross-chartering vessels and space, leveraged lease purchase release of vessels, and formation of flexible consortia have also been developed and used. New approaches to ship and voyage financing have been developed. Practices even include reservation of intra-regional cargo flows to the fleets of the member nations of the region, while trade between the U.S. and individual member nations is claimed to be governed by bilateral or cargo-sharing agreement terms. This type of extended regional cabotage introduces particular hardships on U.S. liner operators dependent on regional cross-trades to balance their fleet capacity utilization.

It is these and other practices that increasingly inhibit U.S. shipping. For example, the major fear of U.S. liner shipping with respect to ratification of the UNCTAD Code of Conduct for Liner Conferences is that it will result in dumping of tonnage onto the U.S. liner trade, which is the only liner trade governed by open conferences. U.S. shipping by and large has its hands tied and cannot respond to foreign restrictive practices, while U.S. free trade policy and regulations allow open unhindered participation of foreign shipping in U.S. trade. For U.S. shipping to compete effectively, it must be able to respond to restrictive or expansive moves of its foreign competitors.

8.2.1. *Opportunities for United States Shipping*

Many traditional premises of international trade, from which the demand for shipping is derived, have been altered. International shipping is increasingly used to expand national, political, and economic interests instead of providing a service to any and all users as part of a free competitive transport industry.

With government-owned shipping on the rise and nationalistic trends permeating the shipping policies of most countries, the U.S. is nearly alone in its support of free trade and shipping. The role of world shipping has dramatically changed, as has the environment in which it operates. While a declining number of OECD members give verbal support to the promises of free trade and shipping, many are simultaneously entering into restrictive agreements with their trading partners. Formation of multinational shipping consortia, cross-chartering, or joint venturing is often used to seal such bilateral or multilateral agreements.

U.S. shipping is at a disadvantage both economically and politically. On the economic front its hands are tied by government regulation and lack of management freedom; politically, it is required to agree to the extension of free access rights to all comers. Many of the participants in U.S. trade are cross-traders who restrict or even refuse participation by U.S. shipping in their own trade. This is a luxury we can no longer afford. Freedom of access or participation must be mutual. Similarly, U.S. shipping no longer needs cost parity—what it does need is parity of opportunity, parity in terms of trade, terms of access, terms of financing, terms of ship investment, terms of ship manning, and terms of taxation.

U.S. shipping cannot compete effectively just because some of its operating costs are equalized, if its operational and management freedom is severely constrained in comparison with that available to foreign shipping. Operating cost parity which excludes bunker cost differentials is really meaningless at a time when bunker costs of U.S. steam-propelled vessels are often 45 percent of operating costs and 40 percent higher than those of a comparable foreign ship. To attain the opportunity U.S. shipping needs for vital growth, parity in all factors of operations must be provided.

U.S. shipping needs a new charter, new rules, and freedom to allow effective management. A meaningful U.S. shipping capacity is today more important than ever before, because the world is moving toward a more restrictive and nationalistic framework in international trade and relations. To respond to these developments and permit the maintenance of our values and implementation of our policies, the United States must have a "credible" shipping capacity. We cannot consider bilateralism or multilateralism in shipping unless we have the ships to perform our part of the agreement. We cannot respond to restrictive practices or imaginative initiatives of our foreign competitors unless U.S. shipping has the freedom to react. To achieve the effective means to react, changes may have to include the ability for U.S. operators to import and export ships, as well as changes in manning constraints, elimination of many operational and ownership restrictions imposed under the antitrust laws, and freedom of route and service selection, as well as various aspects of financing, ownership, and taxation of U.S. shipping.

Many exciting opportunities are open to U.S. shipping, but it will not be able to take advantage of these opportunities and participate in a meaningful way in the expansion of U.S. trade unless it is given the opportunity to renew and expand its fleet and attain the freedom of action and government support that foreign shipping has generally attained.

BIBLIOGRAPHY

General Shipping

ABRAHAMSSON, B. J., "The Marine Environment and Ocean Shipping: Some Implications for a New Law of the Sea," *International Organization*, Spring 1977.

ABRAHAMSSON, B. J., *International Ocean Shipping: Current Concepts and Principles*. Boulder, Col.: Westview Press, 1980.

ALEXANDERSON, G., AND NORDSTROM, G. *World Shipping*. New York: John Wiley and Sons, 1963.

BARKER, J., AND BRANDWEIN, R. *The U.S. Merchant Marine in National Perspective*. Lexington, Mass.: D.C. Heath & Co., 1970.

BRANCH, A. E. *The Elements of Shipping*. 4th ed. London: Chapman and Hall, 1977.

BROSS, S. *Ocean Shipping*. Cambridge, Md.: Cornell Maritime Press, 1956.

COUPER, A. D. *The Geography of Sea Transport*. London: Hutchinson and Co., 1972.

DEVERCHOVE, R. *International Maritime Dictionary*. 2nd ed. Princeton: D. Van Nostrand Co., 1961.

"Future of Liner Shipping." International Symposium in Bremen, September 23–25, 1975. Bremen: Institute for Shipping Economics, 1975.

GILMAN, S. "Optimal Shipping Technologies for Routes to Developing Countries," *Journal of Transportation Economics and Policy*, January 1977.

GRIPAIOS, H. *Tramp Shipping*. London: Nelson, 1959.

HANSON, P. "Soviet Union and World Shipping," *Journal of Soviet Studies*, July 1970.

RAM, M. S. *Shipping*. New York: Asia Publishing House, 1969.

RINMAN, T., AND LINDEN, R. *Shipping—How It Works*. Gothenburg, Sweden: 1978.

Shipping Statistics Yearbook (annual). Bremen: Institute for Shipping Economics.

Tanker Register. London: E. Clarkson and Co., 1970.

UNCTAD. Commodity Survey 1968. TD/B/C.1/50.

UNCTAD. Consultation in Shipping. TD/B/C.4/20. 1975.

UNCTAD. Containers, Pallets, and Other Unitized Methods for the Intermodal Movement of Freight. St/Eca/120. 1976.

UNCTAD. Development of Expansion of Merchant Marine in Developing Countries. TD/B/C.4/42. 1974.

UNCTAD. Establishment or Expansion of Merchant Marines in Developing Countries. 69.II.D.1. 1968.

UNCTAD. *Handbook of International Trade and Development*. 1961.

UNCTAD. International Transoceanic Transport and Economic Development. TD/B/C.4/46.

UNCTAD. Liberalization of Terms and Conditions of Assistance. TD/B/C.3/77. January 1970.

UNCTAD. Maritime Transport and Economic Development. TD/B/C.18/69. September 1969.

UNCTAD. Measures for the Promotion, Expansion, and Diversification of Manufactures and Semi-Manufactures from Developing Countries. TD/B/C.4/73. April 1973.

UNCTAD. Port Administration and Legislation Handbook. ST/E/108. October 1969.

UNCTAD. Program for the Liberation and Expansion of Trade in the Commodities of Interest in Developing Countries. TD/B/C.1/32. 1972.

UNCTAD. Review of International Trade and Development 1969. TD/B/257/Rev. 1.

UNCTAD. *Review of Maritime Transport* (annual).

UNCTAD. Shipping and the World Economy—Report of a Seminar on Shipping Economics. 67.II.D.12.

UNCTAD. Shipping in the Seventies. UN Sales No. 72, II.D.15.

UNCTAD. Technical Assistance in Shipping and Ports. TD/B/C.4/48. February 1969.

UNCTAD. Terms of Shipment. TD/B/C.4/36.

UNCTAD. Trade Expansion and Economic Integration Among Developing Countries. TD/B/85.

UNCTAD. Trade Projections for 1975 and 1980. TD/B.264. 1969.

UNCTAD. Trade Relations Among Countries Having Different Economic and Social Systems. C251/69. July 1969.

UNCTAD. Transportation Modes and Technologies for Development. TD/B/C.5/73. April 1973.

U.S. Congress, House, Committee on Merchant Marine and Fisheries. Third Flag. Hearings before the Subcommittee on the Merchant Marine, 94th Cong., 1st and 2d sess., serial no. 95–35, 1977.

U.S. Department of Commerce, Maritime Administration. *A Statistical Analysis of the World's Merchant Fleet* (annual).

Shipping Economics and Finance

ABRAHAMSSON, B. J. "Liner and Tramp Rates," *Journal of the Israel Shipping Research Institute*, Winter 1972.

ANTHONY, R. N. *Planning and Control Systems: A Framework for Analysis*. Cambridge, Mass.: Harvard University, 1965.

ATHAY, R. E. *The Economics of Soviet Merchant Shipping Policy*. Oxford: Oxford University Press, 1972.

BAIN, G. F. "Transportation, Distribution, and the Naval Architect." Proceedings, SNAME Spring Meeting, 1967, pp. 12–1—12–11.

BENFORD, H. "Bulk Cargo Inventory Costs and Their Effects on the Design of Ships and Terminals," *Marine Technology*, SNAME, Oct. 1981.

BENFORD, H. "Fundamentals of Ship Design Economics." University of Michigan, Report 65–2, January 1965.

BENFORD, H. "The Hidden Costs of Stockpiling," *Seaway Review*, Vol. 7, No. 4, 1978, p. 31.

BENFORD, H. "Measures of Merit in Ship Design." Ann Arbor, Mich.: Department of Naval Architecture and Marine Engineering, University of Michigan, 1980.

BENFORD, H. "The Practical Application of Economics to Merchant Ship Design," *Marine Technology*, Vol. 4, No. 1, January 1967, pp. 519–536.

BENFORD, H. "Principles of Engineering Economy in Ship Design." *Transactions*, SNAME, Vol. 71, 1963, pp. 387–424.

BENFORD, H. et al. "Current Trends in the Design of Iron-Ore Ships," *Transactions*, SNAME, Vol. 70, 1962, pp. 24–83.

BENNATHAN, E., AND WALTERS, A. A. *The Economics of Ocean Freight Rates*. New York: Praeger, 1969.

BENNATHAN, E., AND WALTERS, A. A. *Port Pricing and Investment Policy for Developing Countries*. Oxford: Oxford University Press, 1979.

BRYAN, I. A. "The Effect of Ocean Transport Costs on the Demand for Some Canadian Exports," *Weltwirtschaftliches Archiv.*, No. 4, 1974.

BUXTON, IAN. "Engineering Economics Applied to Ship Design," *Trans. Royal Institution of Naval Architects*, Vol. 114, 1975, pp. 409–428.

CHAPMAN, K. R. "Economics and Ship Design," *Trans. North East Coast Institution of Engineers and Shipbuilders*, Vol. 83, 1966/1967, pp. 31–46.

COHEN, D., AND SCHNEERSON, D. "The Domestic Resource Costs of Establishing or Expanding a National Fleet," *Maritime Studies and Management*, No. 4, 1976.

DEAKIN, B. M. "Shipping Conferences, Some Economic Aspects of International Regulation," *Maritime Studies and Management*, July 1974.

DEAKIN, B. M., AND SEWARD, T. *Shipping Conferences: A Study of Their Origins, Development, and Economic Practices*. Cambridge, Eng.: Cambridge University Press, 1973.

ERICHSEN, S. "Optimizing Containerships and Their Terminals," Proceedings, SNAME Spring Meeting, 1972, pp. 4–1 to 4–15.

FAMA, F. "Efficient Capital Markets: A Review of Theory and Empirical Work," *Journal of Finance*, Vol. 35, May 1970.

FAMA, E. F., "Financial Setup of Utility Industry."

FERGUSON, A. R., et al. *The Economic Value of the U.S. Merchant Marine*. Evanston, Ill.: Northwestern University Transportation Center, 1961.

GARDNER, J. S. "Optimum Investment Scheduling for Natural Gas Pipeline System", Thesis, 1970.

GILMAN, S., "Optimal Shipping Technologies for Routes to Developing Countries," *Journal of Transportation Economics and Policy*, January 1977.

GORRY, G. A., AND MORTON, G. S. S. "A Framework for Management Information Systems," in *Classics in Innovative Management* (a collection of reprints from the *Sloan Management Review*). MIT, 1976.

GOSS, R. O. Economic Criteria for Optimal Ship Designs," *Trans. Royal Institution of Naval Architects*, Vol. 107, 1965, pp. 581–600.

GOSS, R. O. "The Economics of Automation in British Shipping," *Trans. Royal Institution of Naval Architects*, July 1967.

GOSS, R. O. *Studies in Maritime Economics*. London: Cambridge University Press, 1978.

Goss, R. O., "The Turnaround Time of Cargo Liners and Its Effect Upon Sea Transport Costs," *Journal of Transport Economics*, 1968.

Goss, R. O., ed. *Advances in Maritime Economics*. Cambridge, Eng.: Cambridge University Press, 1977.

Goss, R. O., ed. *Studies in Maritime Economics*. Cambridge, Eng.: Cambridge University Press, 1968.

Goss, R. O., and Jones, C. D. "The Economics of Size in Dry Bulk Carriers," HM Treasury, Government Economic Service Occasional Papers, London, 1971.

Grammenos, C., "Bank Financing for Ship Purchase," Bangor Occasional Papers in Economics, No. 16. Cardiff: University of Wales Press, 1979.

Grossman, W. L. *Ocean Freight Rates*. Cambridge, Md.: Cornell Maritime Press, 1956.

Hatley, J. "Ship Operation for Economic Cost of Transport." Ann Arbor, Mich.: Department of Naval Architecture and Marine Engineering, University of Michigan, 1980.

Heaver, T. D. "The Economics of Vessel Size." Ottawa, Canada: National Harbours Board, 1968.

Heaver, T. D. "A Theory of Shipping Conference Pricing and Policies," *Maritime Studies and Management*, No. 1, 1973.

Heaver, T. D. "TransPacific Trade Liner Shipping and Conference Rates," *Transportation and Logistics Review*, Spring 1972.

Heaver, T. D. "The Structure of Liner Conference Rates," *Journal of Industrial Economics*, 1973.

Hirshleifer, J. "Investment, Interest, and Capital," 1970.

Houthaker, H. S., and Magee, S. P. "Income and Price Elasticities in World Trade," *Review of Economics and Statistics*, May 1969.

Jansson, J. O. "Intra-Tariff Cross-Subsidization in Liner Shipping", *Journal of Transport Economics and Policy*, September 1975, pp. 294–311.

Kendall, P. M. H. "A Theory of Optimum Ship Size," *Journal of Transport Economics and Policy*, May 1972.

Kendrick, D. A. "Programming Investment in the Industrial Process," 1967.

Laing, E. T. "The Rationality of Conference Pricing and Output Policies," *Maritime Studies and Management*, Part I, No. 3, 1975; Part II, No. 3, 1976. (See Schneerson's commentary in the latter issue.)

Lipsey, R. E., and Weiss, M. Y. "The Structure of Ocean Transport Charges," Occasional Papers of the National Bureau of Economic Research, Summer, 1974, pp. 162–193.

Locklin, D. *Economics of Transportation* (7th ed., 1972.

MacMillan, D. "Competitive General Cargo Ships," *Transactions*, SNAME, Vol. 68, 1960, pp. 836–866.

McLachlen, D. L. "The Price Policy of Liner Conferences," *Scottish Journal of Political Economy*, November 1963.

Metaxas, B. N. *The Economics of Tramp Shipping*. London: Athlone Press, 1971.

Meyer and Straszheim. "Pricing and Project Evaluation." Washington, D.C.: Brookings Institution, 1970.

Mossim, J. "Theory of Financial Markets," Englewood Cliffs, N.J.: Prentice-Hall, International Series in Management, 1973.

Myers, S. C. "Interactions of Corporate Financing and Investment Decisions— Implications for Capital Budgeting," *The Journal of Finance*, March 1974.

NACHTSHEIM, J. J. "Ship System Economics—Less the Ship," Proceedings, SNAME Spring Meeting, 1972, pp. 1–1 to 1–17.

OECD. Export Cartels. Paris, 1974

OECD. *Maritime Transport* (annual). Paris.

OECD. Ocean Freight Rates as Part of Total Transport Costs. Paris, 1967.

O'LOUGHLIN, C. *The Economics of Sea Transport*. London: Athlone Press, 1971.

OMTVEDT, P. "Report on the Profitability of Port Investment." Oslo, Mimeographed, 1963.

PEARSON, C. C. *International Marine Environment Policy: The Economic Dimension*. Baltimore, Md.: John Hopkins University Press, 1975.

PESTON, M. H., AND REES, R. "Feasibility Study of a Cost Benefit Assessment of Marine Industrial Areas." London: National Ports Council, 1970.

RUGGLES, N. "Recent Developments in the Theory of Marginal Cost Pricing," *Review of Economic Studies, 1949–50*, pp. 107–127.

SCHER, R. M., AND BENFORD, H. "Some Aspects of Fuel Economy in Bulk Carrier Design and Operations." Ann Arbor, Mich.: Department of Naval Architecture and Marine Engineering, University of Michigan, 1980.

SCHNEERSON, D. "The Rationality of Conference Pricing and Output Policies: Commentary," *Maritime Studies and Management*, No. 3, 1976.

SCHNEERSON, D. "The Structure of Liner Freight Rates," *Journal of Transportation Economics and Policy*, January 1976.

Shipping Conference Rate Policy and Developing Countries. Hamburg: Institute for International Economics, 1973.

SIMON, H. A. *The New Science of Management Decision*. New York: Harper & Row, 1960.

STURMEY, S. G. "Economics and International Liner Services," *Journal of Transport Economics*, 1968.

STURMEY, S. G. *The Economics of Bulking Cargoes*. Institute for Shipping Research, Bergen, 1969.

STURMEY, S. G. *Shipping Economics: Collected Papers*. London: MacMillan Press, 1975.

UNCTAD. Economic Consequences of the Existence or Lack of a Genuine Link Between Vessel and Flag of Registry. TD/B/C.4/168. March 10, 1977.

UNCTAD. Level and Structure of Freight Rates, Conference Practices, and Adequacy of Shipping Services. TD/B/C.4/38. 1969.

UNCTAD. "Port Development," 1978.

U.S. Congress, Joint Economic Committee. Discriminatory Ocean Freight Rates and the Balance of Payments. 89th Congress, 1st session, January 6, 1965.

VAN HORNE, J. C. *Financial Management and Policy*, 3rd ed. Englewood Cliffs, N.J.: Prentice-Hall, 1974.

WOODWARD, J. B., et al., "Systems Analysis in Marine Transport," Proceedings, SNAME Diamond Jubilee Meeting, 1968, pp. 7–1 to 7–21.

ZANNETOS, Z. "Persistent Misconceptions in the Transportation of Oil by Sea." *Maritime Studies and Management*, No. 1, 1973.

ZERBY, J. A., CONLON, R. M., AND KAYE, S. L. "Ocean Transport Cost Analysis of Australian Exports of Wool to Europe." School of Economics, University of New South Wales, 1976.

Shipping Organization and Management

DREWRY, H. P., for Shipping Consultants, Ltd. "Organization and Structure of the Dry Bulk Shipping Industry," Study No. 63. London, 1978.

Federal Maritime Commision. "Fact Finding Investigation No. 6: The Effect of Steamship Conference Organization, Rules, Regulations, and Practices Upon the Foreign Commerce of the U.S.," 1965.

KENDALL, L. C. *The Business of Shipping*. Cambridge, Md.: Cornell Maritime Press, 1973.

LARNER, R. "Public Policy in the Ocean Freight Industry," in *Promoting Competition in Regulated Markets*, ed. by A. Phillips. Washington, D.C.: Brookings Institution, 1975.

MARX, D., JR. *International Shipping Cartels: A Study of Industrial Self-Regulation by Shipping Conferences*. Princeton, N.J.: Princeton University Press, 1953.

MOREBY, D. *The Human Element in Shipping*. Colchester, Eng.: Seatrade Publications, 1975.

National Research Council. "The Sea-going Workforce: Implications of Technological Change." Washington, D.C.; 1974.

Shipping Brokerage, Chartering, and Insurance

BES, J. *Chartering and Shipping Terms*, 7th ed. New York: W. S.   75.

CUFLEY, C. F. *Ocean Freights and Chartering*. London: Crosby Lockwood Staples, 1974.

DOVER, V. *A Handbook to Marine Insurance*, 8th ed. London: H. F. & G. Witherby, 1975.

TURNER, H. A. *The Principles of Marine Insurance*. London: Stone & Cox Publications, 1971.

WINTER, W. *Marine Insurance—Its Principles and Practice*, 3rd ed. New York: McGraw-Hill, 1952.

INDEX